A CONFESSING THEOLOGY
FOR POSTMODERN TIMES

A CONFESSING
THEOLOGY
FOR POSTMODERN TIMES

EDITED BY

Michael S. Horton

CROSSWAY BOOKS • WHEATON, ILLINOIS
A DIVISION OF GOOD NEWS PUBLISHERS

A Confessing Theology for Postmodern Times

Copyright © 2000 by Alliance for Confessing Evangelicals

Published by Crossway Books
a division of Good News Publishers
1300 Crescent Street
Wheaton, Illinois 60187

Cover design: David LaPlaca

Cover photo: PhotoDisc

Index: Steven M. Moulson

First printing 2000

Printed in the United States of America

Library of Congress Cataloging-in-Publication Data

Horton, Michael S.
  A confessing theology for postmodern times / edited by Michael S. Horton.
    p.   cm.
  Includes bibliographical references and index.
  ISBN 1-58134-102-4 (alk. paper)
  1. Theology, Doctrinal. 2. Bible—Theology. 3. Catholic Church—
Doctrines. 4. Lutheran Church—Doctrines. 5. Theology—Methodology.
6. Education (Christian education) 7. Modernism (Christian theology)
I. Horton, Michael Scott. II. Title.
BT80.C64 2000
230'.044—dc21   00-008986
                                                            CIP

15	14	13	12	11	10	09	08	07	06	05	04	03	02	01	00
15	14	13	12	11	10	9	8	7	6	5	4	3	2	1	

CONTENTS

THE CONTRIBUTORS

Charles P. Arand, Associate Professor of Systematic Theology, Chairman of the Department of Systematic Theology and Assistant Dean of Faculty, Concordia Seminary, St. Louis.

Richard B. Gaffin, Jr., Professor of Biblical and Systematic Theology, Westminster Theological Seminary, Philadelphia.

D. G. Hart, Academic Dean and Professor of Church History, Westminster Theological Seminary, Escondido, Calif.

Michael S. Horton, Associate Professor of Apologetics and Theology, Westminster Theological Seminary, Escondido, Calif.

Richard Lints, Professor of Theology and Apologetics, Gordon-Conwell Theological Seminary, South Hamilton, Mass.

Edgar V. McKnight, Research Professor and William R. Kenan, Jr., Professor Emeritus of Religion, Furman University, Greenville, S.C.

R. Albert Mohler, Jr., President, The Southern Baptist Theological Seminary, Louisville, Ky.

Richard A. Muller, P. J. Zondervan Professor of Historical Theology, Calvin Theological Seminary, Grand Rapids, Mich.

J. A. O. Preus III, President, Concordia University, Irvine, Calif.

Paul R. Raabe, Professor of Old Testament, Concordia Seminary, St. Louis.

David P. Scaer, Professor of Systematic Theology and New Testament and Chairman, Department of Systematic Theology, Concordia Theological Seminary, Fort Wayne, Ind.

Paul F. M. Zahl, Dean, Cathedral Church of the Advent, Birmingham, Ala.

INTRODUCTION

By now just about everyone has used Jeffrey Stout's colorful comparison of discourses on method to clearing one's throat: It's fine for the first time or two, but if it goes on for too long, people begin to get restless. Books on method in mainline academic circles roughly parallel books on apologetics in evangelical scholarship. And both are in disrepute today for many of the same reasons. For one, there is a growing reluctance in the academy more generally to identify a *Wissenschaft* to which Christian discourse must pay homage. The repudiation of universals for particulars and of the grand narrative for our communal narratives sees the specter of modern foundationalism in any attempt to establish such a *petit*-narrative on the illusory bedrock of methodological certitude. Follow the directions on the package and one can't help but come out with the same results: This sort of thinking has passed, as everyone knows. Christian discourse, which theology at least ought to be concerned with, doesn't require an alien science to dictate its object, epistemological criteria, and ends, any more than its content.

A second reason why books on theological method are themselves preceded by apologies for the practice is due at least in part to the influence of Karl Barth. While we would have some fairly serious disagreements with aspects of Barth's program, he at least fractured the hegemony of neo-Protestant theology, with its marriage of convenience to the natural (and later, human) sciences. Christianity is about Christ, Barth and his disciples said, not about some universal experience, reality, or limit-situation. So he replaced the *analogia entis*— inherently apologetical and concerned with external reference—with the *analogia fidei*, which is inherently hermeneutical and chiefly occupied with internal coherence, thereby pointing the way toward the most dominant forms of narrative theology.

So why another book on theological method? Why don't we just start doing theology and stop talking about how we would go about doing it? If my own parochial intuition cannot judge, I have it on good authority from many colleagues that there are few places today where people are actually engaging in what used to be called "dogmatics"—not even in conservative, confessional circles. And yet there is a growing cottage industry of lay and pastoral journals such as *Pro Ecclesia, Logia,* and *Modern Reformation* which are feeding and expanding the circle of those wanting to engage in this somewhat premodern practice. Many are just coming to confessional convictions of one sort or another from non-confessional backgrounds. While the experts have told them that this sort of thing is dead, boring, irrelevant, and so forth, they go on naively confident that theology has the potential to shape their entire existence and action.

This volume is evidence of that spirit. It is also evidence of an emerging ecumenism of quite a unique sort. This book is the product of a somewhat informal conference held in the summer of 1998, sponsored by the Alliance of Confessing Evangelicals, dedicated to the subject of recovering the practice (indeed, the very idea) of systematic theology in a postmodern context. While "modern" ecumenism stressed a common ground of universal (noncontroversial and therefore banal) consensus and experience, "postmodern" ecumenism doesn't always have to be hopelessly pluralistic but can be hopefully confessional. That means that we can spend a few days with each other trying to understand how theologians and biblical scholars think, speak, and act, from within particular communities of discourse. In this way, such discourse enriches the wider, shared project of defending key evangelical convictions instead of being dismissed or suppressed as a disturber of the peace. By defending our shared consensus in its own particular way, given its own history of exegesis and praxis, each ecclesiastical community represented around the table brings enormous resources to bear without sacrificing any distinctives in order to participate. In order to get us thinking, we commenced our festivities with a provocative and spirited defense of postmodern literary theory as applied to biblical and theological studies.

To this end Professor Edgar McKnight, author of *Postmodern Use of the Bible,* lent his kind services. Let us note up front that this opening contribution to part 2 of this volume does not represent the position of the Alliance itself. By beginning with our challenges, we needed someone outside our circle to set up for us something more than a straw man, to keep us from making our task easier than it really is. Professor McKnight proved he was up to that task, and his criticism and comments throughout the conference were much appreciated, if not always received with thorough acquiescence.

We hope to continue meeting in the coming years, pursuing a locus-by-locus program. So this time, the subject was theological method, under the necessarily general rubric, "A Confessing Theology for Postmodern Times," asking ourselves about the prospects of launching new efforts in systematic and dogmatic theology which take serious account of three factors: 1) our resources (Scripture, as well as our own historical theologies); 2) our challenges (knowing that this is hardly external to the process of interpretation itself); 3) our opportunities (knowing that both naive optimism and narrow pessimism continue to intimidate some from pursuing a critical-constructive path). In the next conference (and therefore volume), we will examine the doctrine of God, where a great deal of activity is now appearing. Challenges to the classical doctrine of God are rife not only in the mainstream academy but increasingly among evangelical scholars as well. So we hope to tackle some of those issues next. So pardon us if we are clearing our throat one more time, but we hope that it will prepare us to speak more concretely in our future meetings and in the volumes that emerge from them.

—*Michael S. Horton*

PART ONE

RESOURCES

1

The Church's Dogma
and Biblical Theology

Charles P. Arand

The era of modernity gave rise to the independent study of the
Bible within the university apart from an ecclesial context.
Coinciding with that shift there arose almost simultaneously the
development of "biblical theology" (a discrete field in biblical studies) as an alternative to the dogmatic/doctrinal theology produced by
the church. Dogmatic theology can denote either a descriptive task of
identifying a theology within the Bible, or a constructive task that
accords with the Bible. The former is more a historical task, the latter an attempt to formulate a modern theology compatible in some
sense with the Bible.

The argument for the divorce between biblical theology and dogmatic theology rested in part on the belief that in the early and
medieval church the Bible "functioned within a dogmatic-ecclesiasti-
cal framework in a subservient role in order to support various traditional theological systems."[1] The Reformation signaled a shift in
emphasis by its appeal to the Bible as the sole authority in matters of
faith, but even it did not make the decisive move toward complete
independence for biblical studies from the ecclesial tradition. The term
"biblical theology" first came into prominence in the seventeenth century among both pietists and rationalists. The pietists wanted a theology based solely on the Bible. The rationalists called for a return to
the simple and historical religion of the Bible apart from the complex

dogmatic and ecclesiastical formulations. In the end, both pietists and rationalists argued for a return to biblical theology.

The field of biblical theology has generally leveled a number of broadly based criticisms or charges against dogmatic theology. My colleague Paul Raabe has enunciated a number of these issues that dogmatics must address. The first has to do with using passages of Scripture as proof-texts for doctrine in a way that may neglect serious exegesis. Here dogmatics must be held accountable to the biblical texts as understood historically and contextually; it must provide biblical explanations for its categories; and it must explain its overall matrix in a biblical way. The second issue flows from the first: Dogmatics must avoid strained attempts to harmonize portions of Scripture that are in apparent disagreement or conflict—failing to take into account the diversity of the scriptural material. Finally, dogmatics should avoid interpreting the Bible in light of the later creeds or confessions, or in light of later Christian orthodoxy, since these represent viewpoints subsequent to and therefore possibly divergent from those found in the New Testament.

One of the greatest contributions of biblical theology as a discipline has been to highlight the richness and variety of materials within the Bible. But if the neglect of biblical theology in dogmatics led to an emphasis on the unity of the Bible so as to homogenize its content, the emphasis on the diversity of the Bible's witness has raised questions about the unity of the biblical message. In biblical studies itself it has led to a sharp distinction between Old Testament and New Testament theology, and between the theologies of individual authors within the biblical books. In doing so it has raised questions about the task of biblical theology, namely, whether or not it involves little more than classifying the discrete theologies of the various authors. Second, the loss of an ecclesial context compelled biblical theology to search for a new philosophical framework (such as philosophical idealism or historical evolution) as a substitute for the church's dogmatic framework within which to integrate the diverse biblical material.[2]

A long overdue but ultimately healthy corrective has been taking place in biblical studies, in which scholars once again acknowledge that the Bible is the church's book. Biblical hermeneuticians such as

Stanley Habermas and James Voelz[3] increasingly push this very point. That is to say, the Bible was a book written from within the church and for the church. If the Bible is the church's book, then one has to ask the church how it intended the Bible to be read, for what purpose, and how it teaches its members to read the Scriptures. It is recognized that the church has taught its members down through the generations how to read the Bible, that is, with the presuppositions and goals appropriate to the Scriptures themselves. This recognition opens a window of opportunity for bringing biblical theology and dogmatic theology once again into conversation. The two need to interact from the start as the basis for any new biblical theology. I would like to highlight a few items that dogmatic theology brings to the table for biblical theology.

THE VALUE OF THE CHURCH'S CREEDAL AND CONCILIAR DOGMA

Throughout its history the church has drawn upon a variety of expressions and terms to describe the nature and function of its dogma (especially as expressed in its creeds and confessions) in relation to the Holy Scriptures. Paul spoke about the "pattern of sound words" (2 Tim. 1:13, NKJV). Irenaeus and Tertullian referred to the *regula fidei* (rule of faith) and "canon of truth" according to which a person could study the Scriptures.[4] In the *regula fidei*, the church set forth the "system" or "framework" that was to guide the interpretation of Scripture.[5] When bishops of the early church delivered the creed to catechumens on Palm Sunday, they often spoke of it as a summary of Scripture.[6] Athanasius argued against the Arians by drawing upon the entire sweep or "general drift" (*scopus*) of Scripture as well as the goal and purpose (*finis*) of Scripture.[7] The distinctively Lutheran confessions see themselves as standing firmly within this tradition.[8] They too claim to be directives, guides (*Anleitung, rationes; Ep R&N*, 6),[9] comprehensive summaries and forms, summary formulas and patterns of doctrine (*Begriff und form, compendiaria forma et quasi typus, SD R&N*, 1), and summaries and models of sound doctrine (*Summa und Forbild der Lehre; compendaria hypotyposi hyposi seu forma sanae doctrinae, SD R&N,* 9); form of teaching sound doctrine (*Form der Lehre, compendaria hypotyposi sanae doctrinae, SD R&N,* 10).

What was the church attempting to say through the various terms and phrases it employed in describing the dogma of church as set forth in the creeds? Put another way, what is the value of church dogma? First, such creedal and confessional statements provide a framework and presuppositions for the reading of Scripture. Second, they summarize the orthodox faith of the Christian church and therefore serve as our confession, made before God and the world, concerning what the church believes, teaches, and confesses to be the message of Scripture. Third, the ancient orthodox church's dogma provides a hermeneutical guide for reading Scripture in a theologically orthodox way. We all read Scripture within a hermeneutical circle, as do all readers whether consciously or unwittingly. Fourth, the church's dogma is intended to teach "the pattern of sound words." This also includes how one is not to speak, thus avoiding the repetition of rejected heresies.

Dogma Provides the Church's Presuppositions for Approaching Scripture

A Christian's exploration or study of Scripture does not involve setting out into an "uncharted territory to explore matters which had never before been encountered."[10] Nor does anyone read the Bible in isolation from other Christians. Every person is a part of a community. Instead, an individual's exploration of Scripture most often begins with an encounter of Scripture as given in the detailed accounts of others.[11] It may be that our parents, pastors, teachers, or friends introduced us to the content and study of Scripture. In their account we receive a summary of Scripture's central message and receive therein some clues as to what we should look for—what is important and what is less central. Their telling of the story thus shapes our subsequent reading. The impression of what they found stimulates those who follow in their footsteps. In a sense, the church's dogma represents the "accumulated insights" of those who have explored the Scriptures down through the centuries.

It is at this point that dogmatics must challenge the unexamined assumptions of biblical scholarship. One of the goals of biblical studies within the universities for the past two centuries has been to free the Bible from the "shackles" of the church and its dogma. One of the contributions of the postmodern critique of the Enlightenment is to lay bare the lie that there is any such thing as a purely objective science. Instead, every reader lives in a community and is shaped by that community's presuppositions, values, and methods.[12] If a person does not employ the presuppositions of the church in reading the Bible, then he or she will simply substitute some other set of presuppositions. The church's confession and dogma provide an honest, "up-front" statement about its presuppositions: "This is what we have discovered in Scripture and this is how we read the Scriptures."

DOGMA PROVIDES A MAP FOR THE READING OF SCRIPTURE

The presuppositions provided by the church's dogma take the form of an overarching framework or overall summary of the Bible's contents. Thus creeds and confessions have often been referred to as doctrinal expositions of Scripture. As documents that set forth the accumulated insights of the church over a period of centuries, the church's confessional and dogmatic writings might be likened to a collection of maps gathered into an atlas. Instead of mapping out geographical features, they map out the doctrinal terrain of the Scriptures.

This metaphor of a map or atlas is useful in understanding the reciprocal relation between the confessions and biblical writings. The confessions reproduce in miniature the doctrinal content of the Scriptures. This involves two elements. First, the confessions draw together into one place the principal sights that are "must sees" in Scripture, as a map might highlight the mountain peaks in a given region that rise to at least 14,000 feet in elevation. Second, the confessions employ certain principles congruent with those of Scripture itself for mapping out the region to be explored.[13]

When Jesus asked Peter, "Who do you say that I am?" Peter responded with a creed-like statement, "You are the Christ, the Son of the living God" (Matt. 16:15-16, NKJV). Peter's confession states the essence of the Christian faith, and the creeds simply unfold its mean-ing. The early councils explicated and defined the creedal faith amid the current heretical distortions. To speak the truth necessarily entails opposing falsehood, and opposing falsehood serves to clarify the truth. It is not surprising that many of these ancient heresies seem to pop up again and again under new dress, since only a finite number of fundamental heresies is even possible or imaginable.

THE CHURCH'S DOGMA AS A HERMENEUTICAL GUIDE

Maps are not intended to replace or avoid the trip through the country they survey. Indeed, there is no substitute for seeing the scenery of the countryside for yourself. Maps are merely a guide for actually taking the trip.[14] Dogma is no substitute for reading and studying the Scriptures themselves. A traveler uses a map and embarks on a journey in order to arrive at a destination. The purpose of dogma is to "send us back into the Scriptures with more reader competence."[15] It takes us to the center of the region. It points out highlights along the way: "Be sure to see this waterfall!" (e.g., don't miss the doctrine of the church). The purpose of dogma is to lead us unerringly to the gospel. But, unlike a simple journey, the confession's trip through the sacred Scripture is also a geographical-mapping operation. It is intended to understand the totality of the region to be explored, to understand the parts of that region in relationship to one another, and in so doing to arrive at the heart and the center of the region—for only then can one understand the region's essence, its essential nature, its very soul. In other words, the confession intends to organize the entire content of sacred Scriptures and in so doing determine the key of the organizational matrix which will provide an understanding of all of the constituent parts. How, for example, does the Trinity relate to christology or to soteriology?

One could also illustrate this point by updating Irenaeus's imagery of the mosaic (Against Heresies, 1.8.1; cf. 1.9,1-4) to the more contemporary imagery of a jigsaw puzzle. Like a jigsaw puzzle, the Scriptures contain many topics or articles of faith that need to be pieced together until they form a coherent picture, with all the pieces taken into account. The creeds and confessions assist in assembling the individual pieces in the same way that the picture on the cover of the puzzle box provides an aid in the assembly of the many puzzle pieces. They do so by providing a "snapshot" of the entire picture in which it is possible to discern the central features of the puzzle as well as the relationship of the various pieces to one another, especially to the central features. Moreover, like a photograph taken with a low aperture setting, the center remains clearly focused. It shows which pieces are placed into the center and which surround it. Irenaeus put it well: "In this way the whole body of truth remains whole, with all the members harmoniously fitted together and without violent clashing."[16]

Dogmatics thus poses a number of questions for biblical studies. For example, is there any theological unity binding together the manifold theologies identified within the Scriptures? In other words, how do we fit the pieces together? If Jesus declares himself to be one with the Father and at the same time declares that the Father is greater than he, how are these texts to be understood? When the Bible refers to the word "God" (*Theos*) is it referring to the divine essence and being or is it referring to the Father? If the former, how should the phrase "Son of God" be understood? If Jesus is merely a man, then "Son" must mean that he is merely an adopted son. If Jesus is God, then what is his relation to the Father who is also called God? Church dogma seeks to clarify with some precision the biblical faith. It forces biblical scholars to grapple with these kinds of "mega" questions.

Dogma and the Writing of New Maps

As summaries of Scripture, the confessions do not exhaust the content of Scripture. There is much in Scripture yet to be explored. Again, to return to our analogy, a map (a world map, for example) will depict the arrangement of bodies of water and land masses with respect to one another and the configuration of boundaries. Unlike a photograph, however, it will not reveal all the detail that can be seen in a landscape. Instead, a map provides a more comprehensive and selective picture. In like manner, the confessions show the arrangement of various articles with respect to one another as well as the basic configuration or parameters of those articles; this does not imply that they exhaust the content or details of a given article or series of articles.

The ecumenical creeds and councils map out the thoroughly explored terrain of the doctrine of christology and the Trinity during the first seven centuries of the church's history. More passages may certainly be brought to bear upon the topic to further illuminate it. The Reformation confessions explore rather thoroughly the contours and content of soteriology. That does not mean, however, that the language of forensic justification or the metaphor of the courtroom is the only way that the Scriptures articulate the gospel. In other instances the creeds speak of a doctrine in brief fashion, such as the Holy Spirit or the church. At the same time, they provide the parameters within which those particular loci might be developed.

When biblical scholars address matters that are discussed in the creeds or that are not discussed in the creeds and dogma of the church, they will do so in a way that does not override the basic doctrinal framework of the confessions but instead will explore how the issue under examination fits within the whole. In other words, theological reflection will take place within the parameters of this framework. For example, the centrality of the kingdom of God in the Synoptic Gospels will be examined in light of the emphasis on the centrality of justification as stressed by the confessions—and that in turn within the context of christology.

As the church enters into new wildernesses of contemporary theology, areas that have not been thoroughly explored, it can use the maps of the confessions as an orientation and guide. New methods and technologies for mapmaking, such as infrared photography and satellite imagery, may provide new insights and reveal new details. They do this, however, in such a way that their findings do not redraw or alter the boundaries of current maps. Instead, their discoveries find a place within those boundaries. The answers they provide must take into account the current features already sketched out on the maps and must be placed into a relationship with those features. The confessions can also be used as a basis or guide for the development of more detailed maps or for different types of maps. Exegesis (mapmaking) will remain an ongoing activity that continually yields new and helpful insights.

Finally, dogma provides a pattern for thinking through and articulating the biblical message. This does not mean that one must simply quote Bible passages or must merely repeat the dogmatic sentences, but it does mean that one learns to think and speak in an orthodox way, in a way that conforms with the orthodox dogma. For example, to speak of the person of Christ in an orthodox way is to give full weight to the "one" and to the "two," one Son of God who is fully divine and fully human. Thus the early church's creedal and conciliar dogma functions like grammar or like the rules of chess. It does not dictate the specific sentences you will utter or the specific moves you will make, but it does determine the pattern for speaking or moving in an acceptable way. As a corollary, dogma also provides unalterable boundaries that are not to be crossed. As Raabe notes, many of the theologies attempted have been proposed before and found to be heretical. For instance, adoptionism continues to be promoted through the sharp distinction between the Jesus of history and the Christ of faith.

The Retrieval of Historic Christianity

In order to bring into mutual conversation biblical theology and church dogma, which dogma and which church's dogma should we include in the matrix?

We might call it a renewed interest in historic or classical Christianity. This can be seen in the Call to Faithfulness conferences sponsored by the Institute for Evangelical and Catholic Theology, the establishment of the journal *Pro Ecclesia,* and Thomas Oden's search for consensual Christianity through a study of patristic exegesis. The Alliance of Confessing Evangelicals itself may fit in with this trend as well. These theologians know that the present, without a past memory and tradition, is self-illusory and finally destructive. David Tracy refers to these neo-conservative approaches as "theologies of retrieval." It is believed that we need to retrieve these resources if we are to maintain a Christian identity and find a Christian unity.

This return to the dogma of historic Christianity, this theology of retrieval, can be done in two different steps. First, theologians can engage in a retrieval of a church body's own theological heritage. This was certainly a hallmark of the nineteenth-century confessional revival. It is certainly helpful in defining one Christian tradition over against another. It is to some extent needed today as we face the increasing balkanization of Christianity arising out of postmodernity. Stanley Grenz's *Theology for the Community*,[17] for example, is a self-consciously Baptist systematic theology. But it may be questioned whether and how much such an effort by itself it can contribute to Christian unity. If there is a hope of making a positive contribution toward the creedal unity of the many and diverse church bodies and groupings of congregations, we cannot select the unique theology of any one particular denomination.

A second move, and an arguably more ecumenical step, is to take it back one step further and inquire into the dogma of the early church. This is needed for two reasons. First, the Protestant Reformers themselves repeatedly insisted that they were saying nothing new and that they were simply reiterating what the ancient orthodox church itself had said. While we often begin our citation of the fathers with Luther or Calvin, they began with Irenaeus, the Cappadocians, or Augustine. Second, our age is increasingly one in which the church must define itself over against non-Christian religious options rather than over against other Christian traditions. That, of course, raises the question, What is Christian? and this raises the need for those groups claiming to be Christian to demonstrate that they stand within the tradition of historic Christianity.

But which dogma of the early church and what understanding of the Bible do we choose? The best place to begin is with the ancient ecumenical creeds, especially the Nicene Creed, since it is officially affirmed by Roman Catholicism, Eastern Orthodoxy, and most Protestant churches. The Nicene Creed was confessed, reaffirmed, and further explicated by the councils of the undivided church that took place from the fourth to the eight centuries. These councils are still recognized by most of Christendom as expressing the orthodox dogma of Christianity. Indeed, when we speak of "historic Christianity," we are referring to the boundaries of the faith expressed by the creeds (Apostles', Nicene, and Athanasian) and by the first seven councils (Nicea, 325; Constantinople I, 381; Ephesus, 431; Chalcedon, 451; Constantinople II, 553; Constantinople III, 680; and Nicea II, 787).

CONCLUSION

In the end, biblical and dogmatic theology need each other. Theology at its best within the church has always involved an integration of the two disciplines. The most rigorous dogmaticians were also the best biblical scholars of their day. (Within the Lutheran tradition, for example, these would include such figures as Martin Luther, Phillip Melanchthon, and Martin Chemnitz.) Conversely, the best biblical scholars in the church never failed to draw the necessary dogmatic conclusions from their studies for the well-being of the church. What has been separated in the last two centuries needs to be brought back into dialogue for the twenty-first.

Notes

1. Brevard Childs, *Biblical Theology of the Old and New Testaments: Theological Reflection on the Christian Bible* (Philadelphia: Fortress Press, 1992), 4.

2. Childs, 6.

3. James W. Voelz, *What Does This Mean? Principles of Biblical Interpretation in the Post-Modern World* (St. Louis: Concordia, 1995).

4. Frances Young, *The Making of the Creeds* (Philadelphia: Trinity Press, 1991), 8-9.

5. See Paul J. Grime, "Confessional Pre-Understanding in the Interpretation of Scripture," STM Thesis (Fort Wayne, Ind.: Concordia Theological Seminary, 1987), 41ff.

6. Cyril of Jerusalem states in his catechetical lectures (V. 12) that the creed comprises "the whole doctrine of the faith in a few lines." It should be committed to memory, he says, in part because "it is not some human compilation, but consists of the most important points collected out of Scripture." *The Works of Saint Cyril of Jerusalem*, vol. 1 (Washington, D.C.: Catholic University Press of America, 1969), 146.

7. Cf. T. E. Pollard, "The Exegesis of Scripture and the Arian Controversy," *Bulletin of the John Rylands Library* 41 (1959): 423. See Grime, "Confessional Pre-Understanding in the Interpretation of Scripture," 36-87.

8. In terms of sources from which the confessions are drawn, it may be helpful to draw a distinction between the creeds of the early church and the confessional writings of the sixteenth century. The confessors recognized that the creeds (especially the Apostles' Creed) can trace their lineage back to the "rule of faith" or "canon of truth" which contained the sum of apostolic doctrine. Irenaeus and Tertullian indicate that these precursors reach back to the processes of handing on the faith orally by the apostles and not directly to the Scriptures. Their summarized content, however, was entirely congruent with Scripture and contained nothing that could not be found in Scripture itself. And so the early church regarded such "a normative over-view as 'apostolic' and as the standard to which appeal was to be made when controversy about the content or interpretation of scripture arose" (Young, *Making of the Creeds*, 9). Both points, derivation and congruence, are captured by Martin Chemnitz: "For there is no doubt that the primitive church received from the Apostles and from apostolic men, not only the text (as we say) of the Scriptures, but also its legitimate and natural interpretation" (*Examination of the Council of Trent* [St. Louis: Concordia, 1971] I, 244).

What might be said of the earliest rules of faith and perhaps even of the Apostles' Creed cannot be said with reference to the sixteenth-century Lutheran confessions, from the Augustana to the Formula of Concord. Without exception, the confessors claim to draw their doctrine from the fountains of Scripture itself (*SD, R&N*, 1, 3, 10). The Augsburg Confession concludes on the note that the confessors are ready to present further information on the basis of Scripture (*AC* 28). The Formula of Concord pledges itself to the same Augsburg Confession "because it is taken from the Word of God and solidly and well grounded therein" (*R&N, 5*).

9. I will use the following abbreviations in this chapter: *AC* (Augsburg Confession); *Ap* (Apology); *FC* (Formula of Concord); *SD* (Solid Declaration); *Ep* (Epitome); *R&N* (Rule and Norm). All quotations from these documents are taken from Theodore G. Tappert, ed., *The Book of Concord* (Philadelphia: Fortress Press, 1959).

10. Alister McGrath, *The Mystery of the Cross* (Grand Rapids, Mich.: Zondervan, 1988), 52.

11. This recognition of postmodernism has provided one of the more incisive criticisms of modernity's attempt to circumvent any and all tradition in order to obtain a purely objective and assumptionless reading.

12. See Paul Raabe's essay (chapter 11 of this book).

13. This would seem to be a particularly important issue in light of the oft-quoted statement that Lutherans subscribe to the doctrinal conclusions of the confessions, but not the specific exegesis. Arthur Carl Piepkorn said of the confessions, "We are not bound to the exegesis of any particular passage which they choose to interpret" ("Suggested Principles for a Hermeneutics of the Lutheran Symbols," *Concordia Theological Monthly* 29 [January 1958], 20). This cannot be taken to mean that it is unimportant in order to determine "how" the confessors arrived at their doctrinal conclusions. If all of the specifics of their exegesis may come in for occasional criticism, the general

principles that they used for arriving at their doctrine become all the more important.

14. This metaphor was originally suggested by Carl Braaten. Unfortunately, he does not develop its potential. While acknowledging its usefulness as a metaphor, Braaten seems to perceive some lack of congruence between the map and the territory that it represents, as if the map had been drawn up by amateur cartographers. This emerges in his insistence that we take the map with us in order to see if it corresponds to reality. See Carl E. Braaten, "The Confessional Principle," in *Principles of Lutheran Theology* (Philadelphia: Fortress Press, 1983), 27-42.

15. See Raabe (chapter 11 of this book).

16. Quoted in Martin Chemnitz, *Examination of the Council of Trent*, vol. 1, (St. Louis: Concordia, 1986), 245.

17. Stanley Grenz, *Theology for the Community* (Grand Rapids, Mich.: Eerdmans, 2000).

2

Sources of Lutheran Dogmatics:
Addressing Contemporary Issues
with the Historic Christian Faith

J. A. O. Preus III

The topic that has been assigned to me is "Sources of Lutheran Dogmatics." But there are at least two ways of identifying sources. We could talk about sources of content, and we could talk about sources of form. Perhaps we could speak in terms of substance and style—what we say and how we say it. I have chosen to address the latter; I will leave the other question to my colleague, Richard Muller, who is much more qualified to deal with the more substantive issues. What he writes concerning Reformed sources finds strong correspondence also among Lutherans.

So, I will speak on the topic, "Sources of Lutheran Dogmatics," with the subtitle, "Addressing Contemporary Issues with the Historic Christian Faith." And I will ask, not only what do our sources say, but also how do they go about saying it?

INTRODUCTION: RECOVERING A CONFESSIONAL IDENTITY

The Lutheran Church today lives and works in an increasingly pluralistic world. Unlike the nineteenth and much of the twentieth centuries, when we found ourselves dealing almost exclusively with other Christian traditions (first Protestants and later Roman Catholics), we now function in the midst of a mind-numbing array of religious options. These range from other world religions (such as Islam, Judaism, and Buddhism) to New Age religiosity and sectarian spirituality. In the midst of this cacophony of competing voices, Christians are becoming increasingly eclectic in their religious faith and piety. At the same time, they are identifying less and less with the theological position of any particular tradition or denomination. This "post-denominational" spirit results further in a de-emphasis on any particular and specific truth claim. People are increasingly cutting themselves off from their history, from what has theologically defined them. To put it bluntly, people today, even in our own churches, don't know and don't care about their own theological tradition. They will simply believe what they find desirable.

A pluralistic culture brings to the forefront the question of the identity of a particular tradition. And, contrary to what many people today think, the matter of identity, namely, "Who are we?" is an important one because, more than anything else, a church's identity shapes not only its present but its future as well. If we do not know who we are, we do not know where we are going, what we are all about, what we stand for. My mother suffered from Alzheimer's disease. Before it ended her life it robbed her of her past, which in turn took away her present. She could not remember who she was because she could not remember her past. Because she could not remember her past, she could not discover her purpose for the present, and she was cut off from her rightful future.

What is our Reformation identity? Historically for Lutherans, it has been defined by ecumenical creeds and confessions as deposited in the Book of Concord. These constitute our confessional heritage. They shape our mission. They provide the norm and touchstone for our faith (what we believe) and our life (the shape of our worship and piety). The Book of Concord sets forth our theological position as well as our theological agenda by making the gospel the alpha and omega for all that we say and do. As Lutherans, we are proud of the doctrine of the confessions, most of all because at the center of it all stands the doctrine of the gospel. We believe that, as true expositions of Scripture, the confessions give all glory to Christ and full comfort to sinners. We proclaim them in a loving and kind way, inviting others to join us in confessing these beautiful articles of faith.

If we wish to be confessional, we must guard against two extreme and equally pernicious positions: *non-confessionalism* and *hyper-con-fessionalism.* Some of us appear to be somewhat embarrassed about our confessions, even at times refusing to go by the name "Lutheran." The same could be said, I am sure, in Reformed, Presbyterian, or Baptist churches. Some seem to be embarrassed about the doctrine of the confessions, feeling it to be a hindrance to church growth. Perhaps they are reacting to the way in which some have wrongly used the confessions as an excuse for not engaging in outreach. Perhaps they are reacting to the content of the confessions itself. Either way, this view cannot be tolerated. It will spell the end of confessional Lutheran theology. Ironically, and tragically, it will only serve to promote some other theology, some "confession" other than Lutheran, which will not be an improvement but rather, ultimately, a loss of the beautiful gospel for which our confessions stand.

At other times, the term *confessional* has come to denote little more than a label for a particular political position. Much mischief has also gone on in the name of "confessionalism." At times it has come to be little more than a label to be used for "putting someone in their place," or to provide an escape from actually listening to what a person is saying. A great deal of unkindness and judgmentalism has gone on under the label "confessional." But there is nothing confessional about meanness of spirit. There is nothing confessional about party loyalty. There is nothing confessional about labeling people unfairly on the basis of a simplistic caricaturing of their viewpoints. In fact, these very activities and attitudes disqualify one from the title *confessional,* for they stand in opposition to everything the confessions stand for and are a glaring contradiction to our Lutheran symbols. It merely adds insult to injury that these anti-confessional attitudes parade themselves falsely under the guise of confessional.

Ironically, the "a-confessionalist" and "hyper-confessionalist" positions share one thing in common: Neither engages in an in-depth exegetical, historical, and theological study of the confessions. Neither consistently uses the confessions as guides for solving the challenges facing the church today. Obviously, both of these extremes must be avoided. Both, ultimately, sell out our confessions. Both end in tragedy.

The Lutheran confessions, with their center in the gospel and their pastoral priorities on the comfort of sinners, provide an excellent model for engaging in theological discourse in our times. We must strive to be neither a-confessional nor hyper-confessionalist, but confessing and confessional Lutherans for our times. It is especially at this point that we need to take a fresh look at our confessional heritage. The Book of Concord has historically normed and shaped our theological positions and priorities. Less obviously but no less importantly, the Book of Concord also shapes a Lutheran mind-set and outlook by showing how we should go about dealing with the questions and issues raised in our own day. Thus, being faithful to the confessions not only involves faithfulness to their theological content in all their articles but also faithfulness to their spirit. This includes matters of theological method, which in turn guides us as we develop positions on issues facing us today.

1. The Development of Deep Theological Thinking

A distinctively Lutheran confessional approach to the theological task finds its definitive expression in the Formula of Concord. In many ways, it is not only a Formula of Concord: It is also a formula *for* concord. That is, it provides an excellent model for dealing with theological controversies as well as for going about the task of doing theology in our day and age, just as it did in the sixteenth century. There are five ways in which the Formula of Concord can help us, not only to say what we say rightly, but also to say it well; that is, not only can it guide us in the content of our conversation—it can also guide us in the course of our discourse. Essential to such discourse is the development of deep theological thinking.

First, those who crafted the Formula focus on issues and not on personalities. They insist on dealing with others on the basis of the *status controversiae* (point at issue) rather than superficial labels or personal or political issues. In focusing on the issues, they do not adopt a simplistic or reductionistic approach. Rather, they recognize the complexities and nuances of a problem that require disciplined and deep theological thinking. They do not caricature positions; they present a fair-minded description of the opponent's position.

Second, the Formula of Concord highlights the importance of the issue at hand. It consciously avoids logomachies or arguing for the sake of arguing. It avoids useless or inappropriate contention. It avoids bickering about matters that are not at issue or are only marginally related to the issue at hand. Instead, when dealing with a given issue, the Formula shows how it affects the core of the church's proclamation—how it affects the preaching and hearing, the administering and receiving, of the gospel.

Third, the Formula sets forth the biblical truth, and in so doing avoids extreme positions on both sides of an issue. In particular, it rejects the approach that counters an error merely by stating the opposite position. Stating the opposite of an error can still be (and often is) error. This has been a particularly disturbing aspect of the various theological debates occurring in our circles. Unfortunately, many of us have fallen into the trap of countering a position we find wanting by putting forward a position that is the opposite. However, the Formula shows us that there never is and never will be a substitute for that difficult, narrow way of letting the Scriptures decide issues for us and, on that basis, formulating positions that stand against the extremes that tempt us on both sides.

Fourth, the Formula engages in biblical exegesis. The Formula's approach begins with a discussion of the biblical evidence and then proceeds to examine the tradition of the church. We would be wise if we would follow the Formula's pattern of always beginning our discussion with the biblical evidence, followed by an examination of the early church fathers, before proceeding to an examination of the various local traditions of our churches.

Fifth, and finally, the Formula affirms the catholicity of the confessional Lutheran church by self-consciously placing itself within the tradition of the wider, historic Christian theology. The Apology to the Augsburg Confession especially seeks to show how its doctrine stands in continuity with the theology of the early church. The confessors were throughout intent on refuting the charge of sectarianism. The

Catalog of Testimonies was appended to the Formula in order to show that its christology is in harmony with the historic Christian faith. This commitment tells us that it is neither prudent nor appropriate to engage in theological discourse without taking into account what the church has always, everywhere confessed. If we ever act as if we have a corner on the truth, or as if we are the teachers to whom the rest of the world must simply listen, we will be acting in a way that is less than wise and less than respectful.

We must be careful not to reduce our theology to a few catch-phrases, facile clichés, or superficial judgments. We must probe deeper into the complexities and profundities of theology, confident in what is clearly true but also aware of what is not so clear. While Scripture is clear, our own reality often is not so clear and often our error is that we interpret our reality poorly. This just as certainly ends us in error.

We must also avoid *ex post facto* justification for positions that have been determined by other than theological factors. Too often, our theology is neither informing nor shaping our practice. Instead, we often adopt a particular position that solves some practical problem or is the latest trend and then seek to find a biblical and theological justification for it—which all too often is strained and artificial.

There is far too much of a "party-spirit" mentality in our conversations, too much division and stereotyping. We need to learn to hear others, beyond what seminary they attended or what denomination they belong to. We need to learn to deal better with issues (*ad rem*). There is also far too much judgmentalism. We must never be content merely to be right (understood in an intellectualistic or rationalistic, that is, superficially doctrinal way) but we must strive to be right in the right way (i.e., truth in love). This is the full meaning of "orthodoxy": right teaching and right practice.

We can never be content with single-issue reductionism of any kind. As important as our intra-denominational issues are, we must not ignore those theological issues that confront the entire Christian church on earth. Without losing our theological focus, we must also address the broad sweep of current issues, not only in North America but in the whole world.

2. The Commitment to Serious Biblical Theology

Second, following the confessional pattern of theological discourse requires a commitment to serious biblical theology. Confessional Lutheran theology has always engaged in an in-depth study of the Bible through the use of the original languages and utilizing the best tools of the day. The key to addressing the problems of our times is to return to serious, thoughtful biblical theology. This is what the Lutheran movement was predicated upon in the beginning. This must be reasserted today. A confessional Lutheran study of the Bible is neither *fundamentalist* nor *radical* in approach.

Our approach to the Bible cannot be a fundamentalist "concordance" approach nor a pietistic emotive approach that focuses on one's feelings, giving short shrift to the text. I am speaking now as a member of the Lutheran Church—Missouri Synod. In my opinion, we haven't done enough to distinguish our approach to the Scriptures from that of the fundamentalists. For the last three decades we have largely defined ourselves in opposition to the "liberals" or the biblical critics. This needed to be done, and we must make no apologies for standing against what history has now shown to be a bankrupt and defunct system. We were right on this, and the new trends in biblical studies are now in the process of putting the last nails in the coffin of the old-style historical-critical method of biblical studies.

We did not, however, take great enough pains to distinguish ourselves from the fundamentalists and the mainstream evangelicals. Thus, we have found ourselves with some strange bed-fellows, all because, on the surface, we appeared to be saying the same things about the Bible. And we have had to pay a high price for this. We have run the risk of losing our center in the gospel of Jesus Christ and our focus on his means of grace. We have flirted with substituting the formal prinicple (Scripture) for the material principle (the gospel).

This shows itself, for example, in our unwarranted openness to the church growth movement, in our rush to cast off our traditional forms of worship, in our understanding of what worship is, in our very understanding of the church, and in many other ways. There is abroad in our synod an anti-sacramental mentality that is foreign to our

Lutheran theological core. It has even been said by some that the Lord's Supper is a hindrance to the growth of the church. This could only be said by someone who comes at the question from a very different theological perspective. It is time to reassert our gospel-centered, sacramental, incarnational, christocentric (not bibliocentric) theology, and to clearly distinguish ourselves from the fundamentalists.

At the same time, it is increasingly necessary to define ourselves in contrast to what commonly goes by the term "postmodernism" today. Of course, this term is used in many different ways. In general, however, it is used in reference to a cluster of assumptions or presuppositions about the nature of reality and about historical texts. It suggests, among other things, that texts (such as the Bible) do not have their own meaning, but that they await the meaning brought to the text by each individual reader.

While the Christian faith centers in a Person, we are also fundamentally people of a text. The Scriptures and their exposition in creeds and confessions remain the source and norm for what we teach and confess. Thus, we will need to face the a-historical challenge of postmodernism.

3. The Necessity of a Confessional, i.e., Historically Christian, Approach to Theology

Third, our commitment to the confessional pattern of theological dialogue necessitates an approach to theology that values its long history. We must learn to articulate and put into practice a substance and style that is genuinely confessional—that is, evangelical and catholic. The Lutheran confessions again provide a model for such an approach. The confessions were gospel-centered to the core. That gospel shaped their entire theology. At the same time, they had little interest in isolating themselves from the wider stream of Christian tradition. For them, the early church fathers were as much their spiritual ancestors and witnesses to the gospel (indeed, more so!) as they were for the Roman Catholics. The Apology of the Augsburg Confession is a virtual patrology of the early church. The writings of Martin Chemnitz, the chief author of the Formula of Concord, reveal an intimate familiarity with the issues, controversies, and theological writings of the entire church, past and present, East and West.

Today, we seem always to be pulled in two opposite directions. In our search for order and stability in the face of the incursions of mainstream evangelicalism, many of us today are looking to Rome and Constantinople. *There* is to be found, many hope, the antidote for the cultural accommodation characteristic of American evangelicalism. Those who lament our catholic (or non-American) tendencies would pull us toward Pasadena or Wall Street. What we need to learn is that the way to combat an error is not to espouse its opposite. The opposite of error is almost always also error. The way to combat error is by espousing what is true, not merely by proposing error's opposite.

A Lutheran confessional position toward other traditions involves *neither a refusal to hear nor an uncritical acceptance* of the truth claims of other Christians.

On the one hand, there are some among us who view the historic, highly liturgical churches with such great suspicion that they propose whatever is the opposite. They would pull us more toward Pasadena or even Wall Street. They promote a view of church and ministry that is clearly anthropocentric. They propound a view of the church that is non- or even anti-sacramental and anti-incarnational, instead suggesting that the church is fundamentally a psycho-sociological organism. For the sake of numbers, they pander to some of the basest instincts of sinful humans, even selling the gospel like a product and turning the church into a corporation modeled on the patterns of Madison Avenue. In their lust after the theology of glory, they are selling out the church, its liturgy, its sacraments, its gospel and, thus, giving in to the secularizing forces of modern America.

We have much in common with the Roman Catholic Church and the Eastern Orthodox churches, and we should not ignore what they may have to teach us, both in terms of growing churches (the Roman Catholic Church is the fastest-growing church in the world) and in terms of enduring under circumstances of opposition and persecution (e.g., the Russian Orthodox Church).

On the other hand, there are those among us who would pull us more toward Rome or Constantinople. The more their opponents call for contemporary worship, the more they insist on the "historic" liturgy. The more some promote the notion of "everyone a minister," the more they promote an extremely high view of the ministry (as if the way to combat a view of the ministry that is too low is to propose a view that is too high). The more "American" some become, the more German the others become. This approach has within it the seeds of destruction, for it ends up promoting the very things against which the Reformation of the sixteenth century rebelled.

4. The Need for Critical Appreciation of the Best of Contemporary Theological Thinking

In the fourth place, our confessional commitment requires that we develop a critical appreciation for the best of contemporary theological thinking. In our assessment of contemporary theological thinking, too often there is an undifferentiated, undiscriminating approach. Either we reject all new ways of thinking or speaking theologically out of hand, or we embrace all new ideas with open, uncritical arms. There must be a better way. In short, we must say yes and no to the truth claims of others: Yes to what is good and right and true; no to what is bad and false and untrue. It is not a question of saying one or the other, nor of adopting an all-or-nothing approach. Not one or the other, but both; this is the only proper approach. Which is worse? To say no to what is true or to say yes to what is false? Both are equally wrong for those who genuinely seek the truth.

Such an approach allows *neither naive openness nor hypercritical reaction.* Far too many today are too naive in their acceptance of the truth claims of others. Too often we allow ourselves to be misled by others' false notions because we are convinced that their motives are pure.

On the other hand, in our approach to contemporary theological claims, we must avoid a hypercriticism which assumes that if any idea is new it is, *ipso facto,* false. No one has a corner on truth. True, biblical ideas are also found, more often than many think, outside our own circles. Our task is to seek the truth wherever it can be found, even if it comes from the lips of those who may also, in other respects, hold ideas that are erroneous. What is true is true, even when spoken by an errorist. Our task is to seek and embrace the truth, wherever it is found. Furthermore, because the claims of others are constantly changing and, in fact, our world is constantly changing, it will not do merely to repristinate what other respected orthodox theologians have said in the past. Of course, we honor them and seek to know how they answered the claims of others in their day, but we also know that it will not be sufficient merely to repeat what they have said. Instead, building on their wisdom, we must speak anew and in new ways the eternal truth in this ever-changing world.

5. The Need for Fresh Theological Thinking

To meet the challenges of contemporary thinking, we need to cultivate the vision, creativity, and courage to articulate fresh, theologically informed answers to today's (and tomorrow's) questions. While the confessions drew heavily upon those who had gone before them, they also answered the questions of their day in the categories of their day with tremendous insight, freshness, and vitality. Lutheran confessional theology must thus lead neither to worn-out church-growth clichés nor to simplistic citation theology.

It is time for us to turn our intellectual and theological resources to answering today's challenges in a way that is uniquely confessional and gospel-centered. Too much borrowing from others promotes a kind of theological dependence which causes churchly paralysis. In addition, it runs the danger of encouraging a patchwork theology that lacks the integration the gospel provides.

At the same time, we can never be content merely to repeat what has already been said. Often, merely citing the fathers is a cover-up for laziness or sloppy thinking. Although what the fathers said provided guidance for the church of their day, and although it can provide a framework for responding to today's questions, merely to quote them comes off as stale. Furthermore, ignoring the historical situation in which they spoke, or in which we now speak, may actually distort their theological position.

6. The Obligation to Critically Evaluate American Culture

A sixth implication of a confessional approach to theological discourse is the obligation to critically evaluate our cultural context. Fresh theological thinking about contemporary issues also requires a fresh perspective on American culture. Writing from my own history, in many ways the Americanization of the Lutheran Church—Missouri Synod (LCMS) has not yet fully happened. We are still not entirely comfortable in our "new land." Perhaps this is good. Perhaps it is best not to become too comfortable in America. However, we can surely do a better job of living in America, of adopting a more positive yet at the same time more critical stance vis-à-vis our American culture. Such a stance involves neither uncritical acceptance nor wholesale rejection of American culture.

Many are too naive in their embrace of American culture. They are unaware of how they have allowed their cultural biases to affect, usually detrimentally, their view of the church. By doing so, they blur the necessary distinction between theology and culture, between the right- and left-hand kingdoms of God. They too easily allow a preemption of the church by the culture and thus compromise the church's ability to pass judgment upon the culture by proclaiming the Law, and to provide what only the church can provide by proclaiming the gospel. There is much to lose by such uncritical acceptance of American culture—everything, in fact.

At the same time, many among us see American culture as the Enemy. They tell us that what is "American" is per se inimical to Christianity. This, they say, is what's wrong with American evangelicalism: It is too American. They posture the church as a "little flock" standing against the world, against the incursion of American individualism, or democratism, or commercialism, or deism, and so forth. Their view is that whatever is American is at all costs to be avoided. And, of course, there is much in American culture that is contrary to Christian faith. Often, however, these assertions are made by people who are not always as alert to their own cultural biases as they claim to be. If it is negative to be too "American," how is it better to be too German or British or Scandinavian?

7. The Commitment to Concern for Broader (Global) Issues

A seventh application of the confessional pattern of theological discourse involves a commitment to concern for the broader, that is, global issues of our time. This disallows parochialisms of any extreme.

One often gets the impression that the LCMS has its own "hot buttons," its own peculiar issues, which concern no one else in the world. This is undoubtedly true of other denominations as well. While we can't deny the importance of those issues that are our own, we also need to raise our gaze above what's going on in our congregations, as if our understanding of the church were exhausted by what is happening on the corner of Fifth and Walnut Streets. These concerns continue to vex us and they must be faced.

At the same time, there are huge, global issues of which we remain ignorant and even unconcerned. We have barely paid attention to the challenges brought by a veritable paradigm shift in the philosophy of language, by the claims of postmodernism, by the debate raging in the world about the uniqueness and universality of Christ, by the landmark work being done on the doctrine of the Trinity, by the shift to post-colonialist approaches to missions—and many more such challenges. We must avoid becoming parochial and thus irrelevant. We have too much to contribute to these debates to keep ourselves ghettoed off to the side, dealing merely with our own peculiar issues.

8. Developing Theologically Informed Practice

Finally, being faithful to our confessional commitments requires that we develop a theologically informed practice. There is great confusion today concerning the relationship between theology and practice. Some see no connection; others see no difference. Both are wrong. There is an inseparable connection, but a crucial distinction, between theology and practice. The key is to honor their connection while valuing their difference. This means that we must allow neither anti-theological pragmatism nor the refusal to acknowledge *adiaphora*—things neither commanded nor forbidden in Scripture.

On the one hand, there are those who fail to see the intimate connection between doctrine and practice, imagining that some practices are theologically neutral. They think substance and style can be separated. This is foolishness. This kind of a-theological—even sometimes anti-theological—pragmatism has led to much mischief in the church. Some have even come to believe that doctrine is a hindrance to the growth of the church. How can this be? Cut off from what drives all practice (that is, some sort of theological or philosophical presuppositions), error is almost inevitable, as countless examples from history clearly show. This is a serious problem in our church and it must be addressed.

On the other hand, there are some who can see no difference between theology and practice. They virtually deny the possibility of *adiaphora*. For them, everything is a matter of conscience, on which, of course, there can be no compromise. Like legalists, they demand complete conformity both in doctrine and in practice. They allow no differences, no diversity of practice, no possibility of regional variations in practice.

In fact, of course, there is a great difference between theology and practice, and it is a grave error to fail to acknowledge this. There is a difference, first of all, in that people do not always "practice what they preach," that is, they are inconsistent with their beliefs. This, of course, is wrong, but it is not false doctrine. Secondly, and more importantly, we must maintain a difference between theology and practice because it is simply a fact that true doctrine can result in different practices, according to circumstances. This is not to say that there are no false practices; there are practices that contradict theology and thus are false. But it is also true that a true doctrine can result in a diversity of true practices, as the history of the church, through all its diverse times and places, shows.

Our Reformation confessions provide us not only with the substance of our confession but also with its form. They tell us not only what to say but how to say it. For this reason, our confessions do double duty as sources for Lutheran dogmatics. They give us the content of our conversation and the course of our discourse. This is the measure of our orthodoxy: that we can say what is right, rightly.

3

Sources of Reformed Orthodoxy:
The Symmetrical Unity of
Exegesis and Synthesis

Richard A. Muller

A part from any doctrinally or theologically motivated claims about the excellencies (or deficiencies) of the dogmatics of Protestant orthodoxy, there is overwhelming historical warrant for the assumption that a proper understanding of the development of post-Reformation theology is of paramount importance to the formulation of Protestant theology in the present. The theological development that we call Protestant orthodoxy is, from a historical perspective, the codification and institutionalization of the Reformation. This older dogmatics is the theological result of the interpretation of the Reformation (typically in terms of its confessional bounds) by its immediate heirs.

During the era of orthodoxy (the late sixteenth and seventeenth centuries) Protestant theology was framed both positively and negatively against the background of both distant and recent theological tradition. On the one hand, many of the exegetical insights, doctrinal formulae, polemical arguments, philosophical assumptions, and methodological directions of Protestant orthodoxy arose out of positive elements in medieval and Renaissance thought that carried through the Reformation and were appropriated directly by late-sixteenth-century Reformed theologians. On the other hand, continuing protest against the ecclesiastical abuses and the exegetical and doctrinal problems of the later Middle Ages, together with continuing doctrinal strife with an unreformed Roman Catholicism, bore fruit in large-scale theological systems such as the Reformers did not themselves produce. Whatever one concludes about the quality and continuing value of the Protestant orthodox theologies, one must recognize that they set the form of Protestant doctrinal system in a fullness and detail available nowhere else. Beyond this historical datum, however, lies the ecclesial question of the suitability, the balance, and the faithfulness of this theology. We look, here, to the sources and materials of Reformed orthodoxy in order to note its relevance, as a body of doctrines and definitions and also as a methodological model, to the church of the twenty-first century.

Of course, much has been said in the last two centuries concerning the deficits of this orthodox theology. Protestant orthodoxy, in general, has been declared "rigid," "dry," and "dead." Reformed orthodoxy in particular has been accused of being "speculative" and "metaphysical," "decretal," "predestinarian," and "legalistic." It is said to deduce entire systems of theology from the central dogma of an eternal divine decree—and to draw its principles entirely from Aristotle. It is called by turns "biblicistic" and "proof-texting," or "rationalistic" and "philosophical." Now, certainly, no theology can be all of these things at the same time, in the same place, and in the same way. In fact, a closer look at the literature of the critique makes it clear that much of the recourse to history and, specifically, to the examination of late-sixteenth- and seventeenth-century intellectual history on the part of modern theologians has been part of an attempt to detach the theology of the immediate heirs of the Reformers from the theology of the Reformation and, then, once the rift is assumed, to claim the Reformers as the forerunners of modernity. This approach has been typical of neo-orthodox theologies, particularly among the followers of Karl Barth, and it has been typical of studies of the history of biblical interpretation.[1]

During the past two decades, historians have reexamined the Reformed orthodox materials from several perspectives: notably, from the perspective of the problem of "central dogmas" in theology; from the perspective of the declared "grounds" or *principia* of the older orthodoxy; and from the perspective of its theological method (namely, the "scholasticism" of the late Renaissance).[2] When examined in terms of the problem of central dogmas (and, I might add, so-called "formal" and "material" principles of Protestantism), the older orthodoxy simply does not oblige the categories—which are largely nineteenth-century in origin. When examined from the perspective of its own stated *principia*—namely, Scripture (the cognitive principium) and God (the essential principium)—the older orthodoxy evidences patterns that are, again, not sympathetic to the claims of its modern theological critics: Specifically, it is not primarily philosophical or rationalistic; it is not fundamentally deductive (whether one looks to predestination, justification, or the person of Christ as the central pivot); nor is it biblicistic and proof-texting in the sense alleged (i.e., it does not arbitrarily extract texts from the Bible for use as the basis of propositional claims unrelated to the original context of the verse in Scripture); nor, indeed, does its "scholasticism" imply either a return to medieval models or a particular theological or philosophical content. The claims made by the modern theologians are either utterly wrong and undocumentable or they are simplistic in the extreme.

What I plan to do here is to add another dimension to the discussion—the dimension of the sources, the very rich and diverse sources of Reformed orthodoxy. When we move past the problems of central dogmas, principia, and the method of this theology to the issue of its actual sources, we come to a conclusion similar to those reached in the other just-mentioned revisionist analyses: Simply stated, the Reformed orthodox theology of the late sixteenth and seventeenth centuries is far too rich and variegated in its sources and in its use of those sources to oblige the rather simplistic claims of the modern theological critics—namely, that it is dry, rigid, dead, deductive, speculative, metaphysical, decretal, predestinarian, legalistic, Aristotelian, biblicistic, proof-texting, rationalistic, and philosophical. For the sake of clarity, I will examine a series of sources in an order that relates to their relative level of normativity and, with each source, comment as specifically as I can in the space allotted on how it was used and integrated into the larger whole of theological thought. Thus, I will examine: 1) Scripture, exegesis, and ancillary disciplines; 2) the ancient creeds and the confessions of the Reformed churches; 3) the church fathers; 4) the theological tradition generally, including the medieval doctors and the Reformers; and 5) the philosophical tradition and reason, specified as logic, rhetoric, and their methodological applications. As a final issue—I hesitate to call it a "source," for both historical and theological reasons—I will note the relationship between systematic or dogmatic theology and practice in the era of Reformed orthodoxy.

I. SCRIPTURE, EXEGESIS, AND ANCILLARY DISCIPLINES

Contrary to much of the "received wisdom" concerning the seventeenth century,[3] the era of orthodoxy was a time of great exegetical, textual, and linguistic development in Protestantism—and, indeed, it was the orthodox exegetes who were responsible for the major monuments to biblical scholarship. One need only mention such vast efforts as Buxtorf's *Tiberias*; the translations of Tremellius, Junius, and Polanus; Weemse's *Christian Synagogue*; Walton's *London Polyglot Bible*; Castell's *Lexicon heptaglotton*; Pearson's *Critici sacri*; and Poole's *Synopsis criticorum* to gain a sense of the magnitude of seventeenth-century efforts to analyze both the text and language of Scripture and the tradition of biblical exegesis.[4] Beyond this, it is no difficult matter to show the intimate relationship between the most detailed exegesis of the age and the development of Reformed orthodox theological systems.

Several specific illustrations of the scope of orthodox-era exegesis are in order. First, the *Annotationes in Novum Testamentum* of the much-maligned and misunderstood Theodore Beza. From the perspective of the age and, most probably from Beza's own perspective, this was his chief work. The *Annotationes* evidence that Beza was as much a proponent of the philological methods of Renaissance humanism as he was an heir of the Reformed theology of Calvin, Vermigli, and others. On the one hand, the *Annotationes* are by far the most sophisticated effort of the age to establish the text of the New Testament and to translate it accurately—while, on the other hand, they are a remarkably finely tooled statement of the exegetical basis of Reformed theology. Beza examined the best codices of the day and then proceeded to analyze the critically emended Greek text over against extant translations—notably the Vulgate, Erasmus, and even Calvin—in order to argue his own conclusions and produce a superior Latin translation. Then, on the basis of his philological and exegetical conclusions, he offered a running annotation on the text. One can get a partial glimpse of both of these aspects of the work by examining the New Testament of the Geneva Bible, which combines accurate translation of the Greek text and marginal interpretations, based largely on Beza's efforts.[5] One can also see the effects of his exegetical work in both the exegesis and the theology of the next several generations of Reformed orthodoxy.

Second, attention can be drawn to the exegetical model proposed by Andrew Willet.[6] Willet's method, identified as "hexapla" in the titles of nearly all of his commentaries, was distinguished by its "six-fold" approach to a text.[7] Willet began with an "Analysis," "Method," or "Logicall resolution," corresponding to the "argument" placed by many sixteenth- and seventeenth-century commentators at the beginnings of chapters. This he followed with "the Genesis or Grammaticall construction where the translations differ," namely, a verse by verse synopsis of the differences between extant translations, noting all of the variant renderings of the Hebrew together with additions found in the ancient versions. Willet's third section, "the Exegesis, or theologicall explication of doubtfull questions and obscure places," is constructed as a series of questions and answers, sometimes quite lengthy. Here, Willet resolves issues of textual variants and various translations by comparison with other biblical texts and with citations found in the church fathers, in rabbinic commentators, and in various ancient and modern translators. The fourth section, "the didactica" or "places of doctrine observed out of [the] chapter" follows the *locus* method of exegesis found in the works of earlier Reformed exegetes such as Bucer, Musculus, and Zanchi by offering positive theological statement of the topics related to the text. The fifth section, "places of confutation," handles theological debates relating to these *loci* (Willet thus not only understands doctrinal theology to be grounded in exegesis, he also models for his readers the movement from exegesis to doctrinal statement). Willet's sixth and final section, "the places of exhortation and comfort," moves his exposition from exegesis of text to homiletical application in a series of moral and spiritual observations on the text.

It is at this point that the criticism of "proof-texting" also falls flat: The theologians of the seventeenth century certainly did accompany virtually all of their doctrinal formulations, even at the level of finely grained propositions on minute points of doctrine, with a battery of citations from Scripture. Yet, when one follows out their citations to the biblical commentaries of the day, one finds that their citations do not represent texts torn out of context but, rather, their citations point toward what one can only call the "assured results" of the best exegetical methods of the age. Indeed, what the reader finds is a close cooperation between the theologian and the exegete, with the theological affirmation of Scripture as final norm of theology worked out in practice as a use not merely of biblical texts but of detailed exegesis in the original languages of Scripture as the basis for doctrinal formulation.[8]

Of course we must remember that none of the theologians of the sixteenth or seventeenth centuries built (or even intended to build) new theologies on the basis of their own exegesis. From its very beginnings, the Reformation assumed its catholicity over against the abuses and dogmatic accretions of late-medieval Roman Christianity. In other words, the Reformers and their successors understood their theology to stand in continuity with the great tradition of the church, particularly with the theology of the ecumenical councils, the church fathers, and the "sounder" of the medieval doctors. Scripture was certainly the prior norm for theology on the basis of which all other norms were to be judged, including the ecumenical creeds and the fathers. Nonetheless, the orthodox theologies of the Reformation and post-Reformation eras accepted the larger part of the Christian exegetical and dogmatic tradition—and rather than reinvent theological system, they reshaped it in terms of the Reformation insights. We therefore pass on to the subordinate norms and sources of Protestant theology.

2. The Ancient Creeds and the Confessions of the Reformed Churches

The ancient creeds, namely, the Apostles', the Nicene, and the Athanasian, plus the decision of the Council of Ephesus and the formula of Chalcedon, were consistent guides for the Reformed orthodox in their identification of fundamental teachings of the faith, in the establishment of a foundation for catechesis (here the Apostles' Creed is of course most prominent), and in their formulation of the doctrines of the Trinity and of the Person of Christ. As theologians of both of the great Protestant confessions recognized in their less-polemical moments, these boundaries were consistently observed on both sides—Reformed and Lutheran—and their differences, however substantial, went beyond the basic definitions: In virtually all of their colloquies, the dogmatic standards of the ancient creeds provided a point of initial agreement.

Beyond the creeds, and marking the specific doctrinal boundaries, are the confessions of the Reformed churches. The Reformed confessions took on, early in the sixteenth century, the appearance of systematic overviews of the faith. Unlike the Lutheran confessions, which tended to be organized around the main points of Reformation-era dispute, the Reformed confessional documents tended to begin with a doctrine of Scripture, to proceed through the basic body of theological topics, and to conclude with the doctrines of church, sacraments, and the last things. Nor are the Reformed confessions less than forthcoming in identifying adversaries of the faith. The relatively irenic Second Helvetic Confession condemns the "peculiar opinions" of the Anabaptists as "against the Word of God," noting specifically the "Jewish dreams" of Anabaptist millennialism.[9] The Heidelberg Catechism identifies the Mass as "nothing else than a denial of the one sacrifice and passion of Jesus Christ and an accursed idolatry."[10] The Belgic Confession indicates that "we detest the error of the Anabaptists . . . who reject the higher powers and magistrates."[11] And the Gallican Confession condemns "the papal assemblies, inasmuch as the pure Word of God is banished from them, their sacraments are corrupted, . . . and all superstitions and idolatries are in them."[12] And, of

course, the confessions uniformly uphold the ancient orthodoxy of the
ecumenical creeds in their condemnation of the archetypal heresies—
Arianism, Manicheeism, Marcionism, Nestorianism, Eutychianism,
and so forth.

The creeds and confessions, therefore, provide by way of affirmation and condemnation both a positive and a negative background
for Reformed dogmatics. There are, of course, numerous theological
systems or synopses of doctrine (some in the form of sermons) from
the era of orthodoxy that take either the Apostles' Creed or one of the
confessions or catechisms as their point of departure: thus, Perkins's
Exposition of the Symbole or Creede of the Apostles; Witsius's
Exposition of the Creed; Ursinus's, Bastingius's, Voetius's,
Groenewegen's, Leydekker's, and VanderKemp's expositions of the
Heidelberg Catechism; and Ridgley's commentary on the Westminster
Larger Catechism, to name just a few. Beyond these overtly confessional efforts, moreover, the large-scale dogmatic projects of the day
were consistently conceived within the creedal and confessional
boundaries—not out of undue deference to these secondary authorities but on the assumption that these churchly standards had been
framed and tested by the study of Scripture and were, therefore, sound
guides to the limits of theological formulation.

3. The Church Fathers

Although in the past it was a little-studied field, an increasing number
of scholars are beginning to examine the ways in which the Protestant
theologians of the sixteenth and seventeenth centuries appropriated
the patristic materials as sources for their theology.[13] These sources
were of profound importance to the Protestant orthodox—as wit-
nessed, among other things, by the numerous gatherings of patristic
materials and editions of church fathers printed during the period and,
indeed, by the invention of the term "patrology" by the eminent
Lutheran theologian Johann Gerhard.[14] On the Reformed side,
Gerhard's work was preceded by the *Medulla theologiae patrum* of
Abraham Scultetus.[15] In form, Scultetus and Gerhard adumbrate the
modern patrology: They offer a brief explanatory prologue on the life

of an author, a list of his works, and an analysis of their contents. It is worth dwelling on the fact that Gerhard was able to identify and name the specific discipline of "patrology" and to write a massive study of the fathers that was organized very much like modern patrologies, not because he was a uniquely creative individual in this field but rather because this field of study had so prospered among Protestants that it could, by Gerhard's time, be perspicuously organized and named as a distinct field of study.

This interest in the fathers does not mean, of course, that the heirs of the Reformation yielded under the pressure of Roman Catholic polemic and accepted tradition as a norm of faith alongside Scripture. Rather, they followed the lead of the Reformers themselves (and, in fact, of a host of medieval predecessors) in identifying Scripture as the sole absolute norm for theology and the church fathers as a subordinate norm or guide,[16] continually to be measured against the results of biblical exegesis. The Protestant orthodox use of the church fathers must be understood as the direct outgrowth of the great Reformers' assumption that the Reformation was the catholic church, that Rome had fallen away, and that the best of the tradition not only could be appropriated by, but belonged by right to, the Reformation and its descendants.

It was typical for Reformed and Lutheran theologians to begin their attempts at rapprochement in colloquy with appeals to their common stance on the Niceno-Constantinopolitan and Chalcedonian formulae and their mutual respect for and reliance on the tradition of patristic orthodoxy. So too was it typical for each side in these debates to frame what they viewed as problematic in the other's theology as grounded on patristic heresy. Thus Lutherans identified the Reformed as "Nestorians" and the Reformed returned the favor by calling the Lutherans "Eutychian."

Perhaps more important than these mutual recriminations was the profound effort of both sides of this debate to frame their respective christologies and their doctrine of the Trinity over against the clearly heretical theories of the Socinians—and, in so doing, to identify their own positive relationship to the normative development of patristic christological and trinitarian thinking beyond a simple affirmation of the ecumenical creeds. The Socinians, those exegetically-grounded ancestors of the Unitarians, were consistently, with good warrant, identified as "Arians." And, of course, it was quite typical of the Reformed to identify their synergistic opponents, whether Roman Catholic or Arminian, as "Pelagians" or, if precise terminology was necessary, "Pelagianizers."

4. The Theological Tradition Generally, Including the Medieval Doctors and the Reformers

It was also characteristic of the era of Protestant orthodoxy that the theologians, whether of the Reformed or of the Lutheran confessions, became masters of the great tradition of the Western church. They were not, in other words, sectarian theologians who blindly grasped onto Scripture as an exclusive basis for all theological insight and then proceeded to trust their own exegetical intuitions—nor were they blind followers and slavish imitators—*epigoni*, as they are often called—of the great Reformers. Rather, in the tradition of the Reformers, these successor theologians took the catholicity of Protestantism seriously, claimed for themselves and their churches the best of the Christian tradition, and appropriated it critically, for the clarification and for the defense of the faith.

Modern critics of seventeenth-century Reformed theology often point out how seldom Calvin's name is cited as an authority. Of course, a careful perusal of the writings of seventeenth-century Reformed orthodox writers does in fact yield a fair number of citations of the writings of Calvin, not only of the *Institutes*, which continued to be printed in multiple editions throughout the century, but also of his commentaries and of his many tracts and treatises. So, too, do the seventeenth-century writers cite other Reformed predecessors, notably Vermigli, Zanchi, and Beza. Nonetheless, it is true that the citations of these significant forebears are not found with the density that twentieth-century theological hagiographers might hope for. Reformed orthodoxy was, after all, the theology of a living church and not merely a carbon copy of the thought of the Reformers. But what we can declare, with some confidence, is that the developing tradition of

Reformed theology in the seventeenth century paid close attention to its roots in the Reformation and was concerned as it encountered new adversaries and new problems—such as the detailed anti-trinitarian exegesis of the Socinians, the denials of divine simplicity and eternity by Vorstius and the Socinians, and the pelagianizing "middle knowledge" theory of the Jesuits and Arminians—to maintain the teachings of the Reformers in increasingly detailed forms.[17]

To this end, the Reformed orthodox also drew on the medieval tradition. Exemplifying the positive use of medieval materials, the Genevan-trained Lambert Daneau wrote a Reformed commentary on the first book of Lombard's *Sententiarum libri quatuor*. Daneau also drew on the thinkers identified by Calvin and other Reformers as *saniores scholastici*—sounder or more trustworthy scholastics—such as Lombard, Aquinas, Bonaventure, and Durandus, to build his own system of theology. Franciscus Junius of Leiden wrote the first major prolegomenon to theology, adapting the categories of the medieval scholastics to Reformed doctrine in order to identify the meaning of the term *theology,* the genus of the discipline, its proper object, and its goal or direction.

Proofs of God's existence also entered the Reformed systems, probably by way of the later editions of Melanchthon's influential *Loci Communes Theologici.* What is important to note here is the development of patterns of argument: While the Reformed theologians of the orthodox era often drew on the causal, cosmological, and teleological models of Thomas Aquinas's "five ways," they also tended to follow patterns of Renaissance logic and to develop the proofs discursively. In addition, given the impact of Renaissance rhetoric on Protestant thought, it is not surprising to find a blending of the logical and the rhetorical, the strictly demonstrative with the more persuasive forms of the arguments. It is typical, in other words, for the Reformed orthodox to mount the proofs in order to persuade atheists of the truth of Christian theism, and to draw on rhetorical forms such as the argument *e consensu gentium* (the common agreement of the heathen), rather than to design the proofs as a foundation for theological system.[18]

By way of example of the defensive and polemical use of the past, in the face of Jesuit, Arminian, and Socinian advocacy of a so-called divine "middle knowledge"—a divine knowledge of future contingents and counterfactuals prior to and outside of the divine willing—Reformed theologians drew on the medieval and late-Renaissance scholasticism of various Thomist, Scotist, and Augustinian thinkers, noting the traditional distinction of God's knowledge into the necessary knowledge of God's self and of all possibilities and the free or voluntary knowledge that God had concerning all actuality. This division of the topic, noted the Reformed orthodox, was exhaustive and necessarily the only division.

5. THE PHILOSOPHICAL TRADITION AND REASON, SPECIFIED AS LOGIC, RHETORIC, AND THEIR METHODOLOGICAL APPLICATIONS

In the era of orthodoxy, albeit to a lesser extent than in the early stages of the Reformation, Reformed theologians remained wary of the wholesale adoption of any particular philosophy. This wariness extended especially to the new philosophies of the day, most notably the philosophies of Descartes and Spinoza. The Reformed orthodox readily perceived that Descartes' principle of radical doubt and his subsequent deduction of an entire philosophy (including the existence of God) from his own self-consciousness was not only contrary to their biblical and confessional norms but was also fundamentally absurd. Spinoza's philosophical monism was condemned as a dangerous form of atheism. With reference to both Cartesian and Spinozistic philosophy, the Reformed condemned the unbridled use of reason as an ultimate norm for the elicitation of truth concerning God, the world, and human destiny. Descartes' philosophy had to be used eclectically—and Spinoza's was utterly rejected.[19]

Of course, Descartes' approach to the physical universe was viewed by the orthodox not only as inimical to biblical truth but also as in violation of the fundamental rule that, whereas logical conclusions are drawn by deduction from general principles, conclusions concerning the physical order must be made by induction from direct examination of particulars. And this point leads us ineluctably to the issue of what, for lack of a better term, must be called "Christian

Aristotelianism." The standard philosophical models and tools used by the seventeenth-century orthodox belonged to the tradition of modified Aristotelianism that had its beginnings in the thirteenth century.

It is important to recognize what this use entailed and what it did not. The Christian Aristotelianism of the Protestant orthodox drew on rules of logic and devices such as the fourfold causality in order to explain and develop their doctrinal formulae—and only seldom, if ever, to import a full-scale rational metaphysics or physics into their theology.[20] Contrary to what is sometimes claimed, the fourfold causality (i.e., first, formal, material, and final causes) does not imply a particular metaphysic. Specifically, it is not by nature "deterministic." One can use the model to delineate the soteriological patterns of the eternal decree of God and its execution in time; one can also use the model to describe the sources and effects of human sinfulness and human moral conduct; or one can use the model to explain how a carpenter makes a table. The large-scale result of Christian Aristotelianism was not, in other words, a fundamentally Aristotelian Christianity: Aristotle would have disowned this hybrid philosophy with its infinite God who created the world out of nothing![21] There was, certainly, less imposition of rational metaphysics on theology in the seventeenth-century orthodox affirmations of divine eternity, omniscience, and immutability than there is in the twentieth-century claims of a changing God whose very being is in flux and who lacks foreknowledge of future contingency!

6. THE RELATIONSHIP BETWEEN SYSTEMATIC OR DOGMATIC THEOLOGY AND PRACTICE

At the outset, I noted that the issue of this final section could not properly be included among the "sources" of Reformed orthodox theology. After all, every one of the stated norms and grounds for the formulation of orthodox Protestant dogmatics consists of objectively given doctrinal or methodological principles, whether Scripture as the ultimate norm, or the confessions and tradition as subordinate norms, or philosophy and logic as ancillary and methodological tools. Nonetheless, the life, piety, and practice of the

church did relate directly to dogmatic theology in the era of orthodoxy. Virtually all of the theologians of the era understood the discipline of theology either as a mixed "speculative" and "practical"
discipline or, indeed, as a purely practical discipline.[22] What they
meant by the inclusion of the term *praxis* in their definitions was that
the entire discipline of theology was goal-directed: Theology, understood as a *praxis* or practical discipline, was directed toward the goal
of human salvation. More specifically, each doctrine taught in the
theological systems of the day (not merely, for example, the doctrine
of God, but each individual divine attribute; not merely the doctrine
of the last things, but each sub-category of the doctrine) was to be
known both for itself as a truth of God and for the sake of the goal
of salvation toward which it directed the human knower. Each
rightly understood (i.e., orthodox!) doctrine would have a direct
impact on piety, on the shaping of faith, on the shaping of Christian
life. The "practice of piety," to borrow the title of a great treatise of
the era, was not an objective source of theological system; yet it was
certainly a rule for the right conduct of theological system. In other
words, it was very clear to the Reformed orthodox that rightly formulated Christian doctrine would relate directly to the life of the
church and of the individual believer and, conversely, poorly or
wrongly formulated doctrine would not.

Not only, therefore, do we see in the era of orthodoxy a direct and
profound relationship between the formulation of doctrine and the
basic exegesis of the text of Scripture, but we also see a direct relationship between the formulation of doctrine and the life of the
church. If, in the normative pattern of theological work, exegesis was
intended to lead directly to the production of sermons, commentaries,
and theological formulations, so too the commentaries and the theological formulae of the full-scale systems were intended to lead the
exegetical result, through a rigorous process of interpretation and formulation, back to the life of the church both as a guide to right preaching and, like preaching itself, as a guide to Christian life. In this sense,
Christian life or "practice" did function among the sources of orthodox theology—at very least it was an index to the success or failure of
the work of the theologian.

CONCLUDING REMARKS

An examination of the sources of Reformed orthodoxy (and, we might add, of Protestant orthodoxy in general) easily and clearly sets aside the stereotypes of this theology. At the very least, the standard claims about central dogmas, legalism, rationalism, and proof-texting biblicism fail because they are simplistic. How simple and, indeed, simpleminded it would be to deduce a theology from one principle; and by contrast, how complex it in fact is to construct that theology out of exegetical arguments nuanced by extensive knowledge of the biblical and cognate languages, attention to the exegetical tradition, and acknowledgment of the significance of creeds, confessions, and the wealth of the tradition. How equally simple it would be to give one's theology over to an "ism"—whether legalism, rationalism, or Aristotelianism; and by contrast, how complex it is in fact to balance out a wide variety of issues, sub-themes, and ancillary sources, to develop a critical perspective on the philosophical tradition that modifies it at crucial points, and to retain the rationality of exposition without ever allowing reason to have principial status. Would that the modern theologies that criticize this older orthodoxy were able to match its expertise in the many theological disciplines! Would that they were able to understand (and master) as clearly and well the hierarchy of sources, with Scripture as ultimate norm, followed by ecumenical creeds, churchly confessions, the wealth of the tradition, and the various ancillary disciplines in a descending order of authority!

We do Protestant orthodoxy a profound historical injustice when we examine it through the tinted glasses of a modern "ism" (like Barthianism or so-called "neo-Reformed theology") that itself all too quickly and easily falls before the criticism of holding a central dogma, of failing to do substantive exegesis on its own or of failing to rely on the exegetical tradition, of refusing the authority of churchly confessions, and of falling prey to a particular philosophical perspective. (Barth's epistemology is more thoroughly subservient to Kant than any Reformed orthodox epistemology was bound by Aristotle.) When we ask, however, the historical question of continuity and development, as illustrated by the present discussion of sources, we find that the standards and principles of the Reformed orthodox remained in continuity with those of the Reformers—and we find, also, that the doctrinal formulations of the Reformed orthodox stood consciously in continuity both with the Reformation and with the tradition of Christian orthodoxy that reached from the patristic era through the Middle Ages. The orthodox writers' use of sources was specifically intended to maintain this orthodoxy in and for their own time.

The final question to be addressed is, of course, one in which historians seldom engage: namely, the question of the importance and usefulness of this Reformed orthodoxy for the present day. I do not intend to play at being a systematic theologian; but I do wish to observe, if only by way of comparison, that few if any modern theologians can claim a comparable grasp of Scripture, biblical languages, confessional norms, the great tradition of Christian meditation, and a coherent method, logic, and use of philosophical categories. Nor can many modern theologians—at least among those well known in our time—claim to bear, in as finely tuned a theology, the standard of orthodoxy both ecumenical and confessional born consistently by the theologians of the late sixteenth and seventeenth centuries.

On the one hand, I fully recognize that a great seventeenth-century theology, such as Francis Turretin's *Institutes of Elenctic Theology*,[23] cannot be directly imported into the twentieth century for use in a classroom. In the first place, Turretin's *Institutes* is a polemical system that does not claim to offer a "positive" exposition of doctrine: Many of its adversaries are long-dead and largely forgotten, and it does not address a whole series of new issues that need to be addressed by theologians in a post-Kantian world that claims also to be "postmodern." Second, Turretin's *Institutes* uses in detail a largely neglected theological vocabulary with which most students and many professors are unacquainted. On the other hand, I am compelled to note that the often-heard comment—that this older theology fails to speak to the modern world and needs to be "translated" into a form relevant to the church—also falls short of the mark. The somewhat archaic sound of a seventeenth-century theology, whether of a continental Reformed theologian in translation or of a Puritan writer in the original English, is hardly more distant from piety and the pulpit than the often-involuted language of a Barth, a Pannenberg, a Moltmann, or a Torrance.

Given that technical theology (whether of the seventeenth or twentieth century) always demands study and, for the sake of its use as a framework for piety and preaching, some "translation" into the living vernacular, the question arises as to which theology, that of the seventeenth or that of the twentieth century, provides the better basis for interpreting the sense of Scripture, for constructing a functional language about God, for thinking and teaching within the context of a confessing church, for addressing the great issues of the identity and the work of Jesus Christ, the problem of sin, and the gift of salvation. The answer becomes quite simple, if only because of the diversity of modern theology in its desire for newness of expression and its frequent refusal to speak the language either of Scripture or of the church.

The "sources of Reformed orthodoxy" are the same today as they were in the seventeenth century—which is to say, a theology that intends in the twentieth century to be both Reformed and orthodox must hold Scripture as its ultimate norm and must take with utter seriousness the task of biblical exegesis—indeed, it ought to cultivate as close a relationship between theological formulation and the best of churchly exegesis as was realized in the era of orthodoxy. It must hold the creeds and confessions of the church as secondary norms, given that they summarize the wisdom of the church in interpreting Scripture and provide salutary boundaries for the roving mind of the theologian. So also must it take with utter seriousness the tradition of the church as the place where the task of formulating doctrine has been done and where the nature of faithful and unfaithful formulation has been clearly delineated. As the older orthodoxy demonstrates, whether in the creeds and confessions or in the broader interpretive tradition, the church must provide the context for theological meditation and formulation unless our theology is prepared (as is the case with much modern theology) to be useless to the church. Individual imagination or vision is simply not a suitable criterion for doctrinal formulation. Even so, theology today can draw a lesson from the way in which the seventeenth century received a tradition of philosophy and logic and, in addition, a tradition of regarding philosophy as a tool or instrument rather than as a fundamental principle of knowing. And finally, theology today can also learn the pattern of faithful movement from Scripture to theology, preaching, and piety that maintained the distinction between these forms of expression but consistently assumed that their ongoing relationship was necessary to the integrity of each form. This balance of and faithfulness to its sources is surely the heart of the lesson that seventeenth-century orthodox Reformed theology holds for the church in the present age.

Notes

1. Cf., e.g., Alister McGrath, *Reformation Thought: An Introduction,* 2d edn. (Grand Rapids, Mich.: Baker, 1993), 129-30; James B. Torrance, "Strengths and Weaknesses of the Westminster Theology," in Alasdair Heron, ed., *The Westminster Confession in the Church Today* (Edinburgh: St. Andrew, 1982), 40-53; idem, "Calvin and Puritanism in England and Scotland—Some Basic Concepts in the Development of 'Federal Theology,'" in *Calvinus Reformator* (Potchefstroom, South Africa: Potchefstroom University for Christian Higher Education, 1982), 264-77; Frederic W. Farrar, *History of Interpretation* (New York: Dutton, 1886; reprint Grand Rapids, Mich.: Baker, 1961); *The Cambridge History of the Bible,* 3 vols., P. R. Ackroyd, C. F. Evans, G. W. H. Lampe, and S. L. Greenslade, eds. (Cambridge: Cambridge University Press, 1963-70).

2. For a summary of arguments and literature, see Richard A. Muller, "Calvin and the Calvinists: Assessing Continuities and Discontinuities Between the Reformation and Orthodoxy, Part I," in *Calvin Theological Journal* 30, no. 2 (November 1995): 345-75; "Part II," in *Calvin Theological Journal* 31, no. 1 (April 1996): 125-60.

3. Thus, Farrar, *History of Interpretation;* Basil Hall, "Biblical Scholarship: Editions and Commentaries," in *Cambridge History of the Bible,* III (Cambridge, England: Cambridge University Press, 1963–1970), 38-93; and Norman Sykes, "The Religion of Protestants," in ibid, 175-198. One has the distinct impression when reading these essays that none of the authors troubled himself to look at any commentaries of the era.

4. See, e.g., Stephen G. Burnett, *From Christian Hebraism to Jewish Studies: Johannes Buxtorf (1564–1629) and Hebrew Learning in the Seventeenth Century* (Leiden, Netherlands, and New York: E. J. Brill, 1996); Peter T. van Rooden, *Theology, Biblical Scholarship and Rabbinical Studies in the Seventeenth Century: Constantijn L'Empereur (1591–1648), Professor of Hebrew and Theology at Leiden,* trans. J. C. Grayson (Leiden, Netherlands: E. J. Brill, 1989); Jai Sung Shim, *Biblical Hermeneutics and Hebraism in the Early Seventeenth Century as Reflected in the Work of John Weemse (1579–1636)* (Ph.D. dissertation, Calvin Theological Seminary, 1998).

5. See Irena Backus, *The Reformed Roots of the English New Testament: The*

Influence of Theodore Beza on the English New Testament (Pittsburgh, Pa.: Pickwick Press, 1980); Marvin Anderson, "The Geneva (Tomson/Junius) New Testament Among Other English Bibles of the Period," in Gerald T. Sheppard, ed., *The Geneva Bible: The Annotated New Testament,* 1602 edn. (New York: Pilgrim, 1989), 5-17.

6. See Peter William van Kleek, "Hermeneutics and Theology in the Seventeenth Century: The Contribution of Andrew Willet" (Th.M. thesis, Calvin Theological Seminary, 1998).

7. E.g., Andrew Willet, *Hexapla in Genesin* (Cambridge, 1605; 2d edn., enlarged, 1608); *Hexapla in Exodum* (London, 1608); *Hexapla in Leviticum* (London, 1631); *Hexapla in Danielem* (Cambridge, 1610); and *Hexapla: That is, a Six Fold Commentarie upon the Epistle to the Romans* (Cambridge, 1620).

8. Cf. the discussion in Richard A. Muller, *Post-Reformation Reformed Dogmatics. II. Holy Scripture: the Cognitive Foundation of Theology* (Grand Rapids, Mich.: Baker, 1993), 525-540.

9. Second Helvetic Confession, xx.5; xi.14.

10. Heidelberg Catechism, q. 80.

11. Belgic Confession, xxxvi.

12. Gallican Confession, xxviii.

13. See, e.g.: Peter Fraenkel, *Testimonia Patrum: The Function of Patristic Argument in the Theology of Philip Melanchthon* (Geneva: Droz, 1961); E. P. Meijering, *Melanchthon and Patristic Thought: The Doctrines of Christ, Grace, the Trinity, and Creation* (Leiden, Netherlands: E. J. Brill, 1983); Luchesius Smits, *Saint-Augustine dans l'oeuvre de Jean Calvin,* 2 vols. (Assen: Van Gorcum, 1957–58); further, Manfred Schultze, "Martin Luther and the Church Fathers," in Irena Backus, ed., *The Reception of the Church Fathers in the West: From the Carolingians to the Maurists,* 2 vols. (Leiden, Netherlands: E. J. Brill, 1997), II, 573-626; Irena Backus, "Ulrich Zwingli, Martin Bucer, and the Church Fathers," in ibid., 627-660; Johannes van Oort, "John Calvin and the Church Fathers," in ibid., 661-700; Irena Backus, "The Fathers in Calvinist Orthodoxy: Patristic Scholarship," in ibid., 839-866; E. P. Meijering, "The Fathers in Calvinist Orthodoxy: Systematic Theology," in ibid., 867-88. Also see G. L. C. Frank, "A Lutheran Turned Eastward: The Use of the Greek Fathers in the Eucharistic Theology of Martin Chemnitz," in *St. Vladimir's Theological Quarterly* 26 (1982), 155-171; and Robert A. Kelly, "Tradition and Innovation: The Use of Theodoret's *Eranistes* in Martin Chemnitz' *De duabus naturis in Christo,*" in Marguerite Shuster and Richard A. Muller, eds., *Perspectives on Christology: Essays in Honor of Paul K. Jewett* (Grand Rapids, Mich.: Zondervan, 1991), 105-125.

14. Thus, Johann Gerhard, *Patrologia, sive de primitivae ecclesiae christianae doctores vita ac lucubrationibus* (Jena, 1653); cf. Johannes Quasten, *Patrology,* 4 vols. (Utrecht: Spectrum; reprint Westminster, Md.: Christian Classics, 1950–86), I, 1.

15. Abraham Scultetus, *Medulla theologiae patrum in quo theologia priscorum primitivae ecclesiae doctorum* . . . (Amberg, 1598).

16. Cf. Friedrich Kropatscheck, *Das Schriftprinzip der lutherischen Kirche. Geschichte und dogmatische Untersuchungen. I. Die vorgeschichte. Das Erbe des Mittelalters* (Leipzig: Deichert, 1904) with Paul de Vooght, *Les Sources de la doctrine chrétienne d'après les théologiens du XIVe siècle et du début du XVe* (Paris: Desclée, 1954), idem, "Le rapport écriture-tradition d'après saint Thomas d'Aquin et les théologiens du XIII siècle," in *Istina* 8 (1962): 499-510, and Muller, *Post-Reformation Reformed Dogmatics, II*, 1-50.

17. On Arminius's Molinism, see: Eef Dekker, "Was Arminius a Molinist?" in *Sixteenth Century Journal* 27, no. 2 (1996): 337-352; idem, *Rijker dan Midas: Vrijheid, genade en predestinatie in de theologie van Jacobus Arminius, 1559–1609* (Zoetermeer, Netherlands: Boekencentrum, 1993); and Richard A. Muller, *God, Creation and Providence in the Thought of Jacob Arminius: Sources and Directions of Scholastic Protestantism in the Era of Early Orthodoxy* (Grand Rapids, Mich.: Baker, 1991), 154-166.

18. See John Platt, *Reformed Thought and Scholasticism: The Arguments for the Existence of God in Dutch Theology, 1575–1650* (Leiden, Netherlands: E. J. Brill, 1982).

19. Cf. Michael Heyd, "From a Rationalist Theology to a Cartesian Voluntarism: David Derodon and Jean-Robert Chouet," in *Journal of the History of Ideas* 40 (1979): 527-542 with Maria-Cristina Pitassi, "Un manuscrit genevois du XVIIIe siècle: la 'Refutation du système de Spinosa par Mr. Turrettini,'" in *Nederlands Archief voor Kerkgeschiedenis* 68 (1988): 180-212.

20. Cf. Martin I. Klauber, "The Use of Philosophy in the Theology of Johannes Maccovius (1578–1644)," in *Calvin Theological Journal* 30, no. 2 (1995): 376-391 with Lynne Courter Boughton, "Supralapsarianism and the Role of Metaphysics in Sixteenth-Century Reformed Theology," in *Westminster Theological Journal* 48, no. 1 (Spring 1986), 63-96.

21. See, at greater length, Richard A. Muller, "Scholasticism, Reformation, Orthodoxy and the Persistence of Christian Aristotelianism," in *Trinity Journal* n.s. 9 (1998): 81-96; in response to Ronald N. Frost, "Aristotle's *Ethics*: The *Real* Reason for Luther's Reformation," in *Trinity Journal* n.s. 8 (1997): 223-241.

22. Richard A. Muller, *Post-Reformation Reformed Dogmatics. I. Prolegomena* (Grand Rapids, Mich.: Baker, 1987), 215-226.

23. Franciscus Turretinus, *Institutio theologiae elencticae*, 3 vols. (Geneva, 1679–85; new edition, Edinburgh, 1847); now available as *Institutes of Elenctic Theology*, 3 vols., trans. George Musgrave Giger, ed. James T. Dennison, Jr. (Phillipsburg, N.J.: Presbyterian and Reformed, 1992–97).

PART TWO
CHALLENGES

4

A Defense of a Postmodern Use of the Bible

Edgar V. McKnight

As a Christian and as a New Testament scholar I am vitally interested in the question of how one does theology in any conventional sense in light of the contemporary revolution in biblical studies, a revolution set in the context of a "postmodern" era. How does one speak of God? How does one deal with dogma? Indeed, my sabbatical project for the 1995–96 school year at the University of Muenster was entitled, "Theology and the Contemporary Revolution in Biblical Studies." In my proposal to Fulbright, I pointed out that theology and conventional academic study of the Bible have proceeded along different and often divergent paths, especially over the past two centuries. Theology has usually constructed systems in conformity with theological and philosophical assumptions, or has sought timeless truths or the essence of things. Biblical study, meantime, has dealt with theological questions secondhand, distancing the text for objective study and dealing with matters amenable to critical and historical analysis. A hiatus developed between theology and biblical studies. Now a literary turn is taking place in biblical study. This turn is taking place at the same time that literary study has entered into a post-new-critical phase in which readers have become an essential ingredient in literature, vital in its "actualization," and texts have become capable of a multiplicity of "actualizations." Recent developments in literary study may be seen as a move from a "modern" concern with epistemological questions to a "postmodern" concern with worlds projected by texts. Because the postmodern turn eschews the attempt to ground the world objectively, the turn in literary studies has to do with imaginative and constructive descriptions of an infinite number of personal worlds.

It would seem that a postmodern turn would bring an end to theology. I would suggest, however, that a fresh examination of the status and practice of theology in light of a literary paradigm might enable us to re-envision theology and the use of the Bible in theology. Before I report on my wider project and sabbatical findings, I must do two things. First, I must admit that my sabbatical project came to be centered on the single question of christology. The title of the work begun in the sabbatical became *Jesus Christ in History and Scripture: A Poetic and Sectarian Perspective.*[1] But more importantly, I must attempt to correlate my agenda with the agenda of the Alliance of Confessing Evangelicals.

The first question is, How serious can confessing evangelicals be about engaging postmodernism? Immediately after Dr. Horton contacted me about the colloquium, I began to "surf the web" to learn more about the Alliance and how the Alliance might possibly relate to what is called a postmodern mentality. Very quickly I found the Alliance home page and read the September–October 1995 issue of *Modern Reformation* magazine, which dealt with postmodernism. Instead of a simplistic condemnation or commendation of postmodernism, I found an evenhanded evaluation of what the new philosophical worldview might mean. One writer sees "a new set of challenges and temptations for biblical Christians," but he also sees that "the postmodern age . . . presents untold opportunities for recovering the historic Christian faith."[2] Another writer cites Stephen Toulmin's book *Cosmopolis* and examines four areas mentioned by Toulmin where "considering the values of postmodernism will be a worthy endeavor." The writer suggests that in these areas the shift away from modern values to postmodern values "involves returning to medieval and pre-enlightenment (read 'Reformation') values."[3] When I read those essays, I felt that my agenda would not be at odds with the agenda of this colloquium, indeed that I would learn by sharing your agenda.

The next question has to do with my academic and theological location. This needs to be made clear so that you can account for and/or discount some of my comments. As I indicated to Dr. Horton in our initial conversation, there is a family resemblance between my location and that of confessing evangelicals; but there is a historical difference as well, because I come out of a tradition that was not part of the fundamentalist-modernist debates of the beginning of this century. Baptists in the South were isolated from the acids of modernity that spewed upon the theological and religious world of the late nineteenth and early twentieth centuries. By the time those debates touched Baptists in the South, they were so numerous that they did not need to belong to the developing evangelical movement that grew out of the controversy. Our agenda, then, was not exactly the agenda of organized evangelical groups. Instead of seeing myself essentially as part of an evangelical movement of this century, desiring to remain faithful to Calvin and Luther and their protest against the Roman Catholic ecclesiastical system, I see myself as part of a radical reformation movement desiring to push the reformation of Calvin and Luther beyond Calvin and Luther.[4]

Is it possible that, from a position beyond the mainline Reformers, the mainline Reformers can be most fully appreciated? Could a radical reformation mentality recoup the theological and doctrinal tradition of the reformation and even the abiding values of the Catholic traditions? That may be essentially the same question as whether Reformation theology can be done from a postmodern location.

In the remainder of the paper, I plan to circle around the question of postmodern biblical study and postmodern theology: 1) I will begin by sketching a reader-oriented postmodern use of the Bible that is not nihilistic but is properly skeptical about final scientific and philosophical foundations; 2) then I will provide a framework for appreciating the dialectic between an absolutized foundationalism existing outside of time, place, and history, and a radical contextual contingency and life world; 3) that dialectical approach will be fleshed out in terms of a non-foundationalist circular poetic and sectarian approach, and 4) the major circles that coexist and form a dynamic relational system or nexus will be examined from today's perspective; 5) as we come to some conclusions and consequences of such a sys-

tem, I will deal with the nature and function of the Bible in such a view;
6) finally, I will attempt to bring all of this to a focus by speaking of
metacritical schemata (not foundations) that provide direction to biblical study and theological construction.

1. A READER-ORIENTED POSTMODERN USE OF THE BIBLE

In my *Postmodern Use of the Bible*,[5] I contrasted a postmodern use
with a modern use and compared my suggestions about a postmodern use with Harry Emerson Fosdick's classic volume, *The Modern
Use of the Bible*.[6] The critical distancing of the text in the historical
approach gradually transformed biblical writings into museum pieces
without contemporary relevance. My book was designed for those
who had become less and less satisfied with the meanings that historical criticism was capable of discerning. The postmodern perspective
that I presented was that of a reader-oriented literary criticism, a criticism that views literature in terms of readers and their values, attitudes, and responses. A radical reader-oriented criticism is postmodern
in that it challenges the critical assumption that a disinterested reader
can approach a text objectively and obtain verifiable knowledge by
applying certain scientific strategies. A radical reader-oriented
approach sees the strategies, the criteria for criticism and verification,
the "information" obtained by the process, and the use made of such
"information" in light of the reader. The reader is no more
autonomous than the text in postmodernism; the reader and the text
are interdependent. The text is actualized by the reader in such a fashion that the text may be said to actualize the reader.[7]

In *Postmodern Use of the Bible*, I gave the most attention to a contemporary poetic or creative use of the language of the Bible. I contrasted an earlier poetic use of language with a later descriptive use of
language, and both of these with a contemporary poetic use. In a first
poetic stage, the articulation of words was able to bring into being the
power common to subject and object. These words of power were not
to be argued about but were to be accepted and pondered, their power
absorbed by a disciple or reader. With a second phase, beginning with
Plato, words became primarily the outward expression of inner

thoughts or ideas. Interpretation was governed by the Platonic idealistic view. The Bible was understood and interpreted within the same Platonic worldview as other literature. Acceptable meanings were confined to dogmatic statements. The Bible and the dogma of the church could be set side by side and found to be saying the same thing by means of strategies of typology and allegory. In the modern form of the descriptive phase of language, a form that we somewhat intuitively take to be normative, the meaning sought is governed by the worldview emphasized in science and mathematics. The critical study of the Bible emphasizes statements that can be made consistent with various critical approaches by means of historical, critical, and/or theological strategies. The need for a conceptual language satisfying to the modern person reflects the worldview of the descriptive stage.[8]

In *Postmodern Use of the Bible*, I suggested that there is a dialectical relationship between the modern and the postmodern, the critical and the postcritical. A postmodern approach is not a premodern approach. A postmodern approach exists only in dialogue with modern or critical assumptions and approaches. The appreciation of the Bible as poetic, then, does not mean we return to a pre-critical or uncritical period. We are in a contemporary poetic stage, after having experienced (and continuing to experience) the descriptive stage of language. We remain entangled with the critical, even though it is relativized. I suggested that interpretation in a conceptual language satisfying to contemporary human beings, and appreciation of the Bible as literature, may be related productively. One may move to interpretative in a conceptual language after experiencing the power of the Bible as language. On the other hand, one may come to the Bible as language and literature against the horizon of the conceptual language of dogma. But in a postmodern perspective, the conceptual language is related to an explanatory system that is quite different from that in a modern paradigm.

2. Contingent Life World and Explanatory System

Anthony Thiselton's book *New Horizons in Hermeneutics*[9] states very clearly the contemporary form of the conflict of paradigms of idealism and realism going back to Plato and Aristotle.[10] The contemporary form, of course, is created by the loss of the ideal of some absolutized foundationalism outside of time, place, and history. Some scholars in the new situation emphasize contextual contingency and historical situatedness. Others continue to emphasize explanatory system. Thiselton combines the two when he speaks of the desire for an open system in which both life world (i.e., experience in this time and place) and explanatory system are provisional. The problem for Thiselton is the "possibility of an open system in which neither contingent life world nor explanatory system has the last word, but contribute to some interactive whole."[11]

In *New Horizons in Hermeneutics,* Thiselton indicates the breadth of his interests by means of a three-fold wordplay. First, reading produces effects upon readers that may enlarge the horizon of readers. The reading of biblical texts, therefore, "can become eventful as transforming biblical reading."[12] Second, new horizons have been opened in the development of hermeneutics as an interdisciplinary study over the past two decades. Thiselton cites in particular "the nature and goals of readers' interactions and engagements with texts" as part of the "revised agenda."[13] Hermeneutics may transform our notion of reading; transforming biblical reading may be one effect of hermeneutical inquiry. Third, the book attempts to open new horizons moving beyond those already established within the discipline of hermeneutics. Thiselton suggests that a metacritical level of reflection accompanies the transformation of biblical reading. According to Thiselton there are three levels of critical reflection: pre-critical, critical, and metacritical. At the pre-critical level, a reader reads texts rather than engaging consciously in the task of interpretation. The reader is mastered by the text. At the critical level, the result of engaged reading is submitted to critical evaluation. The text is mastered by the critic as the critic scrutinizes the text as an object of inquiry. The critic creates distance from the text and from this distance is able to answer questions about how the text works. These two levels are essentially the poetic and the critical. The metacritical evaluation is the process of submitting the critical program of criticism to a yet higher level of critical evaluation. Thiselton describes not only this metacritical level but also a renewed poetic use of the Bible. (He does not correlate these in a circular hermeneutics, as I do.) One aspect of a postcritical or postmodern paradigm is the awareness that paradigms exist, that different worldviews provide the lens through which we see everything. In order to appreciate the impact of this awareness we are being forced to think on a metacritical level. We must think about thinking and knowing, but not from the perspective that we can arrive at the certainty provided either by revelation or by enlightenment rationality. The ideal of objectivity has been replaced with the concept of perspective. Objectivity is an illusion, but total subjectivity is not the only alternative; perspective is a more useful concept. No one focus of observation ever gives a complete picture, so the concept of reality itself is altered when movement is made from objective to perspective. A shift is made from "the absolute" to a plurality of kinds of knowing, and from "right" method toward a multiplicity of methods.

The new vision is a sort of symbiosis. Elements evolve and change together, affecting each other in such a way as to make the distinction between cause and effect meaningless. The diversity, openness, complexity, mutual causality, and indeterminacy of a postmodern paradigm are ingredients for qualitative change, while the earlier mechanistic paradigm is more or less static, viewing matter as driven by a mechanistic force in a totally determined manner. Peter Schwartz and James Ogilvy have spoken of this overall change of pattern as one "from reality as a machine toward reality as a conscious organism." Machines are relatively simple mechanical instruments, but conscious beings are very complex and unpredictable. The world we see is like the human beings we are.[14]

This move toward humanization is an important move. Instead of reducing human beings to older models of the nature sciences, the sciences are being re-envisioned from the perspective of the human world. Foundations for knowledge (to use modern terminology) are being sought that are more basic than the scientific theories and procedures of any one or all of the sciences—foundations are sought in human relations and actions.

The contingent and unpredictable life world and explanatory scientific and philosophical system seem to be diametrically opposed.

They seem to cancel each other out. So how can they coexist and contribute to some interactive whole? They are indeed opposed as explanatory systems have been developed and refined on this side of the Enlightenment—at least one reading of the Enlightenment.

In the essays I mentioned earlier, contained in the September–October 1995 issue of *Modern Reformation* magazine, the work of Stephen Toulmin is cited. According to Toulmin, the modern mentality that cannot abide the lack of certainty is the result of a certain telling of the story of the Enlightenment. In that telling, humanity in the seventeenth century "set aside all doubts and ambiguities about its capacity to achieve its goals here on Earth, and in historical time, rather than deferring human fulfillment to an Afterlife in Eternity—that was what made the project of Modernity 'rational' and this optimism led to major advances not just in natural science but in moral, political, and social thought as well."[15] The story as seen from the end of the twentieth century and the beginning of the twenty-first century is more ambiguous. Toulmin declares that, "in choosing as the goals of Modernity an intellectual and practical agenda that set aside the tolerant, skeptical attitude of the 16th century humanists, and focused on the 17th century pursuit of mathematical exactitude and logical rigor, intellectual certainty and moral purity, Europe set itself on a cultural and political road that has led both to its most striking technical successes and to its deepest human failures."[16]

Toulmin distinguishes two phases of the development of the modern world and modern culture. The first phase was literary or humanistic and involved "respect for the rational possibility of human experience" and "delicate feeling for the limits of human experience."[17] In theology or philosophy during this first phase of development, "you may (with due intellectual modesty) adopt as personal working positions the ideas of your inherited culture; but you cannot deny others the right to adopt different working positions for themselves, let alone pretend that your experience 'proves' the truth of one such set of opinions, and the necessary falsity of all the others."[18] What was offered by sixteenth-century humanists was not proof or repetition of particular philosophical positions but rather "a new way of understanding human life and motifs." Sixteenth-century humanists "like Socrates long ago, and Wittgenstein in our own time, . . . taught readers to recognize how philosophical theories over-reached the limits of human rationality."[19]

The second phase of the development of modernity, according to Toulmin, was scientific and philosophical: "After 1600, the focus of intellectual attention turned away from the humane preoccupations of the late 16th century, and moved in directions more rigorous or even dogmatic, than the Renaissance writers pursued."[20] Toulmin suggests that the birth of modern philosophy and the exact sciences involved not simply a forward movement from the sixteenth century but also rejection of the values of the earlier humanistic scholars. Those earlier scholars were "committed to questions of abstract, universal theory, to the exclusion of . . . concrete issues. There is a shift from a style of philosophy that keeps equally in view issues of local, timebound practice, and universal, timeless theory, to one that accepts matters of universal, timeless theory as being entitled to an exclusive place on the agenda of 'philosophy'."[21]

3. A POETIC AND SECTARIAN APPROACH

I advocate a poetic and sectarian approach that attempts to correlate the local and universal, the time bound and the timeless. By sectarian, I have reference to the radical reformation. The radical reformers and their descendants may be compared and contrasted with the Catholic and Protestant scholasticism and rationalism prevailing in their day. In overly simplistic terms, the Roman Catholic reading of the Bible was constrained by the church as a known, extrinsic institution. The church was a foundational beginning and ending point. The Protestant reading was constrained by particular doctrines that served as foundational beginning and ending points. The radical reformers were concerned with both church and doctrine, but the way they saw themselves as church influenced their reading of the Bible and their concern for doctrine. They existed as church in the present. But that present Christian community was aware of itself as the primitive *and* the eschatological community. The Bible, then, had contemporary and not mere antiquarian relevance. The radical reformers were like the

Qumran community in that they read the Bible as referring to them and their lives in the present. They were like the Jesus of Luke's Gospel, who indicated that the Scripture just read in the synagogue in Nazareth "has been fulfilled in your hearing" (Luke 4:21, NRSV).

Doctrine was important to the radical reformation, but doctrine stood in relation to the life and practice of the church as primitive and eschatological community. A dialectical relationship existed between doctrine and practice, which meant that a doctrine satisfying at one time was unsatisfying at another. The "principle of fallibility" has been defined by the Baptist theologian James McClendon as a principle characteristic of the radical reformers. This means that "even one's most cherished and tenuously held convictions might be false and are in principle always subject to rejection, reformulation, improvement, or reformation."[22] The reading of Scripture has to do with faith and practice, and that faith and practice have essentially to do with mission, liberty, discipleship, and community. In the reading of the Bible and practice of biblical insights within the church, there is a tentativeness, a provisionality. The church is by nature provisional, subject to correction arising from further Bible reading. The church must change, for God is on the move, and the end is not yet.

The "poetic" perspective recognizes the creative contribution that readers of the Bible must make, the contribution that readers make in their reconstruction of Jesus, for example. Contemporary readers are not engaging in a foreign practice. They are recapitulating the creative activities of the early evangelists. But this poetic or creative activity seems to be strange and foreign because of our "modern" scientific approaches. We must, therefore, defend poetic approaches in the academy and in the church. In the book on Jesus that I mentioned earlier, I deal with the question of the church and the critical study of Jesus. I defend the historical-critical study of Jesus as engaged in by historical-critical scholars, but I declare that such study cannot be made the gatekeeper to all truth.[23]

The sort of historical study that makes Christian faith an essential factor is not a study recognized as historical by the world at large. I think that it is probably advisable for Christians to continue to engage in the sort of "skeptical" study that methodologically ignores the sacred in attempting to explain historical data. At the same time Christians need to emphasize that this sort of historical-critical study does not and cannot constitute the gatekeeper to all truth. The church, then, should engage in a historical study that is recognized as histori-cal-critical study by the academy. As the church engages in such study it cannot help but acknowledge to itself and to its fellow historians that, for it, history and the sacred cannot finally be divided (the sacred is not to be simply identified with the history of the world, but the sacred cannot be isolated from the world). If I were to attempt to take such a model and apply it to the study of theology in general and to the construction of dogma in particular, I would try to make the same sorts of distinctions. A distinction can be made—in principle, at any rate—between the theology that presupposes the truthfulness of the Christian religious convictions and assumes the task of clarifying what these convictions are and what they mean, and the critical sort of study that does not presuppose the truth of Christian faith. In a critical or a "modern" epoch, the first-order Christian theology must be accom-panied by a second-order theology that asks whether the claims of this first-order theology are in fact valid. When this sort of study is done, then, what counts are the conditions of truth that are established by the academy. So I see a parallel between a critical study of the Bible as data, and theology as a critical study of theological affirmations as data. But in both instances, we have discovered the limitations of our critical approaches. The historical-critical results will not form the gatekeeper for all truth concerning Jesus Christ, nor will second-level critical reflection on theology form the gatekeeper for a first-order the-ological enterprise.

How is the critical study related to the constructive study in a post-modern epoch? In my book on the study of Jesus, I emphasize that the church's engagement with political, social, cultural, and other this-worldly references in its reconstruction of the historical Jesus may be shaped in ways that impinge upon values that transcend those refer-ences, values that are more ultimate for the church. That is, we can tell the Jesus story as historians conscious of Christian affirmations about Jesus as the Christ, and conscious of the constraints (limitations and requirements) of historical reconstruction. The story of Jesus will be recorded in a way so as not to be inconsistent with the historical context of Jesus. What sorts of actions and teachings can be mapped with historical conviction from the world of Jesus to the life of Jesus? What can be understood from the human historical level that can at the same time be susceptible to transcendent realities?

In his study of Jesus, N. T. Wright lists five specific questions that guide the work of "third questors" (more-or-less traditional scholars who take a non-Bultmannian approach to the study of Jesus). These five questions are historical-critical sorts of questions that impinge upon the church's agenda: 1) How does Jesus fit into Judaism? 2) What was Jesus seeking to *do* within Judaism? 3) Why did Jesus die? 4) How and why did the early church begin? 5) Why are the Gospels what they are? Wright lists a sixth question that leads directly into christology: How is the Jesus we discover by doing history related to the contemporary church and world?[24] You can see that this approach is understandable to the historical-critical scholar—to Jewish scholars, secular scholars, and Christian believers—but it is quite different from the severely historical approach of Bultmann that sets up the criteria of authenticity for sayings of Jesus that result in very little that can be established as authentic.[25]

4. A CIRCLE OF CIRCLES

Let me go further to suggest how a particular theological perspective may serve as the horizon for the non-confessional critical enterprise and for other factors in a non-foundationalist hermeneutic. In place of a foundationalist theory of knowledge we may set a circular theory, whereby knowledge is justified in terms of the nexus of relevant factors, the relationship between the meaning-producing factors. Notice that I use the term *relationship*. Genuine meaning is determined in terms of relationship. Often the term *relative* is used in a pejorative sense. If we do not have a firm foundation, critics say, then everything is "relative" and anything goes. When I use the term *relative* or *relational*, I do not mean anything goes.

The circular or relational approach to meaning can be observed in the relationship of the meaning of a word to the meaning of the sentence in which the word is used. The meaning of the sentence depends on the meanings of the words. The meanings of the words, however, cannot be determined apart from the meaning of the sentence. There is a mutual "causality." But the sentence, in turn, is embedded in larger linguistic and literary units that determine the meaning of the sentence. And literature as a system is related to non-literary systems. So literature, philosophy, theology, are not only circular, but they consist of a circle of circles. Knowledge and philosophy and literature do not exist in a vacuum as they operate in this circular fashion. They exist in relation to life. Thought is not sovereign; it depends on the being of life and experience.[26]

A non-foundationalist, circular approach to the reading of the Bible and the theological task begins somewhere, and the beginning point is important. But the beginning point is not the foundation. Hidden behind that beginning point are "prior" "beginning points."[27] Instead of attempting to reconstruct a postmodern foundation, I suggest the appreciation and utilization of circles which hang together in an interlocking fashion and form a dynamic unity. Changes in one circle will affect other circles and the whole dynamic unity.

One circle is the circle of praxis, the practice of religion in terms of individual piety, congregational worship and service, and involvement in the larger world of God's creation. We are learning about this circle and the primacy of this circle from Third World Christians. They are teaching us that understanding of the Bible doesn't always move in a logical fashion from theory to praxis. Bernard Lategan has studied the interpretation of Romans 13 in the South African context, highlighting reading strategies affirming or resisting what appears to be a requirement of Christians to obey the state.[28] Some of the interpretations that Lategan studied were the work of groups of South African biblical scholars who had seen the effects of official practices of apartheid upon their fellow South Africans. They were concerned with the text of Romans that declares Christians are to be subject to governing authorities, because the Dutch Reformed Church had used that text to support the system of apartheid. The scholars, many of them Reformed, wanted to challenge the interpretation of the Dutch Reformed Church. They often organized their arguments in logical fashion, moving from questions of language, to questions of history, to questions of praxis. But in fact they began with praxis. They knew that apartheid was wrong and needed to be abolished. They began with praxis and developed theory adequate for praxis.

Doctrine is another circle. But this circle is dynamic in and of itself. A first-order task may be considered the teaching of Christian doctrine. The second-order task is the theological task of critically examining and revising that teaching. Different levels are involved in these tasks: biblical theology, systematic theology, and comparative theology, for example. As I have suggested, believers engage in the critical theological task, and that task is correlated with the teaching of doctrine. We cannot arrive at a foundation in the critical task. The results will be pragmatic, helpful for the construction of theology and doctrine. This seems to me to be an important point. The different ways in which scholars try to validate religion and theology are all partial. The classical patterns of exclusiveness and inclusiveness and the contemporary pluralistic patterns—phenomenalist pluralism, universalist pluralism, ethical pluralism, ontological pluralism, confessional pluralism—coexist with particular religions and confessions—even (or especially) confessions that make a claim for finality. In a postmodern epoch we construct some critical position as a heuristic structure, not to serve as an unassailable foundation but to help in the task of teaching doctrine.[29] We develop theory adequate for the praxis of teaching.

But we also move behind the teaching of doctrine to the practice of doctrine. Doctrine is not simply a matter of "getting it right" intellectually. Christian doctrine is intertwined with Bible reading and "the practice of doctrine." Jim McClendon means, by "practice," "a complex series of human actions involving definite practitioners who by these means and in accordance with these rules together seek the intended end." He uses the term *convictions* in his relating of Christian doctrines to practice. Convictions help us relate the critical task to the constructive task. According to McClendon, "convictions are not just beliefs or opinions, but are deeply self-involving. By coming to understand our convictions, we can come to know ourselves as we truly are. For our convictions show themselves not merely in our professions of belief or disbelief, but in all our attitudes and actions. Thus . . . convictions have an affective dimension, while . . . they also have cognitive content, and . . . they entail our intentions as well as our action."[30]

In the practice of doctrine, perhaps, some of the insoluble theoretical aspects of the theological enterprise are subsumed or transformed. At any rate, doctrine and theology are a dynamic circle involved implicitly or explicitly in the comprehensive system of hermeneutics.

From the Roman Catholic side, the New Testament scholar Sandra Schneiders has discussed doctrine or "faith affirmative" in relation to practice, faith, and intellectual insight. In her discussion of how the doctrines of creation and incarnation are related to their subject matter and other kinds of affirmations, Schneiders illustrates something of what Jim McClendon is talking about:

> To affirm that God *created* the universe is not to affirm that God performed the chronologically first act in the causal series that scientists call evolution. . . . To affirm creation is to live in a new world, a world one shares with the Creator. The affirmation of creation is not primarily an intellectual assent to a proposition about reality but a personal engagement characterized by humility, gratitude, reverence, and all those other qualities that define the properly religious attitude of the human being before God.[31]

The faith affirmation of the *Incarnation* is not a matter of reasoning logically from sayings and/or deeds of Jesus to Jesus' divinity. To affirm that Jesus is divine "is to profess having perceived in him something that could be but does not have to be perceived, namely, the definitive historical instance of the full coincidence between divine self-giving and human experience." In his words and deeds we experience Jesus as "disclosive of the self-giving God and therefore affirm his divinity."[32]

If one wishes to begin with the seminal doctrines of the Protestant Reformers, one may. But these doctrines will be correlated with a second level of critical evaluation and a prior level of doctrinal practice. It might be interesting to discuss what it means in practice to affirm the five "solas." This would not provide an argument against considering those important affirmations as dogmatic statements. But it would allow us to deal with the affirmations not in a foundational but in a dialectical fashion.

History and historical study and language and literature constitute circles that cannot be ignored in our era.[33] My work since the 1970s has been an attempt to advance the hermeneutical task through an appreciation of the New Testament as literature.[34] We move backward and forward to other circles from the experience of the Bible as literature. We may check our experience with data from these other circles. Does the language allow our reading? What about history and theology? We may relate the biblical material to our lives by retelling, by transformation into the various artistic forms, by preaching, or by fitting the Bible into theological conceptualizations. An inclusion of the literary circle into the hermeneutic circle of circles does fuller justice to the biblical text and its claims upon our lives intellectually, emotionally, and spiritually.

5. The Functions and Authority of the Bible from a Reader-Oriented Perspective

We will now consider the Bible and its functions and authority from the postmodern reader-oriented perspective—and from the perspective of the radical reformation. I would make participatory understanding (rather than reflexive and investigative thought) primary and then ask about the sorts of truth that are discovered in such participatory understanding.[35] The literary units of the Bible may be seen as growing out of, and expressing in fixed literary form, the historical experiences of the people of God. A reader-oriented literary approach to biblical texts allows modern-day readers to recapitulate the significance of these experiences. Through historical study we can do something with the circumstances of origin of the biblical texts and the historical circumstances of the transmission and alteration of the texts that allowed the significance of the texts to be appropriated by a succession of peoples. The historical facts depicted and the circumstances of origin and transmission uncovered *as such* do not really touch our lives, however. They remain historical data. Through our present-day appropriation of the literature growing out of the historical experiences of the people of God, however, we can experience the sacred. The New Testament text, for example, would be seen as an expression of the various sorts of experiences of the people of God brought into existence through Jesus Christ.[36] The Gospels as wholes and the various units of the Gospels, for example, grow out of and express in fixed written form and in appropriate refraction the historical experience of the church. This experience is an experience of the action of God, the Word of God. Historically, it may be seen in terms of the disciples' experience with Jesus, the primitive church's experience with the tradition and with the continuing act of God in ever new situations, the later evangelists' experiences in yet new contexts, the church in its existential formation and shaping of the material, and even canonization(s).

Schneiders, speaking of the New Testament as a "revelatory text" comparable with the sacrament of the Eucharist,[37] declares that,

> it is sacrament in the fully actualized sense of the word only when it is being read, when it is coming to event as meaning through interpretation. However, the book that preserves and localizes for us the possibility of such events of meaning and that stabilizes the meaning and so gives it continuity in the community is a symbolic object that is fittingly venerated so long as it plays its proper role in the context of the entire mystery.[38]

Schneiders is using a Roman Catholic conceptualization and vocabulary to affirm a radical-reformation appreciation of the Bible as an authoritative text overflowing with meaning, capable of matching the needs and capacities of different generations.

I emphasize in my writings not only the actualization of the text by the reader but also the actualization of the reader by the text. In the process of reading biblical literature, the reader is affected in the same way as are readers of all literature. When the readers allow themselves to appreciate the play of language, there is intellectual and emotional pleasure as readers are able to analyze and synthesize the text on the various levels. But biblical literature is more than the occasion for intellectual and emotional pleasure; biblical literature introduces a transcendent world, and the reader must enter into that world at least momentarily in order to appreciate the text. The world uncovered or revealed by the biblical text is a world that is not created or essentially sustained by human will and effort. It is a world properly spoken of as a given, or a gift, that parallels the world of the achievements of humankind. Those who see the world as essentially a human quest are jolted by the picture of the world as a gracious gift. The reader's world may not only be challenged by the world of the text; it may be changed. We call that conversion. The conversion I am interested in is not simply the call for decision in an evangelistic sense. It is not only personal and internal. It is a lifetime project, involving conversion on different levels. Bernard Lonergan speaks of the different dimensions of our human drive to achieve meaning: intellectual, moral, psychological, affective, sociopolitical. Different New Testament texts may address different dimensions of this drive. Lonergan speaks of conversion as the foundation for religion that is concrete, dynamic, personal, social, and historical.[39]

6. A Metacritical Biblical Schema

I will conclude by suggesting a metacritical biblical perspective that allows us to coordinate the various sorts of critical factors in interpretation with the various religious factors, a perspective that allows us to coordinate Scripture as literary and/or historical source and Scripture as religious and/or theological canon. The distinction between the Bible as revelation, providing the unquestioned premises for theological reflection, and the Bible as data to be critically evaluated, became clear in the Enlightenment. But in Augustine we see a foretaste of this distinction and we see a way out of the dilemma created. The broadest context for the interpretation and exposition of Scripture is the enjoyment of God. Augustine clearly establishes this in his treatise *On Christian Doctrine*. In that treatise, he makes a distinction, first of all, between signs and things and then between things to be used and things to be enjoyed. A sign signifies what it causes to come into someone's mind as a consequence of itself; words are signs. A thing differs from a sign in that a thing is something in itself, not used as a sign of something else. Things, however, may either be used (like signs) or enjoyed: "To use [a thing] is to employ whatever means are at one's disposal to obtain what one desires." To enjoy a thing, on the other hand, is to "rest with satisfaction in it for its own sake" (1.4.4). For Christians, then, signs and things to be used function in relation to higher realities, in relation to objects for enjoyment. The Scriptures are not on a par with these things to be enjoyed. They are to be used in relation to these things. "The end of the law, and of all holy scripture," says Augustine, "is the love of an object which is to be enjoyed, and the love of an object which can enjoy that other in fellowship with ourselves" (1.35.39). For Augustine, then, love of God and love of a neighbor are the primary hermeneutical guides. There is a coordination of conventional signs and things to be used with the true objects of enjoyment, but the true objects of enjoyment for Augustine are the superior schemata.

Peter Brown has summarized the basic procedure of biblical exegesis from Augustine's perspective. The first question the interpreter must ask, says Brown,

> is not "what"—"what was the exact nature of this particular religious practice in the Ancient Near East?" but "*why*"—"why does this incident, this word and no other, occur at just this moment in the interminable monologue of God; as so, what aspect of his deeper message does it communicate?" Like the child who asks the basic question: "Mummy, *why* is a cow?" Augustine will run through the text of the Bible in such a way that every sermon is punctuated by . . . "why? . . . Why? . . . Why?"[40]

Since, according to Augustine, the end of the text, the "why" of the text, is the "love to God for his own sake" and "love to one's self and one's neighbor for God's sake," the rule for interpretation follows: "To carefully turn over in our minds and meditate upon what we read till an interpretation be found that tends to establish the reign of love" (3.15.23). A reading that uses signs in a purely conventional fashion may establish an appropriate meaning for many texts, but not for all texts. Augustine gives a principle to apply in such cases: "Whatever there is in the word of God that cannot, when taken literally, be referred either to purity of life or soundness of doctrine, you may set down as figurative. Purity of life has reference to the love of God and one's neighbor; soundness of doctrine to the knowledge of God and one's neighbor" (3.10.14).

Notes

1. Edgar V. McKnight, *Jesus Christ in History and Scripture: A Poetic and Sectarian Perspective* (Macon, Ga.: Mercer University Press, 1999). Let me say something about how my agenda changed during my sabbatical work. I had intended to work on three different parts of a program on "Theology and the Contemporary Revolution in Biblical Studies." The first part was to be a review of the history of the Enlightenment and biblical criticism to indicate the hiatus between the Enlightenment view of critical certainty and the actual practice of local, particular, and ad hoc (instrumental) study.

   The second part was to move from general theoretical considerations to the formulation of a literary-oriented system of theology that would satisfy the current demands of theory and praxis. The history of theology offers instances of dynamic systems involving experience, practice, and theological formulation, formulation that involves a dialectic between heterodoxy and orthodoxy. The position that I intended to develop in my project parallels the practices of the radical reformers, for whom doctrine stood in relation to the life and practice of the church as primitive and eschatological community. This dialectical relationship that existed between doctrine and practice meant that a doctrine that was satisfying at one time became unsatisfying at another time.

   The final part was to be an examination of biblical materials in light of their role in theology in general and doctrine in particular. I intended to develop the thesis that the needs of theology and doctrine are not met simply by historical and/or dogmatic exegesis of passages to determine their explicit teachings on matters such as God and Messiah, sin and salvation. Instead of intellectual justification, a literary-oriented theology would begin with experience and praxis. Experience of biblical literature may function more obliquely in the lives of readers than does conventional theological formulation, much as play functions in the lives of children. But literary experience is not limited to the superficial and momentary. Social, psychological, ethical, intellectual, and other sorts of functions or goals are carried out in the pleasurable experience of both reading and play.

   The focus of my project changed as I progressed. I centered upon the single question of christology: How does one do study of Jesus Christ today? What and how does the Jesus Christ of history and Scripture "mean" today?

2. Gene E. Veith, "Postmodern Times: Facing a World of New Challenges and Opportunities," *Modern Reformation* 4, no. 5(September–October 1995): 16.

3. Rick Ritchie, "Post-Age Due: Has Anyone Noticed the Difference Between 'E.R.' and 'Marcus Welby'?" *Modern Reformation*, 4, no. 5 (September–October 1995): 21.

4. Elsewhere I have suggested that the attitude of the radical reformation as reflected in the recommendation of John Robinson to the Pilgrims before they left for America is akin to the postmodern attitude: "I cannot sufficiently bewail the condition of the Reformed Churches, who are come to a Period in Religion and will go at present no further than the instruments of their Reformation. The Lutherans can't be drawn to go beyond what Luther saw; whatever part of His will our God has revealed to Calvin, they will rather die than embrace it; and the Calvinists you see, stick fast where they were left by that great man of God, who yet saw not all things. . . . I beseech you remember it is an article of your church covenant, that you be ready to receive whatever truth shall be made known to you from the Written word of God." Quoted in Daniel Neal, *History of the Puritans*, part 2, chap. 2, quoted in Ernest A. Payne, *The Fellowship of Believers* (London: The Cary Kingsgate Press, 1952), 74.

5. Edgar V. McKnight, *Postmodern Use of the Bible* (Nashville: Abingdon, 1988).

6. Fosdick's book enabled readers in the first part of this century to make the pilgrimage into the "modern" era and to understand the Bible in an idiom informed by critical and historical assumptions and approaches. The exchange of the historical context for the dogmatic context transformed biblical study into a different discipline both spiritually and intellectually. (In theology, the foundation became religious experience—thought to be universal and perennial.) Eventually those who opposed the "modernistic" historical-critical study found it useful. Some of the most exciting historical-critical study has been done by evangelicals who come to their study against the horizon of vital Christian faith. With these evangelicals there is something of an intuitive meshing of theological and religious values and historical study.

7. In reader-response criticism, the conclusion is reached that there is no absolutely neutral language of literature to serve as a foundation for readers' responses. This is paralleled by the conclusion in philosophy that there is no absolute foundation that can be used in the determination of knowledge. For conventional historical-critical proponents, a New Testament hermeneutic informed by non-foundationalist reader-oriented literary approaches is suspect because it renders problematic the firm mooring of history. For the postmodern literary critic, however, a reader-oriented hermeneutical approach to biblical literature is suspect as well. In fact, in a review of my *Postmodern Use of the Bible*, one critic warns readers that my work could be seen by radical postmodernists as a "sheep in wolf's clothing" because I utilized literary criticism, including the strategies developed with the close reading of New Criticism, for constructive purposes (A. K. M. Adam, "Review of *Postmodern Use of the Bible* by Edgar V. McKnight," *Catholic Biblical*

Quarterly 52 [1990], 758-759). The "wolf's clothing" is a result of post-modern questioning of assumptions of conventional critical approaches (such as the independence of fact and meaning from value and interpretation, the stability of texts and even the autonomy of the self and the nature of reality). The sheep-like quality? The refusal to acknowledge that the questioning of such assumptions must conclude with a nihilistic skepticism. My refusal to conclude with a skeptical and nihilistic deconstruction may be rationalized as it is situated in the literary and hermeneutical traditions. I suspect that my non-skeptical perspective is a result of my earlier work in hermeneutics. My Oxford dissertation with John Macquarrie demonstrated the hermeneutical core of every level of structures of relationship. (It was published with the title *Meaning in Texts: The Historical Shaping of a Narrative Hermeneutics* [Philadelphia: Fortress Press, 1978].) The dominant American brand of deconstruction is a result of a bypassing of the hermeneutical tradition of Schleiermacher, Dilthey, Heidegger, and Gadamer. The deconstructionist critic is then merely a distanced observer of the "scene of textuality" who refines all writing into "free floating" texts. The continually unsituated deconstructionist critic is characterized by a forever new or unmastered irony. A mastered irony does not ignore the valid insight of deconstruction but does not remain forever unsituated. When reader-oriented interpretation comes to biblical texts through the hermeneutical tradition, it seeks to situate possibility in an actual worldly relation; it is a sheep in wolf's clothing.

8. Poetry kept alive the metaphorical use of language even in the scientific descriptive phase. A contemporary approach to the Bible as literature, then, may allow us to recover a function that was lost in a descriptive phase. In contemporary use of poetry, however, the original sense of magic disappears. No longer is there the idea of the possible forces being released by words of power. This does not mean that poetry really loses its power. The power is transferred from an action on nature to an action on the reader or hearer. This may be particularly appropriate for biblical material, whose literary aspects are coordinated with a rhetorical function. It has been suggested, in fact, that the genre of the Bible as a whole is that of proclamation, a mode of rhetoric.

9. Anthony Thiselton, *New Horizons in Hermeneutics* (Grand Rapids, Mich.: Zondervan, 1992).

10. In my work following *Postmodern Use of the Bible,* I became interested in the theological use, moving to the Bible as language and literature against the horizon of the language of dogma, and then moving back to theology in general and dogma in particular. How could I construct some framework to allow relationships to be established between theory and practice, theology and biblical study, modern historical approaches and postmodern literary approaches? I recognize that it appears that I was searching for some overarching totalizing scheme that could be validated in some final fashion. In fact the insight that such totalizing schemes are not possible freed me to experiment, to find some scheme that would be satisfying at that particular juncture in my pilgrimage. I ended up with examination of the different moves in philosophy, theology, literature, and biblical study in relation to the classical

debate between idealism and realism, between Plato and Aristotle and their disciples. I saw the different methods of explanation as different ways of correlating these major paradigms as they have been transformed in philosophy, theology, literary study, and biblical study.

11. Thiselton, *New Horizons*, 401. In Thiselton's own work he leans in the direction of explanatory system. At any rate, Thiselton denies that the inevitability of pluralism is the same as the belief that each life world is self-contained and incapable of metacritical ranking in terms of the transcontextual theory. He indicates that few confusions have more seriously damaged the contemporary debate than the confusion between recognizing the inevitability of contextual pluralism at the level of establishing critical norms, and the mistaken assumption that to attempt to move in the direction of a provisional and corrigible metacritical ranking of such norms is thereby to deny this inevitability (613).

12. Ibid., 1.

13. Ibid.

14. Peter Schwartz and James Ogilvy, *The Emergent Paradigm: Changing Patterns of Thought and Belief* (Menlo Park, Calif.: SRI International, 1979).

15. Stephen Toulmin, *Cosmopolis: The Hidden Agenda of Modernism* (New York: Free Press, 1990), ix.

16. Ibid., x.

17. Ibid., 27.

18. Ibid., 29.

19. Ibid., 99.

20. Ibid., 23.

21. Ibid., 24.

22. James W. McClendon, Jr., and James M. Smith, *Convictions: Defusing Religious Relativism* (Valley Forge, Pa.: Trinity Press International, 1994), 112.

23. The limitations of historical-critical methods as such were noted by those engaged in those methods. Ernst Troeltsch himself was very aware of limitations. But in a "modern" context with "modern" assumptions, alternatives were not available to satisfy both our critical and religious itches. Adolf Schlatter in the early decades of this century and Peter Stuhlmacher in the present time attempted to solve the problem by collapsing conventional historical method and a faith perspective or method that explicitly recognizes the sacred as involved in history. According to Schlatter, criticism is required because a revelation that discloses God apart from and separate from human beings does not exist. Criticism, however, should be exercised by observing the historical events that lie behind the traditional texts, events in which the certainty of God for individuals and for humankind as a whole is produced. The method of the historical exegete must be appropriate to the objectives of both the biblical text and the believing exegete. When we try to explain religion from the perspective of the world apart from God, we immediately set

ourselves in radical opposition to the subject matter of the biblical text that will not be explained from the perspective of such a world but which asserts the idea of God loudly and persistently. (Schlatter, "Aetheistische Methoden in der Theologie," in U. Luck, ed., *Zur Theologie des Neuen Testaments und zur Dogmatik: Kleine Schiften mit einer Einfuhrung* [Munich: Chr. Kaiser Verlag, 1969], 148-149.)

Peter Stuhlmacher recapitulates the arguments of Schlatter against the background of the work of Bultmann and his students. If historical method is necessary, Stuhlmacher says, and the method is to deal with life-giving and life-sustaining forces, with the witness of God made perceivable in the historical linguistic documents, then historical method must be more than or different from the conventional historical method. It must be method that has a capacity for dealing with the purpose of confrontation with the biblical texts and their world. Stuhlmacher suggests that the principle of perception must be used alongside the conventional principles of correlation, criticism, and analogy. Through the power of the principle of perception, Stuhlmacher declares that we may regain the possibility of discovering in history something new and without analogy. (*Vom Verstehen des Neuen Testament: Eine Hermeneutik,* Grundrisse zum Neuen Testament, vol. 6 [Goettingen: Vandenhoeck and Ruprecht: 1st edn. 1979; 2nd edn. 1986]).

24. N. T. Wright, *Jesus and the Victory of God,* vol. 2 of *Christian Origins and the Question of God* (Minneapolis: Fortress, 1996).

25. Marcus Borg speaks to readers who are interested in what neutral observers of the first century would have concluded about Jesus and what can be said from a religious perspective. The four- or five-stroke sketch of Jesus painted by Borg views him as a religious ecstatic, healer, wisdom teacher, social prophet, and movement founder or catalyst. These are categories we are familiar with. Borg's portrait is not distinctly Christian; it is one that is understandable to contemporary people in general. Readers are able to use these frameworks for purely historical research, but they are able to bring these understandings to bear on their religious experience. Borg himself indicates that his historical portrait of Jesus has made a difference to him religiously. Instead of a concentration upon dogma, he sees faith as believing in the following sense: "to give one's heart, one's self at its deepest level, to the post-Easter Jesus who is the living Lord, the side of God turned toward us, the face of God, the Lord who is also the Spirit" (*Meeting Jesus Again for the First Time: The Historical Jesus and the Heart of Contemporary Faith* [San Francisco: HarperSanFrancisco, 1994], 137).

26. The limits of knowledge and the failure to establish some final foundation for knowledge have been applied in dramatic fashion in literature in the skeptical deconstruction associated with Jacques Derrida. Skepticism, however, is not the only possible conclusion. Skepticism results from the assumption that foundationalism is the only route to knowledge, or that the only kind of knowledge that counts is that which is based on foundationalism. The reader-oriented approach that I have advocated is a non-skeptical approach resulting from the assumption that knowledge is always related to life and that the sort of knowledge that really counts is knowledge grounded in life.

27. We may begin with dogma, but dogma is not the foundation—we do not reduce the Bible to dogma. If we already know what the Bible has said or can say to us, we are unable to hear a new word in our reading of the Scripture. We may begin with history, or sociology, or anthropology, or psychology, but we do not reduce the Bible to any object of scientific research. We may begin with readers in communities of faith with confidence that the Bible speaks, because it has spoken, but this is not a foundation.

28. Bernard Lategan, "Reading Romans 13 in a South African Context," in Bernard Lategan, ed., *The Reader and Beyond: Theory and Practice in South African Studies* (Pretoria: Human Sciences Research Council, 1992), 115-133.

29. Anseln Kyongsuk Min has analyzed the competing positions and advocated a position he calls "the dialectical confessionalist pluralism of solidarity" or simply "dialectical pluralism." This dialectical pluralism "is confessionalist in that it understands religion to be a matter of existential commitment, discipleship, and transformation that includes but also transcends objective rationality and thus more a (salvific) way of existing to be confessed in faith and praxis than a theory to be understood in detached reflection. . . . As such, this pluralism encourages each religion to confess its distinctive beliefs and claims including the claim to finality. . . . [I]t does not relativize the absolute claims of religions or demand . . . renunciation of such claims as a condition of interreligious dialogue. Rather, in deference to the confessional character of religion, dialectical pluralism leaves it up to each religion to maintain or modify its ultimate claim on its own terms in light of the dialectic of its inherited tradition and the challenge of the pluralistic situation" ("Dialectical Pluralism and Solidarity of Others: Toward a New Paradigm," *Journal of the American Academy of Religion* 65 [1997], 588).

30. James W. McClendon, Jr., *Systematic Theology: Doctrine* (Nashville: Abingdon, 1994), 29.

31. Sandra Schneiders, *The Revelatory Text: Interpreting the New Testament as Sacred Scripture* (San Francisco: HarperSanFrancisco, 1991), 49.

32. Ibid.

33. In our postmodern world, we recognize the limitations of historical study. We recognize that our historical tools as such are unable to uncover the connection of the eternal with the finite in historical experience. This is not due to a lack of connection! It is due to a methodological assumption of the historical approach itself. I have already suggested ways that the historical-critical and constructive (or poetic) operate.

34. Biblical texts are linguistic structures. The same linguistic and literary principles at work in the case of literary masterpieces are at work in the case of biblical writings. Readers can come to the biblical text as they come to other literature and exercise their creativity and faith. A rich difference of opinion exists today over the relative importance of the text and reader and the best ways conceptualizing the activities of the reader in actualizing the text. But there is unanimity of opinion that the reader is necessarily and legitimately involved in the process of reading.

35. From such a perspective, the debate over whether the New Testament text is the occasion for profound philosophical and theological thought or for experience (sometimes denigrated as superficial "feeling" and "enjoyment") would be transformed. It is possible that debate over the foundations of history, Scripture, and experience would be transformed.

36. In *Meaning in Texts,* I dealt with the historical shaping of a narrative hermeneutics and Wilhelm Dilthey was a central figure as he sought to discover the life that had expressed itself in literary works. Dilthey saw the literary text as stamped by life—as one stamps a coin. I suggest that the New Testament text is stamped or imprinted by the life of religious experience.

37. Schneiders, *The Revelatory Text,* 40. Schneiders quotes from "Dei Verbum" [Dogmatic Constitution on Divine Revelation of Vatican Council II] in Austin P. Flannery, ed., *Documents of Vatican II,* vol. 1 (Grand Rapids, Mich.: Eerdmans, 1984), vi:21.

38. Ibid., 43.

39. See Bernard Lonergan, "Theology in its New Context" and "The Dimensions of Conversion," in Walter E. Conn, ed., *Conversion: Perspectives on Personal and Social Transformation* (New York: Alba, 1978), 3-21.

40. Peter Brown, *Augustine of Hippo* (Berkeley: University of California Press, 1967), p. 253.

5

The Vinyl Narratives: The Metanarrative of Postmodernity and the Recovery of a Churchly Theology

Richard Lints

Richard Lints

INTRODUCTION

There is a tree in central Florida. It is maybe ninety feet high and huge around the base and has a crown that stretches across almost as many yards as the tree is tall. From the top of this tree, when the wind is still, you can see almost to the Caribbean. The trunk looks about as much like that of a live oak as one might wish. The bark is deeply grained and covered with that pea-soup-green-colored stuff you see on trees in hot, wet places. It's a big, nice tree, a good place for the tree house that adorns it.

But it's not made of wood.

The trunk and branches are formed out of pre-stressed concrete wrapped around a steel-mesh frame. The bark and green stuff that cover much of it are painted on. The leaves, all 800,000 of them, are made of vinyl.

This tree—Disneyodendron eximus (out of the ordinary Disney tree—in corporate parlance) holds the Swiss Family Island Tree House, an attraction in the Adventureland part of Walt Disney World's Magic Kingdom.

The Swiss Family Island Tree House, shaded by its vinyl leaves, is a representation of the tree house built by the Swiss Family Robinson in the 1960 Disney movie of the same name.

The movie—based on Johann Wyss's takeoff on Daniel Defoe's *Robinson Crusoe*—is one in which, as in all "Disney versions," art and history are transformed by dilution. So we have a fake tree, holding a fake tree house, representing a fake story told in a different medium from, but alluding to, a classic piece of literature, in an amusement park visited by 30 million people a year, most of whom are, like myself, enchanted.

These are the opening words of cultural critic Stephen Fjellman's book *Vinyl Leaves: Walt Disney World and America*.[1] Immediately after these opening words he shouts (though he is writing), "What is going on here????"

The Vinyl Narratives of Postmodernity

As Fjellman reflects on that disconcerting question, he suggests that Walt Disney World is not simply an isolated amusement park but rather is one of the many "narratives" of postmodernity that have reshaped American culture. It is not simply a place but a story of the way we would like to be. It is an all-encompassing narrative we embrace willingly as we become by design one of the story's characters, with our identity intimately wrapped up with the story itself. I want to suggest that, like the vinyl character of the leaves on the tree, the story it embodies is a "vinyl narrative." It is an artificial construct made to look like the real world in many ways, but at critical junctures it deviates from reality in order to achieve a set of higher purposes. It makes a covenantal promise with each of its consumers. The words of its central refrain, "If you can dream it, we can do it," is a covenantal promise. It holds out the eschatological hope of a world without problems, with nothing but pure, unadulterated happiness.[2] Part of the very enchantment of the park is that, interwoven in our interaction with the theme park is a story of huge deception. Like others, Walt Disney has created new symbolic worlds that often have little or no relation to reality. Technically, we know these phenomena as "virtual reality." Jennifer Allen says of Walt Disney World, "They can be forgiven a certain amount of hubris because the laws of reality do not operate here."[3] Disney World is a utopia—which can be yours for a price. It is a world of unrealistic expectations that nonetheless can be fulfilled. It is a world where the streets are always clean, where everyone has a smile, and where the triumph of human creativity has reached apparent perfection.

In other words, it is a story, like other postmodern stories, which would prefer to endlessly postpone the truth question. To use George Lindbeck's categories, it is a cultural-linguistic system of the very profoundest sort.[4] Disney has sought to call the American public to a concern with the internal logic of its own faith in progress and happiness. The world of Disney defines its own language and thought-forms and practices within which consumers find their purpose and meaning. The marketing task is about self-definition and truth is defined intratextually—not as a relationship between text and some "world out there," but as a relationship between a set of products to be sold and a set of desires that will allow any price for satisfaction. It is a story, like other postmodern stories, that tells us that all our desires are worth satisfying and yet implicitly tells us which desires are more important than others and then "commodifies" those desires. The gratification of those desires must be purchased.

Disney World is a world created for us, which in turn recreates us in its own image.[5] No one person or group of people is at fault here; we are all at fault. We buy the image because we want it. It is the raw desire for happiness which drives most transactions in these vinyl narratives. As Woody Allen claimed in his sordid trial defending his affair with his adopted step-daughter, "the heart wants what it wants."[6] We are so enchanted by Disney World that we believe the heart gets what it wants.

In all of this we too often naively suppose that the world has changed but we have remained relatively unchanged. The world may be filled with technological innovations undreamt about fifty years ago—cyberspace-related toys, space-travel gadgets, and advanced medical tools—but the reality is that the greater change has occurred in how we relate to that world, what we think about ourselves, and last but surely not least, the ways in which religious faith has been transformed.

The striking fact of modernity and its cousin, postmodernity, is the ways in which they have reordered our inner consciousness, the ways in which the gadgets of our age have exerted enormous pressure to reshape the categories of our mental life. This is to say that we think differently about the world we live in *because of* the world we live in. We believe the vinyl narratives because, after all, "the heart wants what it wants."

In this respect let me suggest with Peter Berger that the fundamental change in modern consciousness is the movement from fate to choice.[7] The vast array of things now possible through modern technology makes it appear that an individual can pretty much do anything. We are no longer bound by the fates of history. The power of our tools creates so many more choices than could have been conceived of by any earlier civilization.

But the choices created by our tools represent only a small slice of an enormously larger array of choices that are part of the taken-for-granted fabric of modern life: choices of occupation, of place of residence, of marriage, of the number of one's children, of one's vacation destination—the list could go on with regard to the external arrangements of life. But there are other choices, inner choices, that deeply touch the consciousness of individuals: life-style choices, religious choices, and moral choices.[8]

The more choices, the more reflection. The individual who reflects becomes more conscious of himself. He turns his attention from the objectively given outside world to his own subjectivity. As he does this, two things happen simultaneously: The outside world becomes more questionable, and his own inner world becomes more complex. People become more suspicious of any solution which appears as the "only" one. The hegemony of truth itself comes under severe scrutiny.

And ironically, the greater amount of reflection on our own inner subjectivity results in far less reflection about "ultimate matters." Fjellman reminds us,

At Walt Disney World, the world of commodities presents itself in an onslaught of discrete, disconnected packages, and the pursuit of these packages—each designed to fill some artificially constructed need—leaves minimal space in our lives for coherent critical thought about what we are doing. We are encouraged to pay attention only to those things that are amusing and fun.[9]

It is this critical dynamic of human identity that is at the heart of the postmodern challenge. The vinyl narratives of our times suggest that reality is eminently moldable into our own image, that our image is profoundly flexible and ought to be shaped according to our deepest desires, and finally that those desires are most fruitful when empowered with choice. This is the metanarrative of postmodernity, contrary to the expressed distaste for all metanarratives by the postmodern prophets.

THE VINYL NARRATIVES OF THE EVANGELICAL MOVEMENT

The cultural captivity of the modern evangelical church is by now a well-chronicled story. It is not mine to repeat that story here. What I do want to do is suggest the myriad ways in which the evangelical movement has been tempted to buy into the vinyl-like character of its own narrative. The following, then, is more suggestive than exhaustive.

The increased use of drama in worship may well serve to communicate the gospel in a medium intelligible to many contemporary citizens of our culture, but it often does so without recognizing the unintended consequences of such use. The medium reinforces the "story-like" character of the Christian life, but a story rooted in the imaginative constructs of our time. It is an artificial medium whose primary intent is to amuse. Its hidden assumption is that the world unfolds before the audience as the human author imagined it. Its message is that the world can be like this if you want it be. It is Walt Disney-like in the sense that the world is conceived not as simply "out there to be understood" but rather as an unusual puzzle that can be put together in any variety of ways. Drama is a medium that reinforces the artificial character of truth.

Let me also suggest that the very populist character of the evangelical movement has made it susceptible to the vinyl-like character of the postmodern narratives. The theological vision of the evangelical movement has been created in large measure by popularizers, individuals with no other perceivable gift than the ability to communicate effectively. This vision is given legitimization by popular vote, usually in the form of large conferences organized by one of our modern "circuit riders." And it survives by the creation of simple slogans: "the Bible alone," "inerrancy vs. infallibility," "the evil of secular humanism," etc. It is often sustained by Christian talk radio, whose medium reinforces the notion that everybody's opinion matters (but ultimately doesn't matter, because the talk show host gets the final word!). In all of this, evangelical communication techniques often work on the assumption that there is no fixed world out there, simply a nebulous reality looking for a peculiar "spin" to be placed on it.

In many evangelical churches the Bible is studied primarily with the aid of inductive Bible study materials.[10] The fundamental question asked of the text is, "What does it say to me?"[11] Implicit is an assumption about the essential clarity of the text and its accessibility to any person who would briefly consider it. The practice of the inductive Bible study may encourage individuals to read the Bible as they have never done before, but it will also encourage them to read the text according to their own subjective interests.[12] The Bible becomes captive to the whims of the individual, freed from external constraints. The text may say whatever the individual wants it to say, and the church is doomed to having as many interpretations of the text as there are interpreters. In desiring to have no mediators between the Bible and ourselves, evangelicals have let the Scriptures be ensnared in the web of private subjectivism. By avoiding the aid of the community of interpreters throughout the history of Christendom, there has been a reinforcement of the power of the biases of our own individual situation. We often refashion the text in our own image—a thoroughly postmodern thing to do.

The evangelical movement is largely trans-ecclesiastical. An evangelical Presbyterian often feels closer to an evangelical Methodist than to a liberal Presbyterian. The effect of this is that the evangelical Presbyterian (and Methodist) sense their identity lies not in the church but in the nebulous theological heritage called evangelicalism, a heritage that is neither Presbyterian nor Methodist, no more Baptistic than it is paedo-baptistic, no more charismatic than it is non-charismatic, no more dispensational than it is non-dispensational. This parachurch orientation of its theological vision effectively cuts the movement off from an ecclesiology rooted in concrete traditions, traditions in the church in which issues such as soteriology, baptism, ongoing revelation, and the covenant were of central importance. Where there is little "tradition," there will inevitably be no "church" to nurture a theological center.

Let me also suggest that along with the conviction of the malleability of reality in accord with our present situation comes the ironic twist that our present context often reshapes us in its own image. The consumerist character of modern church life is a subject upon which there has already developed a healthy consensus and skepticism. Robert Wuthnow has argued eloquently that, in their more candid moments, evangelicals admit to being thoroughly materialistic (while deploring this trait in their children).[13] They believe in the proverbial bottom line. They shoulder greater and greater personal economic obligations and fret about how to pay their bills. These are matters of sheer necessity, they tell themselves. But they also enlist hearts and minds. Gainful employment does supply us with meaning and purpose for living. But in our modern context, work has become a means of self-expression, and no less so for evangelicals than for non-evangelicals. Careers have replaced callings both inside and outside the church. Having money is too often the key to happiness. Correspondingly, financial setbacks destroy self-esteem. We associate freedom with having a shiny new automobile capable of doubling the speed limit, and with having an IBM Thinkpad, a townhouse in the city, a Sony CD system, a Lexus coupe, or whatever the latest symbols of material wealth may be.

Compare the sermon seventy-five million Americans hear each Sunday morning with the daily bombardment of television commercials to which they are exposed, or the "do this or get fired" pressures they experience at work. Put a few thousand dollars in their pocket and send a young couple out to make a down payment on a new car: How much is some vague religious teaching about stewardship going to matter, compared with arguments about sportiness and acceleration?

Wuthnow argues that Christian faith is, as a result, an ambiguous presence in the evangelical church-going population. It sends mixed signals about work, telling us to work hard—but not too hard. It counsels us to be diligent with our money, but seldom instructs us in how to be diligent. Indeed, it raises our anxieties about money while discouraging us from talking openly about those anxieties. It warns us against the excessive materialism that pervades our society, but offers little to keep us from the temptations of materialism. Feeling ambivalent about the role of wealth, evangelicals therefore go about their lives pretty much the same as those who have no faith at all. At least from one perspective, it would seem that evangelicals have not resisted the vinyl narratives of our age.

THE CHALLENGE OF RECOVERING THE REDEMPTIVE METANARRATIVE

The challenge for us churchly theologians is, of course, the impact of this metanarrative on our apprehension of the divine metanarrative. Religious activity where it exists in this world increasingly has been compartmentalized into a private experience.[14] Berger notes, "religion has become privately meaningful and publicly irrelevant."[15] Religious faith has increasingly ceased to be the glue that holds the world together for believers. It is simply one piece of a very large puzzle. Or, to use my language, it is simply one vinyl narrative among many. The modern religious narrative is vinyl precisely because it appears as artificially constructed, intended not as an integrating story for the rest of reality nor as a metanarrative originating in a transcendent source, but rather as one story among others about a distinctive compartment of our imagination and desires.

The church runs an enormous risk if it interprets its task in light of any of these vinyl narratives. If its *raison d'être* emerges from the vinyl narratives of postmodernity, then it will inevitably downplay the redemptive presence of the living God in the world today. But it is that redemptive presence of God by which the church gains its prophetic power to speak with real hope to a dark world, and not simply with the illusionary type of hope of the eschatological kingdom of Disney World. And it is only by regaining the connection to the redemptive narrative of Scripture that the church will understand the redemptive presence of God. And this is why one of the greatest dangers to recovering a churchly theology is the vinyl-like character granted to all the narratives in postmodernity—including the church's narrative.[16]

Not wanting simply to bemoan the state of evangelicalism (increasingly an easy target, especially for those of us who have become skilled in the use of cynicism in the modern academy), let me turn my attention to a consideration of the opportunities that lie at our feet in the postmodern moment. My central interest at this point is the postmodern challenge to the age-old conviction that the church's story is the story of God's redeeming presence as narrated in and through the Scriptures and which therefore interprets all of reality. The postmodern opportunity is precisely the reawakening of the modern consciousness to the power of stories.

The Christian's hope is inextricably bound up with the story of God's redemption in history, which gives meaning to the past, explains the present, and provides guidance for the future. If the power of the church in our age too often lies in its usurping of the tools and structures of postmodernity, then lost is the conviction of the redemptive presence of the living God as narrated in and through the Scriptures. Consequently, the redemptive story of the Scriptures which mediates that presence becomes inconsequential to the life of the church, and the church thereby inevitably looks for other narratives to tell its story. This is the danger of the postmodern era.

The redemptive narrative of Scripture is not simply a story of ancient events. It is a story which, if true, continues to interpret all of life through its structures. In particular it interprets the church by giving it a theological vision through which God's redemptive presence is understood. And we must remember that the church is not a nebulous entity in the New Testament. The church has particular shape, structure, and spiritual location. Its privileges and responsibilities are spelled out in great detail.[17]

As the apostles address particular churches or groups of churches, they address them with a common theological framework, which is to infuse the people with a new "way-of-looking-at-the world," i.e., a theological vision.[18] We must also recognize that the church was the community which provided the plausibility structures for that "way-of-looking-at-the-world." It reinforced it and provided it with "oomph"[19]—i.e., with power and meaning in the life of the individual. The living community of faith brings to life the story of eternity, so to speak.

This is to say that theologians do not need simply to build bridges with churches: They need to be consumed with the church, fallen and frail as it is. Theologians need to see ecclesiology as the context for their endeavors. They must think of their mandate as arising from the church—not vice versa.

GOD'S REDEMPTIVE *PRESENCE* AND ITS REDEMPTIVE *NARRATIVE*

If the church is the context for theology, what holds the church together? It is the presence of the risen Lord. And it is the preaching of the Word and the celebration of the sacraments through which the Spirit has chosen to make this presence manifest. This presence is intimately rooted in the history of redemption, and it is that story which is the church's story as well: It is the metanarrative of the church.

It is the story of God's redemptive presence that connects the past, present, and future, and thereby connects us with the Living God.[20] At the beginning, God spoke creation into being. His presence throughout creation is everywhere assumed, and yet he remains distinctly separate from his creation. God created by the power of his Word and gave life and breath to his creatures by his Spirit. In this, as at all other critical junctures of redemptive history, there is a manifest presence of the triune God—Father, Son, and Spirit.

It is imperative that we understand that God's presence is an ordered presence at the beginning. It is a presence whose boundaries are set by God himself. He determines the nature and purpose of creation and the manner in which it will reflect him. The two cultural mandates—to be fruitful and multiply, and to be stewards of the garden—are reflections of the character of God himself. It is also God who determines the relationship between his creatures and himself. He is the one who defines good and evil, and he is the one who places Adam on probation in his presence.

In Genesis 3, when sin is introduced, God's presence becomes a threat to the existence of Adam and Eve and the serpent. It is a threatening presence. As a result, the original couple are removed from the immediate presence of God and are cast out of the garden. The flaming swords guarding the garden are the evident reminders that Adam and Eve shall not return into God's immediate presence except through judgment. Cain is further punished for his sin by forever losing his home, ever to be a pilgrim on a journey.

With the renewed presence of God to Abraham in Genesis 12, there is a recovery of the fellowship of the garden, yet deepened in ways unforeseen earlier. God promises to be with Abraham, to make of him a great nation, and to give him a land flowing with milk and honey. God promises a presence, a people, and a place. In all of this, he renames Abram, reminding him that it is ultimately God who redemptively establishes purpose and identity. God's words are accompanied by his promises to be fulfilled in actions. Word and deed go hand in hand.

We reach another redemptive climax in the call of Moses. God shows himself present to Moses in the burning bush. During Moses' entire life God manifests himself in unique miracles, showing himself to be not only the Lord of nature but also the Lord who will use nature for the redemption of his creatures. The Red Sea is parted and the people are baptized into Moses as the one who will take them to the promised land. But in God's providence Moses does not actually take them into the promised land. He looks at Canaan from the other side of the Jordan, foreshadowing the future Redeemer who will take God's people into the promised land of God's presence eternally. At Sinai, Moses is given a glimpse of God's direct presence—but only of God's backside. God determines that Israel will hear him when they listen to Moses. A tent of meeting is constructed, where God will be present to Moses and over which the pillar of cloud will rest, signifying God's abiding presence.

When the people finally are taken into the promised land, it is not until David's rule that the land is entirely brought under Israelite rule. As Moses was not permitted to enter the promised land, so David is not permitted to build the temple where God's name will rest. That task is left to the son of David, Solomon. When the temple is built, God's redemption is actively and graphically acted out in the sacrificial cultus. The people are reminded, however, that the presence of God is still largely protected—the Holy of Holies is entered into only once a year, and then only by the high priest. God's presence is mediated and severely restricted.

The climax of God's redemptive promise occurs with the coming of God himself in the flesh. The apostle John tells us that, in Christ, God has come to tabernacle in our midst. The fullness of God dwells in Christ, and in our union with Christ in his death and resurrection we are given new life, the breath of God's Spirit. The veil of Moses is lifted from our faces when we come to Christ, and now we see God face to face—in Christ. Christ is both God and the mediator of God's presence for his people.

The church in its proclamation and in its celebration of the sacraments has become the mediated presence of God in the world. The church is not identical with God, as Christ himself was; but the church is the vehicle God has chosen, like the tabernacle and the temple, where the presence of God is made manifest.

The life and breath of the Spirit is given in and through the body of our Lord—in his death and resurrection. It is extended to us spiritually in the calling of the church, in its proclamation of the gospel and its practice of the sacraments as the tangible signs and seals of the gospel. Though we still "see" God "through a glass darkly," we wait expectantly for that day when his presence will no longer have to be mediated for us.

We await the day when God himself will reside in the midst of his people. On that day, he will wipe away all our tears, and no longer will there be a sun or a moon, for the Lord will be our lamp. We will know in the fullness of our experience that the Lord is genuinely the Alpha and the Omega. He is the one who makes sense of the beginning and who is the end.

It is this story that transforms not only our particular beliefs but our entire orientation in the world. It is an entire "way-of-looking-at-the-world." And it is the church that ought to tell anew the story by which that collective history is recounted, and to be the community in which its enduring influence is most keenly felt. This redemptive narrative establishes the church's identity by establishing its own place in redemptive history. In knowing the past, present, and future, the church is to know itself anew. Importantly, the church is to know God's redeeming presence, which holds the past, present, and future together. The hope of the church is that eternity is to be spent basking in the glorified presence of God, forever and ever and ever. That is the goal toward which redemptive history is headed. And it is that hope that we hold out before a world caught up in the vinyl narratives of postmodernity.

CHALLENGING THE ASSUMPTIONS AND CHANGING THE STRUCTURES

Substantively, we may affirm that contexts often pave the way for the reevaluation of ideas. If theologians are going to make an intellectual difference, we must also get about the business of figuring out how to create structures and contexts which do not buy so easily into the assumptions of our age. We need to begin "thinking" about the church theologically (i.e., as God sees it) and trying to "live out" some of the theological models of Scripture. Theologians cannot simply defend the "doctrines" of the church but must strive for a church whose identity is the narrative of redemptive history. Theology should not simply reside in the church. The church's integrating center should be God's presence as it is narrated by the story of redemption. Some preliminary examples and suggestions are in order.

Vinyl narratives are notoriously stories within generations and not across generations. The church buys into this shallowness of its own narrative when it ministers by segmenting the generations. Instead of thinking of "age units," might the church return to thinking of "family units"? Why not try keeping families together more in the life of the church—during Sunday school, during worship, and during shared meals, for instance? Might the church think of ministry across the generations rather than simply within the generations? The church needs to develop ways to let older folks be a part of the lives of younger folks, and for younger folks to be involved in the lives of even younger folks. The church ought to be nervous if any one generation in the church is involved only with their peers. This is not simply a pragmatic concern; it is to think about the practice of the church theologically.

In the vinyl narratives of our age, meals are always of the fast-food variety. The investment of our lives in others across the table has been replaced by thinking of meals as simply a means to satisfying one's personal hunger. In that light, might the church encourage people to eat meals together, not simply as a means to meet some new people but as a celebration of the covenantal aspects of shared meals? Families are often so busy that they cannot eat together themselves, and thus there is little permanence in modern family life. Sometimes churches are no different. Blocking out time to share a meal among families and in families will have very profound spiritual consequences. It will not slow the world down, but it just may be one way to remind the congregation (and the family) of the covenant that does in fact bind them together. Think of the profound impact this would have upon our practice of the Lord's Supper as well.

In many of our postmodern vinyl narratives, the heart is deceived into thinking that it gets what it wants. The context of that deception is often that the individual is supreme and thereby is the rightful source of all final choices.[21] Theologians need to remind the church (and themselves as members of the church) that in a kingdom the king has final authority. The church is not a divine democracy. Not everyone gets a vote. And as the old adage suggests, a benevolent dictator is in fact the simplest and most efficient form of government. Theologians do not, nor do pastors, nor do congregations govern the church: God does. We all need to be reminded that the major decisions facing the church have already been made, and therefore the day-to-day logistical decisions must not be so emphasized as to lose sight of the eternal principles that have already been laid down for us by our Lord. This means helping people understand that their central stake in the church is not their right to express their opinions nor to vote in a congregational meeting.

All of these suggestions are not matters to be left to church consultants. These are the tasks of theologically-driven pastors and pastorally-minded theologians. Abstracted from the life of the church, theology often loses its heart and soul. The confessions of the church will inevitably become merely statements of doctrines which protect the church from the outside world, defining simply who belongs "in" and who belongs "out," rather than giving identity to the church by giving to the church an entire "way-of-looking-at-the-world-and-living-in-the-world." Theology has become simply one of the many competing (and abstract) narratives of our age, even (and especially) for church-going folk. And theologians have become technicians and engineers, specialists who are called upon only to answer the really abstract and esoteric questions. If it is true that the church abandons theology only at great peril to herself, it is also true that theologians abandon the church only at great peril to theology.

When theologians lost sight of the foundational institution of God's activity in the world (that is, the church) theology lost the most important forum for the praise of God and thereby lost the means of applying the Bible's theological framework in the contemporary world. The loss of theology's churchly identity was accompanied by the loss of accountability structures for that theology.[22] And as theology became less accountable to the church, it became abstract and removed from the worship of God and the mission of the church.

How is theology in this redemptive-historical sense to return to a church which often does not want it? It must first become convinced that it is good to return. This cannot be accomplished without much greater biblical/theological thinking on the very identity and calling of the church and on this context as the primary context for the theologian's vocation.[23] There must also be an increasing willingness of theologians to speak from within the church and not merely to the church. Instead of evangelical theologians, there must develop Baptist theologians, Presbyterian theologians, and Congregational theologians.[24] The professional theological community must also cease from settling the boundary questions for the community of faith; churches must be urged to more faithfully fulfill this function. The confessional character of the concrete churches cannot be determined at an interdenominational seminary, and it cannot be determined on the pages of a professional academic journal. These questions must be determined in the church and for the church. Theologians must also cease thinking of the church as abstracted from the everyday living, concrete realities of parish life. Theology is to be lived out on the pages of actual history, reflecting the God who has acted out redemption on the pages of actual history.

It ought to be evident to most readers that the context of theological education has greatly influenced theology. Theology today finds its home in the universities and their related cousins, the seminaries. Pursued in the outpost of the modern university, it is not surprising that theology's criteria of success would emerge from that secular context rather than from within the worshiping community.

Theology has become a technical discipline with a language peculiar to itself. And inevitably it became associated with a select group of universities and was built around the paradigms of that school: Berlin or Munich or Tübingen in the last century; Yale, Chicago, and Claremont in our own time. This school-based character of theology also became an institutional sanction for theological diversity as well as conceptual abstractness. The strong and separate identities of the select and prestigious universities (and often our own seminaries) effectively authorized an identity independent from the churches.

If theologians are called to think theologically about the concrete structures of the church in which theology is given life, it may also be said that theologians ought to challenge the intellectual structures that give plausibility to the vinyl narratives of postmodernity. In our day this means in part that confessing churchly theologians must emphasize a metanarrative in a time when all metanarratives of transcendence are suspect. The notion of an overarching story by which all other stories make sense has been declared bankrupt by our contemporary secular prophets. But the attempt to deny all metanarratives is of course itself a metanarrative, and if any lesson has been learned in the philosophical academy of the twentieth century, it is that arguments of relativism are almost always self-referentially incoherent.[25] Nor is there any reason to suppose that the vinyl narratives of postmodernity are superior to all others simply because they are the most common. Postmodern consciousness is merely one of many historically available forms of consciousness.[26] Reading classical literature reminds us of this truth all too often.[27]

We need to affirm that there is a foundation to our knowledge of the divine: the self-disclosure of God in the Scriptures, which is not open to a thousand different interpretations.[28] The foundation is not centrally to be interpreted by us but is to interpret us.

If we are honest, we must admit that there is an inherent dislike for this disclosure of the divine in each and every human being, and it is this dislike that leads too often to a thousand different interpretations. We must expect that there will be different cultural instantiations of unbelief: Unbelief does not have to look the same to be the same. If the lesson of the nineteenth-century secular prophets was that we are capable of creating God in our own image, the twentieth century has given us good evidence that we do this all the time. The heart (and the postmodern heart especially) will always be restless until it finds the living God of the universe. And so we might need to reconceptualize sin for our time, not in terms of breaking a law (since the postmodern knows no binding laws) but in terms of idolatry—chasing after things that will not satisfy our deepest longings. We are controlled in our world by an implicit affirmation that all our desires are worth satisfying. Christians need to make the apologetic case that all our desires are *not* worth satisfying, and that many of our desires are conflicting ones. The greatest and deepest desires—for significance, for security, for eternity—can be satisfied only through God's redemptive grace in Christ.

To the postmodern flattening of all truth claims, we must affirm that it is God who is universal, and not the human interpretation project. All perspectives are not equal, if there is a God who creates every living thing. His perspective finally and ultimately is what counts. Put positively, I am arguing for the centrality of biblical theology not simply as one of the theological sub-disciplines but as the integrating center for all the theological disciplines and (most importantly for it) as the integrating center of the church's identity. Biblical theology—i.e., redemptive history, the story of God's redemption from Genesis to the consummation—ought to be the heart of the church. Without it we will be forever defined by the vinyl narratives of postmodernity. But ironically, it is the challenge of postmodernity that may well reawaken us to the power of the metanarrative of redemption. And for that we thank the Lord for his strange providence.

Notes

1. Stephen Fjellman, *Vinyl Leaves: Walt Disney World and America* (New York: Simon and Shuster, 1993).

2. At least for those with enough money to pay for it.

3. Jennifer Allen, quoted in Fjellman, *Vinyl Leaves,* 204.

4. George Lindbeck, *The Nature of Doctrine: Religion and Theology in a Postliberal Age* (Philadelphia: Westminster, 1984). It is less than clear whether the typological institution of Disney World also bears some remarkable similarities to Lindbeck's experiential-expressivist characteristics. This might suggest the fluidity of the categories themselves.

5. This is Peter Berger's argument in *The Sacred Canopy: Elements of a Sociological Theory of Religion* (New York: Doubleday, 1967).

6. Woody Allen, quoted in Jean Bethke Elshtain, "The NewTape File II," *First Things* (April 1993): 12.

7. This argument is laid out most clearly in Peter Berger, *The Heretical Imperative: Contemporary Possibilities of Religious Affirmation* (New York: Doubleday, 1979).

8. The abortion debate is cast in these terms, as is the contemporary controversy over sexual preferences. Choice becomes the operative mental category in modern life.

9. Fjellman, *Vinyl Leaves,* 247.

10. Most of the major evangelical publishing houses have several lines of Bible commentaries structured along inductive study methods.

11. I am indebted to my colleague T. David Gordon for the following line of argument. This is most clearly spelled out in his unpublished paper, "The Hidden Assumptions of Small Group Bible Study."

12. Cf. Elliott Johnson, *Expository Hermeneutics* (Grand Rapids, Mich.: Zondervan, 1990), chapter 1.

13. Robert Wuthnow, *God and Mammon in America* (New York: Free Press, 1994).

14. For a perceptive analysis of evangelicals in the business community, see Laura Nash, *Believers in Business* (Nashville: Thomas Nelson, 1994).

15. Berger, *Sacred Canopy,* 133.

16. This has not happened because there was some grand intellectual conspiracy in the last century or our own that determined forever the course of the church's identity. No, rather, the confluence of very complex factors, some ideological and some not very ideological at all, created the context in which it seemed only "natural" that all narratives should in the end prove to be no more than vinyl. The historical and philosophical precedents to this post-

modern metanarrative have been told elsewhere. Let me suggest Richard Rorty's sympathetic treatment of these matters in his seminal work, *Philosophy and the Mirror of Nature* (Princeton, N.J.: Princeton University Press, 1981). Believing that Nietzsche is the patriarch of postmodernism, one could also fruitfully peruse Merold Westphal, *Suspicion and Faith: The Religious Uses of Modern Atheism* (Grand Rapids, Mich.: Eerdmans, 1994) for the same story. Michael Horton, *The Divine Drama: Redemptive History and the Nature of Christian Doctrine,* 1998 (unpublished) tells the story in great detail and very much in sympathy with the line of argument I am following.

17. Ed Clowney suggests three reasons why the church as a doctrine of the New Testament has been largely neglected in our day: 1. Americans who have attended church since childhood take the shape of the church for granted. 2. There is normally a distaste for institutions and organizations and therefore the suspicion that those who want to talk about the church are organizational types who confuse denominational loyalty with loyalty to Christ. 3. There are more important things to study. See his *Living in Christ's Church* (Philadelphia: Great Commission Publications, 1986), chapter 1.

18. See my *The Fabric of Theology* (Grand Rapids, Mich.: Eerdmans, 1993) for a greater elaboration of this concept of a theological vision.

19. "Oomph" is a technical term common among linguistically-challenged theologians!

20. It is that connectedness of time of which evangelicalism is so desperately in need. Evangelicals are fragmented and live fragmented lives because they have cut themselves off from time and from the one who created time.

21. Talk radio, where everyone gets to voice their opinion regardless of its validity, is the characteristic genre of this particular narrative in our time.

22. John Muether reminded us a decade ago of the dilemma of settling boundary questions outside of the church. Two of the most notable heresy trials in modern evangelicalism occurred outside the context of the church: Ramsey Michaels at Gordon-Conwell Theological Seminary, and Robert Gundry in the Evangelical Theological Society. Not surprisingly, these trials have been very messy. See Muether, "Contemporary Evangelicalism and the Triumph of the New School," in *Westminster Theological Journal* 50 (1998): 339-347, for further comment on this problem.

23. See the very fine article of Edmund Clowney, "The Biblical Theology of the Church," in D. A. Carson, ed., *Biblical Interpretation and the Church: Text and Context* (Exeter, England: Paternoster, 1984), 13-87. Clowney points evangelical theology in the proper direction, toward a more full-orbed ecclesiology.

24. See my *Fabric of Theology,* chapter 4, for the use of tradition in facilitating this reorientation of evangelical theology.

25. See Alvin Plantinga, "Reason and Belief in God," in *Faith and Rationality,* Alvin Plantinga and Nicholas Wolterstorff, eds. (Notre Dame, Ind.:

University of Notre Dame Press, 1986), 16-93, for an extended explanation of self-referential incoherence.

26. I take this to be Peter Berger's central argument in *A Rumor of Angels: Modern Society and the Rediscovery of the Supernatural* (New York: Doubleday, 1969).

27. This is one reason why reading is such an endangered activity in our time. A powerful argument to this effect can be found in Sven Birkerts, *The Gutenberg Elegies: The Fate of Reading in an Electronic Age* (Boston: Faber and Faber, 1994).

28. Though modest in its argument, Nicholas Wolterstorff has at least raised the possibility that there is a conceptual space required for God to speak. See his *The Divine Discourse* (Cambridge, England: Cambridge University Press, 1997).

6

Overcoming the Schizophrenic Character of Theological Education in the Evangelical Tradition

D. G. Hart

How many conference papers have started with the opening line of Charles Dickens's *Tale of Two Cities* about the best and worst of times? The answer, of course, is too many. But assessing the current status of evangelical theological education inevitably brings to mind Dickens's overused sentence. In many respects, times have never been better for seminaries. Yet, other considerations show a very different picture, one that casts evangelical theological education in an unflattering light. To paraphrase Homer Simpson, applying Dickens's line to evangelical theological education is a cliché because it is true.

First, the good news: Evangelical seminaries are big and growing. Of the accredited theological schools in North America, sixty-three may be identified as evangelical, with enrollments upwards of 30,000, and evangelical schools account for almost half the number of seminary students in the United States and Canada. The five largest seminaries in the United States accredited by the Association of Theological Schools (ATS), the chief regulating body of North American seminaries and divinity schools, are evangelical. Whereas fifty years ago the big names in evangelical theological education were either fledgling institutions or unaccredited because they were regarded by mainline Protestants as crassly sectarian, today evangelicals have become the largest proponents and beneficiaries of formal, accredited theological education, if numbers prove anything.

But statistics are not the only measure. The scholarship produced by faculty at evangelical seminaries has also advanced considerably since the days when neo-evangelical leaders identified the life of the mind as pivotal to the transformation of American culture.[1] For instance, in his book on evangelical biblical scholarship Mark A. Noll devoted one chapter to the recent achievement of evangelical study of Scripture, most of which is conducted at evangelical seminaries. On the basis of academic pedigree, professional participation, and publications, Noll concluded "that in many measurable features contemporary evangelical scholarship on the Scriptures enjoys considerable good health."[2] Even more recently, Noll paid evangelical seminaries higher praise, though it may have appeared back-handed since it came in his book on the "scandal of the evangelical mind." In a sustained critique of evangelical anti-intellectualism, readers may be forgiven if they did not notice Noll's commendation of evangelical seminaries for doing "their job well," enjoying "brilliant biblical scholars," and offering "a rich theological harvest."[3] In other words, if Noll's assessment of evangelical intellectual life is at all accurate, evangelical seminaries can take some comfort from the knowledge that they are not responsible for the scandalous mental capacities of contemporary evangelicalism.

Nevertheless, another side of evangelical theological education exists, one that might prevent the pride that so often accompanies scholarly achievement. That side reveals that evangelical seminaries do not have a clear sense of purpose, which is a problem different from lacking a clear theological identity. The evidence backing up this conclusion is partly impressionistic but is still telling. It concerns the recent advertisement campaign for Regent College, an evangelical school in Canada. These ads, calling Regent the "UnSeminary," literally make it look as if theological education is a day at the beach. One ad shows students reading along the surf in beach chairs, while another reveals a family of four dressed in beach attire, complete with video camera. The caption reads "study hard" and then adds, "and don't forget the beach ball." The specific pitch is for summer school, where students may study with such "internationally known and spiritually sensitive" instructors as Madeleine L'Engle, J. I. Packer, and Bruce Waltke while also taking in Vancouver's Stanley Park, barbecuing salmon, and riding the gondola up Grouse Mountain. A similar ad for the law school at the University of British Columbia might generate protests within the Canadian legal profession for vulgarizing legal studies. But in the world of evangelicalism, where such vulgarity has been part of the tradition ever since George Whitefield manipulated audiences by publishing his diaries, all things are possible, including making theological education fun.[4]

The other symptom revealing evangelical theological education's poor health concerns the rising appeal of distance education on the Internet. As the recent ATS meetings on technology in theological education suggest, machine-based theological education is not the sole concern of evangelicals. Still, what does it say about evangelical theological education that its most advanced school, at least from one perspective, is Bethel Seminary—which offers an M.Div. through the Internet—not the seminary with the most widely published faculty or owning the best theological library? And this is not a hypothetical question, since *Christianity Today* has resoundingly touted technologically delivered theological education as the wave of the future.[5] Aside from the many problems attached to the "Internet Seminary," as some call it—from cost to quality of education—the one aspect of Bethel's recent venture into on-line distance education that should give all theological educators pause is the fact that most of the students enrolled in Bethel's electronic M.Div. are already pastoring churches. A recent study of Bethel's program shows that extension programs have a great appeal to pastors who are too busy to enroll in a conventional course of instruction.[6] The real question is not whether pastors are too busy but rather why they need to study at seminary if they are already in the ministry. Could it be that evangelical theological education is superfluous because it is actually unnecessary for ministering Word and sacrament? This raises a further question about the integrity of the evangelical theological education enterprise. Could it be that seminary enrollments and the scholarship of evangelical biblical scholars and theologians mask a great sinkhole in the basement of evangelical theological education? In other words, evangelical seminaries may be suffering from a state of schizophrenia where they encourage more and more students to enroll in their institutions and hire better and more widely published faculty, and yet all the while they are less certain about their reason for existence.

THE UNSEMINARY TRADITION

Of course, the schizophrenic character of evangelical theological education is not new. Evangelicals have a long history of hostility to seminaries and their graduates even while founding theological schools. The best evidence of such opposition is well documented in Nathan O. Hatch's book on pre-Civil War evangelicalism, *The Democratization of American Christianity*. There he argues that the political and cultural changes wrought by the American Revolution provided a setting that revealed the darker side of the Protestant soul once freed from the restraints of state-controlled churches and universities. In this new environment, evangelicals inverted "the traditional modes of religious authority." Rather than "revering tradition, learning, solemnity, and decorum," as Calvinist clergy did, according to Hatch, "a diverse array of populist preachers exalted youth, free expression, and religious ecstasy." Evangelicals assumed that "divine insight was reserved for the poor and humble rather than the proud and learned."[7]

This inversion of traditional religious authority tapped three evangelical convictions, all of which have profoundly shaped contemporary theological education and learning among low church American Protestants. The first was an anti-creedal impulse that repudiated all theological formulations, whether historic or novel, as a device to keep the theologically illiterate in their place. Since Calvinism was the chief theological formulation in the United States, upstart evangelicals such as Arminian Baptists and Methodists took aim at Reformed orthodoxy's soteriology because it made God active and people passive. Still, evangelical hostility to Calvinism was rooted in a profound contempt for all traces of systematic thought, whether Reformed, Arminian, Lutheran, or Socinian. As one Kentucky pastor who joined the Disciples put it, "we are not personally acquainted with the writings of John Calvin, nor are we certain how nearly we agree with his views of divine truth; neither do we care."[8]

Closely connected to anti-creedalism was anticlericalism. Just as no theological opinion was better than any other, so the holder of that doctrinal conviction, whether living or dead, was no better than any other believer. Of course, we may have some sympathy with certain aspects of these low church convictions, since some Protestant clergy in the new nation were part of the political establishment and so were implicated in all of the inconsistencies and tensions that have bedeviled state churches since Constantine.[9] Still, having conceded the political dimension of antebellum evangelical anticlericalism, its egalitarian presumptions remain. Indeed, both anti-creedalism and anticlericalism manifested a proud and radical egalitarian streak that threatened any attempt to discriminate among social arrangements or cultural expressions. According to Daniel Parker, a Kentucky Baptist, "[T]he preaching manufactories of the east appear to be engaged in sending hirelings to the west, and should any of those *man-made, devil sent,* place-hunting gentry come into our country, and read in our places, we shall likely raise against *them* seven shepards [*sic*], and eight principle [*sic*] men."[10] Chances are that seminary graduates in the Northeast who were learning about polite manners had little interest in going into Parker's country.[11] Still, the point stood. For evangelicals, creeds and clergy were bad because they came between God and man, thus smacking of Romanism.

The only men evangelicals recognized as having some authority were the prophets and apostles who wrote the Bible. In other words, anticlericalism and anti-creedalism were simply different ways of expressing the third prong of the evangelical attack upon religious authority, namely, *sola scriptura.* Yet the words of the men contained in holy writ were different because they were divinely inspired. Thus, the not so subtle evangelical political philosophy was that divine was good, human was bad. To put it another way, the only legitimate authority in this world was God's, a presumption that made rebellion against a king alright but posed a few dilemmas when the ox being gored was headship in the home. Not only did Bible-onlyism threaten all earthly authorities, but ironically it made the individual sovereign.

Without the communion of the saints to guide—a fellowship that would typically extend to clergy of the present and worthies of the past—everyone could interpret the Bible for themselves.[12] So deep was the conviction that people should not submit to any human authority that evangelicals read and distributed a book as old as the Bible as if it were the news running off the penny press.[13]

The legacy of evangelicalism's challenge to all religious authority was and still is especially baleful for theological education. Hatch writes that religion has more appeal at the grassroots level in the United States than in any other Western democracy. In other words, evangelical preachers carved out a firm place in the realm of popular culture and mass movements, hence the popularity of such figures as Billy Graham, Robert Schuller, and Pat Robertson. But in the arena of high culture—"in the best universities, in the arts, and in literary circles"—Protestantism's influence is non-existent.[14] As such, evangelicals have no real foundation for intellectual life because, unlike mainline Protestants, "They will not," in the words of Hatch, "surrender to learned experts the right to think for themselves." In fact, the egalitarian gyroscope at the center of evangelicalism conflicts fundamentally with the hierarchical ways of the academy, where advancement and rank depend on publishable demonstrations of scholarly expertise.[15] In another essay, Hatch writes that the populist and democratic orientation of evangelicalism has resulted in the movement's failure to sustain "serious intellectual life." He adds that, "evangelical scholars are far more likely to speak and write to a popular evangelical audience than to pursue serious scholarship."[16] Evangelical seminaries have the advantage of teaching and studying a topic dear to most low church Protestants—the Bible. But even here evangelical egalitarianism kicks in and makes the conclusions of the seminary professor no better than what the folks "share" at the Wednesday Bible study. The sovereignty of the individual reader trumps all hierarchies, whether academic, theological, or ecclesiastical.

In the early nineteenth century, strange-looking and often disreputable figures (by early Victorian standards) promoted the evangelical inversion of religious authority. Hatch's book covers specifically the early Methodist circuit riders, backwoods Baptists, the first Disciples of Christ, Mormons, and some African-American Protestants. One temptation for Protestants living at the end of the twentieth century is to conclude that egalitarian evangelicalism poses little threat to contemporary theological education since its descendants are more likely to be found on cable TV than behind a lectern. Still, if Hatch is right about the legacy of antebellum evangelical Protestantism, then its impulses are alive, well, and often not far from the surface in the classrooms, board meetings, and libraries of evangelical seminaries.

Take, for instance, the case of seminary faculty. Are church members likely to regard professors as doctors in the church whose judgments and insights, though by no means infallible, are worth hearing if only because of their proficiency and expertise in a specific theological discipline? (Whether evangelical seminary faculty are serving the communions of which they are members is another matter.) A good indicator here comes every time seminary boards of trustees and faculty collide. Do the non-academic board members show any deference to faculty, or are they more likely to think their opinion is just as informed as that of the professor of Old Testament? Or, to take another example, how does the seminary curriculum fare at the hands of evangelical egalitarianism? How much do the courses in systematics, biblical studies, and church history really matter to a pastor's ministry, or are they merely prerequisites to clear the hurdles posed by ordination exams? Do ministers really need to know all of that obscure stuff to be effective? In other words, do students come to seminary to conform to and be shaped by a theological tradition, or is a seminary degree a credential that allows graduates to take calls where they will conform to and be shaped by the expectations of the people?

Scariest of all is what the radical politics of evangelicalism do to the graduates of seminaries who go into the ministry. (Now, of course, not everyone who enrolls at seminary is there to prepare for the ministry of the Word—but more on this later.) It is one thing to challenge the cultural authority of cosseted academics, but it is another to demean the special office of the minister of Word and Sacrament. But this is exactly what happens when the doctrine of the priesthood of all believers, i.e., the sovereignty of the individual, obscures the doctrine of vocation. No doubt, many of the farmers who listened to early nineteenth-century Baptist and Methodist itinerants would have made fun of an Andover Seminary graduate moving to the piece of property next door and trying his hand at raising chickens and growing tobacco after at least thirteen years devoted to book learning. By the same token, the Boston merchants to whom Unitarianism appealed in roughly the same period—a kind of highbrow egalitarianism—would have also been dismissive of a minister from Park Street Church lecturing on the development of the nation's banking system. But why then is the vocation of the ministry different? Why doesn't it also have its own aspects of expertise and professional customs and responsibilities? In other words, why does egalitarianism extend only to religious knowledge and practice, when evangelicals allow for hierarchies to flourish in the worlds of business, sports, technology, and above all, the parachurch?

Still, evangelical egalitarianism continues and raises the most poignant of all questions: Why go to seminary? One way of answering this query is to refer back again to the history of nineteenth-century evangelicalism. An irony of that history is that, come mid-century, Baptists and Methodists succumbed to the temptation of calling learned and respectable ministers and founded their own seminaries. The added irony, at least in the case of Methodists, is that, once they founded their first seminary, they lost their rank as the fastest-growing denomination in the United States. Of course, a variety of factors account for this occurrence. Still, by moving in the direction of a theologically trained ministry, no longer appealing was the tradition of circuit riding that had allowed Methodists to establish churches faster and in more remote places than any other denomination. Roger Finke and Rodney Stark, whose assumptions in their book *The Churching of America* are debatable, speculate that the reason for the founding of Methodist seminaries, simply put, was status envy. "The larger, more affluent Methodist congregations," they argue, "desired educated clergy on social par with Congregationalists, Episcopalians, and Presbyterians." Furthermore, Methodist pastors themselves desired "the social status and increased pay that a well-educated clergy could obtain."[17] Rather than having a clear sense that the ministry is something that requires sustained training and "book learning" because of the difficulties involved in both understanding the Bible and shepherding God's flock, if nineteenth-century Methodists are representative, evangelicals tend to pursue theological education for the wrong reason: It yields a credential that connotes professionalism and the respect that comes with an advanced degree, but it is not necessary for the ministry, because ultimately no one individual's understanding of the Bible is better than another's.

Again, the temptation to attribute this problem to the nineteenth century and not to the current evangelical seminaries meets firm resistance from the history of theological education since World War II. For instance, George M. Marsden's history of Fuller Seminary shows that a desire for respectability and prestige was part of the original motivation behind the founding of neo-evangelicalism's most ambitious theological school. As Harold John Ockenga stated at Fuller's first convocation, Western civilization was in the balance, and the task of saving that civilization depended not on the work of "ordinary Christians alone" but also on Christian intellectuals. And Ockenga's plan as the first president of Fuller was to hire for its faculty men who would have the time to rethink and restate "the fundamental theses and principles of western culture."[18] In Marsden's words, the mission of Fuller involved "much more than just training pastors and missionaries." It also included "a *cultural* task, the task of saving Western civilization."[19] Just how the "Old Fashioned Revival Hour" gospel quartet's numbers at Fuller's first convocation figured in preserving the cultural heritage of Bach, Beethoven, and Mozart must not have been entirely clear to those who gathered in Pasadena to hear Ockenga.

Still, the point remains. When evangelicals have taken up the task of theological education they have done so with mixed motives. No matter how much their aim has been to do something noble, whether training ministers who will save souls or scholars who will redeem Western culture itself, they have also gone into theological education to counter the image of cultural backwardness. And if this seems like an uncharitable interpretation of Fuller's founding, we need to remember that, as part of the neo-evangelical movement, the men who began that seminary were specifically provoked by fundamentalism's "uneasy conscience." Carl Henry, who wrote a book by that title, was painfully aware of conservative Protestants' anti-intellectual and socially backward reputation.[20] To be sure, Henry and his colleagues wanted to help. They wanted to improve the United States and Western culture. But they also wanted to escape the negative perceptions of fundamentalism. Theological education, then, was a way to gain respectability.

But Fuller is not alone in harboring mixed motives. Evangelical seminaries across the board bear some responsibility for pandering to the insecurities of conservative Protestant students who hope a theological degree will give their convictions credibility. Some critics of evangelical theological education, such as David Wells, have identified the D.Min. degree as a telltale mark of the worldly professionalism and upward mobility infecting conservative Protestant churches.[21] Yet just as telling may be the M.A.R., a degree that has enabled evangelical seminaries to grow at an enormous rate. Rather than being content with training pastors and seeing that as the highest of all tasks a theological school can have, evangelical theological educators have yielded to the temptation to expand their influence and their budgets by offering degrees to men and women who have no interest in pastoral ministry. And with the M.A.R. have come other degree programs such that, at least in the case of Westminster in Philadelphia, M.Div. students make up only a third of the student body. (And even here, not all M.Div. students are going into the ministry of Word and sacrament, thanks to the advent of the "M.Div. degree with an emphasis in counseling.") Closely following the expansion of degree programs has been the notion of "kingdom work," an idea that bestows redemptive significance upon all vocations by telling lawyers, bankers, professors, and other professionals that their work is intimately bound up with the coming of God's kingdom.

Thus, the quest for respectability through theological education comes full circle and reinforces the evangelical inversion of religious authority. Evangelical seminaries attract students insecure about the Christian faith and unwilling to study without the promise of an advanced degree, and they give these students a healthy dose of biblical and theological knowledge. In turn, the schools send out graduates with the confidence that the secular vocations into which they now take that theological knowledge are making a difference for Christ and his kingdom. All the while, seminaries have added a new wrinkle to evangelical egalitarianism and its challenge to any sort of theological or ecclesiastical hierarchy. Unlike the nineteenth century, when the laity did not know as much theology or Scripture as seminary graduates who went into parish ministry, now the laity who take advantage of the evangelical seminary's many degree programs have as much theological training as ministers and believe that their vocations have as much redemptive import as that of officers in Christ's church. In other words, even when evangelicals excel at theological education, at least numerically, they can't escape their egalitarian roots. The ethos at most evangelical seminaries encourages the idea that theological education should not be the exclusive domain of clerics or potential clerics. Seminaries should be open to everyone, and with the advent of distance learning on the Internet, theological education is literally within the reach of every household with a telephone and personal computer. In evangelical hands, the advanced theological degree becomes one more instance of American mass education.

A CONFESSIONAL ALTERNATIVE?

Finding an alternative to evangelical theological education is not that difficult. Here I use the example of Reformed education, since that is my own confession. Reformed theological education historically has been more comfortable with theological education and so provides a different model.[22] Benjamin B. Warfield, for instance, defined the purpose of a seminary as an instrument of the church designed to provide prospective ministers with "nothing less" than a "serious mastery of the several branches of theological science." "When we satisfy ourselves with a less comprehensive and thorough theological training," he warned, "we are only condemning ourselves to a less qualified ministry."[23] J. Gresham Machen's aims in founding Westminster in 1929 perpetuated Warfield's vision. According to Machen, a seminary should train a minister not to be a "jack-of-all-trades" but a "specialist" in the Christian religion. Rather than equipping ministers with the practical skills required for parish ministry, a seminary, Machen wrote, "should provide those particular things which can best be learned . . . in school."[24] In other words, Machen and Warfield advocated advanced theological training for seminarians. In contrast to the egalitarian impulse of evangelicalism, Machen insisted that "a theological seminary is an institution of higher learning whose standards should not be inferior to the highest academic standards that anywhere prevail."[25]

In at least four ways Reformed seminaries are, or at least should be, different from their evangelical competitors—if Warfield and Machen are right. First, Reformed theological education is hierarchical, in contrast to evangelicalism's egalitarianism. Reformed seminaries should be characterized by advanced scholarship that mirrors the academic pecking order. Though it is not always the case, we generally deem those professors with greater seniority and longer bibliographies as more learned. Where Reformed seminaries differ from the modern academy is that they include pastors within the ranks of the learned. The Reformed tradition has produced its share of egghead pastors because book learning is part and parcel of what ministers do. For this reason, Reformed seminaries should have no trouble giving prospective students a reason to pursue theological education. The average Christian's understanding of the faith is not good enough for pastoral duties. Some interpretations of Scripture are better than others, especially those whose system of doctrine we believe the Bible reveals. Students, then, go to seminary not to receive a credential that yields credibility but to become familiar with a tradition of theological reflection that they will ultimately preserve and defend, often in contrast to anti-creedal, Bible-only evangelicals.

Second, Reformed seminaries assume students and faculty have lives away from seminary. Theological education should not be a totalizing experience where it functions as family, church, and neighborhood. Seminaries are schools, and their place is not to duplicate the liturgical aspects of congregational and family life, nor is their place to nurture students either emotionally or spiritually. God ordained the family and the church, not the seminary, to be the context in which God's people are disciplined. Though evangelical theological education has a great appeal to believers in search of fellowship and accountability, Reformed theological educators should know enough about the doctrine of vocation to understand that seminary lasts only three or four years, but families, churches, and communities last a lifetime.

Third, seminary assumes the prior work and authority of the church, a point very much related to the second. Ultimately, presbyteries or classes train and ordain candidates for the ministry. Seminaries, ideally, only provide the book learning necessary to sustain licensure and ordination exams. They are only schools; they are not courts of the church that determine the orthodoxy of graduates. Too often in the world of evangelical theological education, students do an end run around the church. Having blossomed spiritually in a parachurch campus ministry and having assumed a position of leadership, many evangelical students go off to seminary to train for the ministry with very little experience in a congregational setting and without the oversight of the church. Ideally, Reformed seminaries work in close cooperation with churches to avoid such a scenario. But to the extent that Reformed theological education produces candidates for the ministry who have no accountability to a church, then they have usurped work to which the church alone is called.

Fourth, Reformed theological education assumes a high view of the nature and work of the church—another point closely bound up with the others. Not only do Reformed seminaries have a clear sense of purpose in educating students into a specific theological tradition, they also have a clear sense of what theological education is for: It is for ministers of the Word who have a special and holy calling to fulfill Christ's Great Commission to disciple the nations. The ministry of the Word and sacraments is not something that any believer may do; rather, it is something that only the vocation of the ministry may do. In evangelical conceptions of the church and special office, ministry is something to which all believers are called, and this helps to explain why attending seminary makes no sense for many evangelicals. But Reformed (and Lutheran) theological education is premised on a clear conviction that theology students are heading for the ministry and that as ministers they will be "stewards of the mysteries of God." Being a good steward of those mysteries requires hard study of the book in which those mysteries are revealed, as well as the reflections of godly and learned men who have studied that book. In other words, the hierarchical academic conventions of Reformed theological education are grounded in Reformed ecclesiology. While evangelical egalitarianism balks at all hierarchical arrangements, whether in church, society, or academy, the Reformed tradition has an easier time with academic hierarchies because it has a better understanding of the legitimate ecclesiastical authority inherent in God's ordained means for restraining evil and building up his church.

Still, these are themes of Reformed theological education in the abstract. We are, obviously, far removed from the days of Old Princeton and Young Westminster. Though the ideals survive within contemporary Reformed theological education, they have certainly taken some abuse. Reformed seminaries still seek to promote high academic standards and still show signs of ecclesiastical affiliation. Yet, one sobering statistic shows how far Reformed seminaries have come—or gone—depending on your perspective. The conservative wing of Reformed Protestantism in the United States now has eleven seminaries serving communions whose membership numbers 600,000, *if* you include the Christian Reformed Church. Without the CRC and Calvin Theological Seminary, conservative Presbyterians and Reformed have ten seminaries for approximately 325,000 church members: two Westminsters, three Reformed, Covenant, Knox, Greenville, Mid-America, and Reformed Presbyterian.

This is a sobering statistic, because it reveals just how big Reformed theological education has become, thanks to its autonomy from the church. If Reformed seminaries were only training ministers, many of the existing institutions would fold. Of course, these seminaries still train ministers and the core of their curricula is the M.Div. course of study. But students going into the ministry of any kind, not simply Presbyterian or Reformed communions, are a minority at Reformed seminaries—which means that Reformed theological education grows increasingly removed from the church and applies the rhetoric of kingdom work to non-ministerial vocations. Just how long the market will sustain so many seminaries is an obvious concern. But even more disconcerting is what the effects of such theological education will be on the church. Could some correlation exist between a diminished estimate of special office and the expansion of Reformed theological education? If so, the continued expansion of Reformed seminaries seems not so much a blessing, but a curse.

CONCLUSION: WHAT ARE SEMINARIES FOR?

Two questions need to be answered if seminaries want to avoid the schizophrenia that lurks within the evangelical tradition of theological education. The first concerns the nature of theological education itself. Theological educators, pastors, and church members need to remember that seminaries don't have a legitimate monopoly on theological education, though such a monopoly does exist. That so many people equate the word *seminary* with the words *theological education* is an unhealthy situation not only for seminaries but also for churches and families.

For instance, Presbyterians are supposed to take theology seriously and believe that theology is important for all believers, not just church officers. They also have at their disposal a wonderful way to learn theology, namely the Westminster Shorter Catechism, a teaching device that the covenantal responsibilities of parents should only reinforce. In other words, theology and the teaching of it should be going on in families and in congregations. Yet, too many Presbyterians rely on seminaries for theological education and assume that only graduates of seminaries are theologically trained, because of the professionalism and degree-mongering that dominates American higher education. Few people are questioning the culture of dependence that the seminaries' monopoly of theological education has created and how seminaries have weakened the natural channels of theological education that exist in the home, the school, the congregation, and the sheer spontaneity of believers gathering together to read a book of theology.

The seminaries' stranglehold on theological education relates directly to one of the common complaints of seminary faculty, that is, that students are not sufficiently prepared for the traditional seminary curriculum. This lack of preparation not only involves being unfamiliar with the subtleties of Cornelius Van Til's presuppositional apologetics, but also a general theological, biblical, and historical illiteracy. This concern echoes the complaint of J. Gresham Machen almost seventy-five years ago. Machen himself knew firsthand the benefits of theological education at home, having had to memorize the *Shorter Catechism* and all the kings of Israel and Judah at his mother's knee. He wrote of Princeton Seminary students, for instance, that they came "for the most part from Christian homes; indeed in very considerable proportion they are children of the manse. Yet when they have finished college and enter the theological seminary many of them are quite ignorant of the simple contents of the English Bible."[26] Machen blamed this ignorance on two institutions—the pulpit and the home.[27]

But the problem was not simply illiterate seminary students; it was far more profound. Machen thought that liberalism had spread to such a great extent in the church because of the theological ignorance of the whole church. In his classic book *Christianity and Liberalism*, he wrote, "An outstanding fact of recent church history is the appalling growth of ignorance in the church. . . . The growth of [such] ignorance is the logical and inevitable result of the false notion that Christianity is a life and not a doctrine; if Christianity is not a doctrine then of course teaching is not necessary." The remedy for this evil, Machen believed, was "primarily . . . the renewal of Christian education in the family" and also "the use of whatever other educational agencies the church can find."[28] Surely seminaries are institutions the church may put to good use. But seminaries alone cannot provide theological education. The church needs not only people with M.Div.'s and M.A.R.'s but, more importantly, people who know and love the catechisms of the various confessional traditions. In fact, one of the reasons why seminary graduates may have such a hard time finding an outlet in the church for what they have learned is that theology has become the exclusive domain of the seminary, with the congregation and home existing as mere bystanders.

What we need, then, is an expansive view of theological education, seeing it not simply as the task of the seminary but also as the responsibility of church officers and parents. The seminary should be regarded as only one piece in the larger puzzle of theological education. Theological education doesn't begin at seminary. It begins in the home, is enlarged and reinforced in the church, and then is refined and polished at seminary. Seminaries don't need more programs. They need more families and churches to do what they are called to do.

The second question facing evangelical seminaries concerns the purpose of seminary education. If theological education happens in a variety of settings, then seminaries do not have to be in the business of mass theological education. They should narrow their training to that necessary for ministers. Going to seminary, then, should be part of one's training for the real kingdom work of ministering the Word and sacraments. It is the regimen necessary for holding special office, not the requirement for church membership.

Of course, such a narrow view of seminary education will dramatically cut down on enrollments. Ironically, however, it will also increase the seminary's influence, that grail none higher than which most seminary administrators can conceive. Without a clear sense of the seminary's function, theological educators will continue to suffer from the schizophrenia that has afflicted evangelical theological education. If seminary education is for everyone, then it ends up being so common that it is worthless. But if seminary education is special because it is connected to a special calling, then seminaries may enhance their reputations and be able to make up for lost tuition revenue by generating more gifts from donors who value the unique work that seminary graduates perform as Christ's undershepherds.

Still, the main reason for narrowing the range of seminary education is not to elevate the image of seminaries; rather, the real reason should be a concern for the church of Jesus Christ. Training ministers used to be the sole task of seminaries. And who could think of a higher calling? To train men who, when preaching, are proclaiming "the very Word of God" (Second Helvetic Confession, Art. 1), who, when celebrating the sacraments, are communicating the "benefits of redemption" (WSC 88) and who, when administering the "keys of the kingdom," are opening to believers and shutting to unbelievers "the kingdom of heaven" (HC 83), is indeed a noble and weighty undertaking. But this is no longer the case, and as a result the church and seminaries both suffer. As important as orthodox theology is, having all seminary faculty affirm *ex animo* the whole of the

Westminster Standards without reservation will not settle the problems that afflict evangelical theological education or the evangelical church. One can hold to a view of inerrancy that would make Warfield proud, or a view of justification by faith that would warm the heart of R. C. Sproul, but if he has a low view of special office then he will not have a proper regard for graduates of theological seminaries, because he will not understand how essential the work of ministers is to God's saving purposes. Only by making the training of ministers their primary aim will seminaries recover a clear sense of purpose and a fixed rationale for existence.

In 1931 J. Gresham Machen said to Westminster's graduating class,

> Remember this, at least—the things in which the world is now interested are the things that are seen; but the things that are seen are temporal, and the things that are not seen are eternal. You, as ministers of Christ, are called to deal with the unseen things. You are stewards of the mysteries of God. You alone can lead men, by the proclamation of God's Word, out of the crash and jazz and noise and rattle and smoke of this weary age into green pastures and beside the still waters; you alone as ministers of reconciliation, can give what the world with all its boasting and pride can never give—the infinite sweetness of the communion of the redeemed soul with the living God.[29]

This is a view of the ministry that is missing in evangelical theological education, that ministers alone are called to lead men and women out of this weary world into the rest and peace of communion with God. Without such a high view of the institutional church and the work of ministers, the training that goes on in seminary will look irrelevant and unappealing in the face of so many more visible and better-paying callings, especially when gussied up with the appellation "kingdom work." Whether evangelical seminaries can ever acquire such a conception of the ministry, given their historic egalitarian ways, is certainly debatable. But if Reformed and other confessional seminaries want to avoid the schizophrenia afflicting evangelicals, they need to reject the egalitarian impulses of the

American Revolution and recover that understanding of the church that lies at the heart of the Protestant Reformation.

Notes

1. On the prospects of evangelical scholarship just after World War II, see George M. Marsden, "The State of Evangelical Scholarship," *Christian Scholar's Review* 27 (1988): 347-360.

2. Mark A. Noll, *Between Faith and Criticism: Evangelicals, Scholarship and the Bible in America* (San Francisco: Harper and Row, 1986), 141.

3. Mark A. Noll, *The Scandal of the Evangelical Mind* (Grand Rapids, Mich.: Eerdmans, 1994), 20, 21, 7.

4. On the less savory aspects of Whitefield's career, see Harry S. Stout, *The Divine Dramatist: George Whitefield and the Rise of Modern Evangelicalism* (Grand Rapids, Mich.: Eerdmans, 1991).

5. See Timothy C. Morgan, "Re-Engineering the Seminary: Crisis of Credibility Forces Changes," *Christianity Today* (Oct. 24, 1994), 74-78.

6. See Donald L. Tucker, "Redefining the Meaning of a Campus: Theological Education at a Distance" (Ed.D. dissertation, University of Pennsylvania, 1988).

7. Nathan O. Hatch, *The Democratization of American Christianity* (New Haven: Yale University Press, 1989), 35.

8. Robert Marshall and J. Thompson, quoted in ibid., 174.

9. For a perceptive critique of Constantinianism, see Stanley Hauerwas, *After Christendom? How the Church Is to Behave If Freedom, Justice, and a Christian Nation Are Bad Ideas* (Nashville: Abingdon, 1991).

10. Quoted in ibid., 178.

11. For an example of some of that advice from theological faculty to seminarians, see Samuel Miller, *Letters on Clerical Manners and Habits: Addressed to a Student in the Theological Seminary at Princeton* (New York: G. and G. Carvill, 1827).

12. See George M. Marsden, "Everyone One's Own Interpreter? The Bible, Science, and Authority in Mid-Nineteenth-Century America," in Nathan O. Hatch and Mark A. Noll, eds., *The Bible in America: Essays in Cultural History* (New York: Oxford University Press, 1982), 79-100.

13. See ibid., 174-179.

14. Ibid., 211.

15. On the hierarchical ways of the academy, see Louis Menand, "The Limits of Academic Freedom," in Louis Menand, ed., *The Future of Academic Freedom* (Chicago: University of Chicago Press, 1996), 3-20.

16. Nathan O. Hatch, "Evangelicalism as a Democratic Movement," in George Marsden, ed., *Evangelicalism and Modern America* (Grand Rapids, Mich.: Eerdmans, 1984), 79.

17. Roger Finke and Rodney Stark, *The Churching of America, 1776–1990: Winners and Losers in Our Religious Economy* (New Brunswick: Rutgers University Press, 1992), 155.

18. Harold Ockenga, quoted in George M. Marsden, *Reforming Fundamentalism: Fuller Seminary and the New Evangelicalism* (Grand Rapids, Mich.: Eerdmans, 1987), 62.

19. Marsden, ibid., 62.

20. Carl F. H. Henry, *The Uneasy Conscience of Modern Fundamentalism* (Grand Rapids, Mich.: Eerdmans, 1947). On Henry's thought, see Marsden, *Reforming Fundamentalism*, 76-82.

21. See David F. Wells, *No Place for Truth, or, Whatever Happened to Evangelical Theology?* (Grand Rapids, Mich.: Eerdmans, 1993), chapter 6.

22. For a "big-tent" approach to evangelical-Reformed relations, see John M. Frame, *Evangelical Reunion: Denominations and the One Body of Christ* (Grand Rapids, Mich.: Baker, 1991). For an interpretation that highlights differences, see D. G. Hart, "The Tie That Divides: Presbyterian Ecumenism, Fundamentalism, and the History of Twentieth-Century Protestantism," *Westminster Theological Journal* 60 (1998), 85-107.

23. Benjamin B. Warfield, "Our Seminary Curriculum," in John E. Meeter, ed., *Selected Shorter Writings of Benjamin B. Warfield, I* (Nutley, N.J.: Presbyterian and Reformed, 1970), 373.

24. J. Gresham Machen, "Comments on Professor Cole's Article," *Religious Education* 22 (1927): 120.

25. J. Gresham Machen, "Westminster Theological Seminary: Its Purpose and Plan," in Ned B. Stonehouse, ed., *What Is Christianity? And Other Addresses* (Grand Rapids, Mich.: Eerdmans, 1951), 226.

26. See J. Gresham Machen, *What Is Faith?* (New York: Macmillan, 1925), 22.

27. Ibid., 21.

28. J. Gresham Machen, *Christianity and Liberalism* (New York: Macmillan, 1923), 176-177.

29. J. Gresham Machen, *What Is Christianity? And Other Addresses,* edited by Ned B. Stonehouse (Grand Rapids, Mich.: Eerdmans, 1951), 238.

7

Reformist Evangelicalism:
A Center Without a Circumference

R. Albert Mohler, Jr.

R eform has always been central to the self-understanding of
American evangelicalism. Ambition to reform American
Protestantism was the energizing dynamic and motivating cause for
the emergence of the so-called "new evangelicalism" as it burst upon
the national scene in the 1940s and '50s. Outraged by the encroach-
ments of liberalism, evangelicals sought to salvage the mainline
denominations. At the same time, however, the evangelicals were frus-
trated with their own historical roots in fundamentalism.

As the title of George Marsden's history of Fuller Theological
Seminary suggests, a central aim of the evangelicals was *Reforming
Fundamentalism*.[1] These early evangelicals wanted to forge a new
evangelical identity and tradition, leaving behind the vestiges of the
older fundamentalism. Now, as a new century begins, some evangelicals seek to reform evangelical theology in the same manner. These
"reformist evangelicals" are seeking nothing less than a total realign-
ment of evangelical theology in a direction more in keeping with postmodern thought. Their success or failure will determine the future of
evangelicalism as a movement—and may mean the end of the evangelical movement altogether.

The history of American evangelicalism is one long narrative of a
search for identity. It seems that every decade or so evangelicals
involve themselves in a new fit of identity crisis. In the early days, pio-
neering founders such as Harold John Ockenga and Carl F. H. Henry

established the identity of evangelicalism. This early understanding of evangelicalism rooted its identity in orthodox Protestantism without separatistic fundamentalism. The founders conceptualized this movement, known as the "new evangelicalism," with a focus on both the center and the boundaries of the incipient movement. The structure of this essay takes as a foundational understanding a mathematical model of "set theory" which identifies several different types of sets. Some sets are bounded, that is, they are identified by the definitional issues at the boundary—who is in and who is out. Other sets are defined as "centered sets," and take their definition from core commitments. Some sets are both centered and boundaried. Then there is the "fuzzy set," which mathematicians describe as the set not well identified either at the center or the periphery.

The early evangelicals in the movement suggested that fundamentalists had made three critical mistakes that these new evangelicals would correct. The first mistake was withdrawal, represented by the fundamentalist doctrine of separatism. Fundamentalist separatism, a quite interesting phenomenon, is still with us in some forms. For instance, some fundamentalist manuals on separation offer a series of test questions on the topic. Some of these questions—such as, "Is it allowable for you to ride with a Southern Baptist pastor to a Bill Gothard seminar?"—are discovered to be trick questions for, as it turns out, one should neither be going to a Bill Gothard seminar nor be in the car with a Southern Baptist!

The mistake of withdrawal was accompanied by a second mistake, the restriction of theological concern. In the view of the new evangelicals, the fundamentalists had severely restricted their theological vision. The evangelicals joined the fundamentalists in their advocacy of biblical inerrancy, Chalcedonian christology, and substitutionary atonement. Nevertheless, in the view of the evangelicals, the fundamentalists were missing some of the most significant theological battles of the era.

The third fundamentalist mistake was the elevation of secondary matters to an unwarranted primacy, illustrated most centrally in the elevation of dispensational eschatology to a place of first-order significance. The evangelicals were determined neither to divide nor to dissipate their theological energy over such issues.

The early evangelicals were at pains to define their differences with fundamentalism without conceding the high ground of biblical authority and theological integrity. The question was how inclusive this movement should be. This was an early concern, and it endures. One way of understanding how the founders handled this issue is to look at the history of *Christianity Today* under its founding editor Carl F. H. Henry. One of the early debates on the board of *Christianity Today* came at Henry's insistence that scholars such as F. F. Bruce and G. K. Berkouwer be included on the contributing board of the magazine. Neither of these figures affirmed biblical inerrancy, and yet Henry argued that both were basically cobelligerents on the conservative side of the great theological battle.[2]

Henry's goal was to rally "an international, multi-denominational corps of scholars articulating conservative theology."[3] The objective of these founders was to establish a firm center, and yet the boundaries were kept less clear. The pressing energies of a fight against liberalism and the hope for a larger culture-shaping coalition formed and forged these early evangelical leaders in such a way that they put a primary emphasis upon the center while acknowledging the task of boundary-making. But they were never quite clear about where the boundaries should lie. As a result they achieved the coalition, and over the next twenty-five years what George Marsden calls an "evangelical denomination" came together.[4] This evangelical empire, centered first in Wheaton, Illinois, then in Colorado Springs, and now perhaps in Orlando, is seen in its institutional embodiment in such organizations as the National Association of Evangelicals, the virtual empire of publishing houses, journals, magazines, schools, colleges, and seminaries, and an entire universe of parachurch ministries.

Coalitions always come at a price. In this case, the price was a loss of theological precision and unity. One of the early and urgently publicized themes of the new evangelicalism was its diversity. Looking back at the primary sources, an observer is struck again and again by how diversity was trumpeted as one of the hallmarks of the evangelical movement.

Behind all of this was the desire to build a great evangelical coalition. In 1967, Henry warned that if evangelicals did not settle the identity issue and, in doing so, coalesce, "They may well become by the year 2000 a wilderness cult in a secular society with no more public significance than the ancient Essenes in their Dead Sea caves."[5]

By the 1960s, this awkward but growing coalition was showing signs of strain. This led in the '70s to fissures that openly threatened the survival of the movement. A younger generation of evangelicals shaped by the cultural context of the '60s pushed for a new evangelical direction. At the same time, the evangelical coalition seemed to be missing some important partners. Carl Henry lamented the Southern Baptist failure to join the National Association of Evangelicals.[6] At the same time, the doctrine of biblical inerrancy was becoming a flash point. In the Southern Baptist Convention and among other evangelicals, inerrancy itself was never a naked issue.[7] It always represented something far larger in scope as well as significance. The foundational issue is, and ever will be, the nature of truth—the understanding of divine revelation.

As this fissure became ever more open, and as the flash point grew to the point of explosion, the issue of inerrancy became a virtual crusade, a very important defining issue. In this controversy, Francis Schaeffer became the pamphleteer, Harold Lindsell became the pathologist, and Carl Henry served as the professor. They sought to bring evangelicalism back to a clear affirmation of biblical inerrancy. In hindsight the effort came too late to salvage the evangelical coalition on a unified understanding of Scripture. The movement would not be saved from itself and reclaim the high ground of the total truthfulness of Scripture.

In Henry's *God, Revelation and Authority*, his massive *magnum opus*, the professor sought to lay it all out in a magisterial form.[8] Even so, the result was not to bring evangelicals together in a unified affirmation of biblical inerrancy. The differences were already too dramatic. William Abraham, for instance, responded to *God, Revelation and Authority* by saying that it was not the wave of the future, but "3,000 pages of turgid scholasticism."[9]

In the 1970s, Fuller Theological Seminary rewrote its confession of faith, eliminating an affirmation of biblical inerrancy. *Christianity Today* moved ever further to the left, simultaneously shifting from a more scholarly perspective to a kind of middlebrow view (and now to a popular perspective) with pragmatic psychotherapeutic concerns gaining primacy.[10] Likewise, many of the colleges and seminaries of the evangelical denominations and coalition continued to move toward theological accommodation with modernity.

By the 1980s, James Davison Hunter could trace the pattern of "cognitive bargaining" among the rising generation of evangelicals, suggesting that this generation was both making and justifying theological concessions in light of the demands of modernity.[11] Again, while the inerrancy controversy itself was a flash point, it was hardly a conclusive battle. Interestingly enough, the inerrancy controversy produced significant victories in only two denominations, neither closely identified with the National Association of Evangelicals: the Lutheran Church—Missouri Synod and the Southern Baptist Convention.

Hunter identified three primary areas of doctrinal decline or accommodation: the doctrine of revelation, the entire structure of supernaturalism, and the integrity of the gospel. The most crucial issue was the exclusivity of the gospel of Jesus Christ. Clearly, both the center and the boundaries were growing fuzzy and imprecise. Hunter, reflecting a sociological perspective, explained that evangelicals are constantly "re-drawing the boundaries of faith."[12] Looking at evangelicalism in the 1970s and '80s, Martin Marty, an outside observer, suggested that this is the natural quandary for any system of orthodoxy placed within the cultural context of conflicting orthodoxies and cultural pluralism.[13]

With the center and the boundaries both growing more fuzzy and imprecise, the call came to define evangelicalism to an even greater degree in terms of its diversity at the expense of its unity. The metaphors used by many of the historians of evangelicalism indicate just how this came to pass. Timothy Smith began talking about the "evangelical mosaic," and then came to see the mosaic metaphor as too fixed and shifted to the metaphor of an "evangelical kaleidoscope," not only infinite in its variety but with permutations and changes ever occurring.[14] Robert K. Johnston said that evangelicalism could be defined only in terms of "family resemblance."[15] Nathan Hatch argued that there is no such thing as evangelicalism anymore.[16] Donald Dayton and others suggested that the term "evangelical" was such an essentially contested concept that it was of no further use. Insofar as there was any use to the category, Dayton contended, it should be defined by its pluralism and not by its unity.[17]

Even more significantly, this period saw open calls for the reorientation of evangelical theology as well as for the reformulation of evangelical identity. In his pivotal book *Beyond Fundamentalism,* theologian Bernard Ramm suggested such a shift from a traditional Reformation model of theology, with its understanding of propositional truth, to a more Barthian model.[18] Ramm's work, with its incipient postmodernism throughout, became a manifesto that is even now celebrated by those who consider themselves reformist evangelicals.

The period of the 1980s found evangelicals engaged in another feverish fit of self-examination. Again, the issue was as basic as evangelical identity. If one looks back to the 1980s, especially the period from 1985 to 1990, one cannot help but notice all the books, articles, and conferences published on this subject, along with colloquia, gathered papers, sections of the American Association of Religion, and peripheral discussions in the Evangelical Theological Society. And yet, all this came to an end without any greater theological clarity.

Coming behind Bernard Ramm was a growing reformist movement that included four different groups or forces. First were evangelical historians, arguing that evangelicalism itself had never possessed clear borders. Second were evangelical theologians, chafing at confessional limitations and embarrassed by evangelicalism's historic cognitive claims. Third were evangelical college and seminary administrators, convinced that holding to evangelical distinctives would doom their institutions to an academic ghetto. Fourth were evangelical pragmatists and parachurch organizations, determined not to let theological convictions get in the way of growth and perceived cultural influence. Of course, behind all of these were larger shifts in the socio-cultural context.

By the late 1980s, some of the still-living founders called for a conclusive and determinative answer to the question of evangelical identity. The most significant event representing this impulse was the "Evangelical Affirmations" convocation held at Trinity Evangelical Divinity School in May 1989. Carl Henry and Kenneth Kantzer, two former editors of *Christianity Today*, called together a group of evangelicals to settle once and for all what evangelicals believe. The fifth paragraph of an invitation letter from Henry and Kantzer is quite illuminating:

> The objective is not to formulate a new creed, but to voice consensus on doctrinal priorities of special contemporary importance in view of both religious and cultural trends. These include the full reliability and inerrancy of Scripture, doctrines of creation, redemption and judgment, the person and work of Jesus Christ and other cardinal theological emphases that shed light on contemporary thought and life. We wish to call the Christian churches to a virile alternative to the cognitive and moral relativism of our time.[19]

As the conference came to order, Carl Henry addressed the gathered evangelicals with this challenge:

> The term "evangelical" has taken on conflicting nuances in the twentieth century. Wittingly or unwittingly, evangelical constituencies, no less than their critics, have contributed to this confusion and misunderstanding. Nothing could be more timely, therefore, than to define what is primary and what is secondary in personifying an evangelical Christian.[20]

The meeting failed to produce what Henry had envisioned. The conference adopted a statement known as the "Evangelical Affirmations," which located the central theological threat to evangelicalism outside and not inside the coalition. The statement claimed that evangelicals are united on such issues as Chalcedonian christology, the exclusivity of the gospel, the infallibility and inerrancy of the Bible, and the historicity of such biblical events as the Adamic Fall. Nevertheless, significant compromises of these basic doctrines were already apparent.

The document centered evangelical identity in the historical tradition of the Apostles' Creed. Looking back at the conference, Kenneth Kantzer explained, "The future of evangelicalism we can safely leave in the hands of God. Our concern at the 'Convocation on Evangelical Affirmations' was of a different order. We sought first to determine what we mean by 'evangelical.' What are its boundaries? Who are in and who are out? Is there any consensus as to what constitutes an evangelical?"[21]

The answer given by the convocation, though impressive, was hardly the last word on the matter. So far as those who would become known as reformist evangelicals were concerned, it was indeed not the last word but the last gasp of a disappearing and outdated evangelical paradigm. It is clear in retrospect that those who framed the conference and who wrote the affirmations did not fully understand that the threat was within evangelicalism as well as without.

In a most timely fashion, a bombshell appeared in the pages of *Christianity Today* just one year after the "Evangelical Affirmations" conference. Robert Brow, in an article entitled "The Evangelical Megashift," suggested a fundamental reorientation of evangelical theology.[22] Aptly named, the article presented a bold proposal, indeed a complete shift of evangelical theology away from an Augustinian-Reformation foundation and toward a postmodernized, Arminianized, synthetic new model. Declared obsolete were doctrines such as substitutionary atonement, the penal understanding of the Cross, forensic justification, alien or imputed righteousness, the doctrine of hell, a dual destiny in eternity, the exclusivity of the gospel, and the classical doctrine of God.

Such doctrines as God's omnipotence, omniscience, sovereignty, and holiness were now, Brow said, all to be redefined in terms congenial to the contemporary worldview. We can see now in retrospect the incredible bravado with which Brow penned this article. He was quite certain that his proposals were the wave of the future, since "a whole generation of young people has breathed this air."[23]

There is no question, of course, that an entire generation of persons, both young and old, has indeed "breathed this air." The question is whether the air is breathable. Brow's article uncorked a bottle that is not easily sealed. This movement came to be represented by an impressive array of theologians and philosophers such as Richard Rice, John Sanders, William Hasker, David Basinger, and, perhaps most significantly, Clark Pinnock.

Pinnock, former student of Francis Schaeffer, former Southern Baptist, former Calvinist, and former defender of classical orthodoxy, has undergone a progression of serial permutations in his theology.[24] He now champions what he calls the "openness of God," a radical reconstruction of theism much like that called for by Brow. As a matter of fact, Pinnock was later to cite Brow's article as the catalyst for the publication of his volume, *The Openness of God*, which Pinnock cowrote with several other authors.[25]

This radical reconceptualization of theism involves a rejection of virtually everything in classical theism with a declaration that classical theism is based on an unbiblical understanding of God derived largely from Greek philosophy. Taking the form of a broadside that would make Adolf Harnack blush, Pinnock's proposals sought to dehellenize the doctrine of God. He rejected God's foreknowledge and omnipotence, while redefining his sovereignty in terms of partnership with creation. Pinnock explicitly said that God's sovereignty is an *ad hoc* sovereignty. God is "endlessly resourceful" and he is always ready with plan B if plan A fails.[26] In Pinnock's "creative love theism," the historic doctrine of the Trinity is tossed aside in favor of a social understanding of the Trinity.[27] The ontological Trinity is discarded.

In terms of the doctrine of providence, all that is left is a process model, regardless of the protestations otherwise of Pinnock and his coauthors. God's will is effective, Pinnock contends, only insofar as he is able "to anticipate the obstructions the creatures can throw in His way and respond to each new challenge in an effective manner."[28] So, rather than having a sovereign God, we have an "effective" God whose sovereignty demonstrates his effectiveness at being able to anticipate the obstructions creatures will throw in his way.[29]

Pinnock called also for a reconceptualization of the gospel, rejecting what he called the "fewness doctrine" of salvation and replacing it with what he preferred to call a "wideness in God's mercy."[30] This new "wider hope" theology is, unfortunately, far wider than Scripture allows. The adoption of inclusivism is tied to an embrace of the historic heresy of annihilationism, in which Pinnock is joined by other well-known evangelicals, including John Wenham and John Stott.[31]

Some years earlier, Pinnock had redefined his understanding of Scripture. Theology professors have a good number of choices of Pinnock material to use in teaching the doctrine of Scripture. These include one volume that serves as a wonderful defense of biblical inerrancy (still in print) along with another volume that virtually takes everything back.[32]

According to Pinnock's new understanding of biblical inspiration,

> Divine inspiration should not be over-supernaturalized. There is no reason to deny that inspiration is at least in part a perfectly natural response to the need to perpetuate revelation, and that many of the people involved in writing Scripture depended upon the familiar Charisms enjoyed in the believing community even today. I think we have exaggerated the supernaturalness of inspiration.[33]

Where does this leave Clark Pinnock? Too evangelical for the liberal mainline and too liberal for confessional evangelicals, Pinnock bemoans his consignment to a theological "no man's land," while beckoning both sides to join him in what he considers to be the middle ground.

Another reformist evangelical of significance is Stanley Grenz, professor of theology at Carey Hall, Regent College. Grenz argues that evangelicals must claim the postmodern moment as an opportunity for evangelical advance. He celebrates what he calls the "post-fundamentalist shift," not only in the culture but also in evangelicalism itself. He is a leading proponent of a revised evangelical theology, leaving behind the creed-based paradigm and moving to what he calls a "spirituality based" model of systematic theology.[34]

Behind Grenz is George Lindbeck's "New Yale School" theology, which argues that truth is located essentially within a cultural-linguistic system.[35] "Theology," Grenz says in agreement with Lindbeck, "is a second-order enterprise."[36] The Bible draws its authority essentially from the community of faith rather than vice versa. Like Schleiermacher, Grenz suggests that culture itself is an important source of theology. "Theology," he says, "is a practical discipline, not a system of propositional truth."[37] Of the doctrine of Scripture, Grenz writes, "Sufficient for the launching of the systematic theological enterprise is the nature of theology itself as reflection on community faith. And sufficient for the employment of the Bible in this task is its status as the book of the community."[38] This means that theology is no longer based on a claim of infallible divine revelation but on the self-conscious reflections of the believing community. The Bible is not defended as inerrant or even inspired, but is granted a privileged position because it is the "church's book." In this shift, the authority is found in the congregation rather than in the Scriptures.

Roger Olson of Baylor University's George W. Truett Theological Seminary has emerged as another of the most vigorous proponents of reformist evangelicalism. A former colleague and writing partner of Grenz, Olson offered a significant manifesto for a new evangelical consensus in an article appearing in (where else?) *Christianity Today*.[39] Olson laments that the familial and familiar unity evangelicals knew in the 1960s and '70s has been breaking up ever since. And yet, Olson maintains, all the theological debates within evangelicalism over the past two decades do not really amount to much. "The various positions in these evangelical debates do not themselves call into question our core commitments, but the rhetoric of the debates often implies that they do," he writes.[40]

Olson is precisely wrong. It is indeed the core commitments that are at stake. Olson laments what he sees as a two-party system in evangelicalism. Traditionalists see evangelicalism in terms of its boundaries, he suggests, whereas the reformists see evangelicalism more as a "centered" set. The traditionalists see the need for firm confessional boundaries, while the reformists intentionally will seek to draw no such boundaries. The reformists are willing to risk "ambiguity about boundaries, who is in, and who is out—they insist on keeping the boundaries open and relatively undefined."[41]

Beneath all of this is a postmodern conception of truth, which is inevitably relativistic. Olson acknowledges a different understanding of doctrine—a different understanding of doctrinal progress—than that held by traditional evangelicals. He argues that for traditionalists doctrinal progress represents digging deeper into the historic sources, and bringing out their contemporary relevance, while for the reformists, doctrinal progress is discovering new light breaking forth from God's Word. Olson casts his lot with the proponents of the openness of God—at least in moral support if not in absolute agreement.

Olson makes some astounding statements. "The reformist idea that doctrinal affirmation is second-order language is simply true," he contends. "No doctrinal formula or theological system is identical with divine revelation itself."[42] He also mischaracterizes the traditionalist affirmation of doctrinal continuity: "Some theological formulations are so closely tied with the church's understanding of what God has revealed that they function as being equivalent to divine revelation."[43] This clearly violates the principle of *sola scriptura* and cannot be affirmed by evangelicals.

Olson suggests three individual affirmations as central to evangelical identity:

1. The trustworthiness of Scripture.
2. The deity of Jesus Christ.
3. The necessity of grace for salvation.[44]

Olson argues that no one who denies any of these points can be an authentic evangelical, but he offers no specificity as to what any one of these may mean. Indeed, Olson would reject any attempt to offer such specificity. Most mainline liberals would affirm these three points, at least in some nuanced form.

Olson calls for a careful distinction between core affirmations and secondary doctrines. But here again, his "core affirmations" are undercut by his relegation of doctrinal clarity as a purely secondary matter. An example offered by Olson is the doctrine of the sovereignty of God. He suggests that the core affirmation is God's ultimate ability to intervene in and control nature and history. Then he goes on to say, "It will not matter—as a test of fellowship—

whether he or she believes in God's meticulous control of all events or opts for a broader understanding such that God is 'in charge, but not always in control.'"[45]

He passes along a sympathetic reference to Paul Tillich, suggesting that reformists live by the motto "that all truth is God's truth wherever it is found."[46] But this is a disingenuous statement if left unclarified. By what standard is a claim judged to be true? Olson offers no answer. This is in the context of postmodernism—a new context he celebrates.[47]

I am firmly convinced that postmodernism is basically the new disguise of modernity, perhaps the end state of modernity.[48] Therefore, I fail to see with great hopefulness the opportunity that Olson here champions. If indeed the core of the postmodern understanding is the "death of the metanarrative," or if, as the French post-structuralist Jean-Francois Lyotard said, "the incredulity of the post-modern mind of meta-narratives" leaves recourse only to petit-narratives, then it is quite difficult to see how we are on the verge of a bold new opportunity for the Christian metanarrative—the gospel.[49]

Olson warns of an impending civil war among evangelicals, and he suggests that to overcome or avoid this fate we must establish a restated center. While listing three affirmations elsewhere in the article, he also offers four unifying themes of evangelical Christianity:

1. Scripture as the highest authority for faith and practice.
2. The supernatural involvement of a personal God in nature and history.
3. The experience of conversion by God's Spirit through Jesus Christ as the gateway into authentic Christian existence.
4. The primary task of theology as serving the church in mission and service.[50]

Again, this set is so reductionistic that it could encompass most sectors of Protestant liberalism. In a very significant article published in *The Christian Century*, Olson explains to mainline Protestants what postconservative evangelicals really believe.[51] Olson seems to agree with postliberals that the biblical narrative is "history-like" rather than history.[52] He rejects what he calls a "wooden approach" to Scripture, "preferring to treat it as a Spirit-inspired realistic narrative."[53] Olson explains that postconservative evangelicals reject the exclusiveness of the gospel and embrace inclusivism. It is possible, he says, that many who never heard the gospel will be saved.[54]

Interestingly, and very urgently, the reformists also reconstrue Jesus' divinity in relational terms. "Most post-conservatives feel free to move away from the language and concepts of Chalcedon while preserving its central intent," he writes.[55] This contrasts markedly with the Evangelical Affirmations conference, where the statement adopted (with only two dissenting votes, according to Kantzer) contended that all evangelicals would affirm without question the christological formulations of Chalcedon and Nicea.[56]

Reformist evangelicals champion an intentional alliance with postliberals, claiming that both have overcome the oppressive legacy of the Enlightenment by breathing the new air of postmodernity. Olson has issued repeated calls for a coalition of postconservatives and postliberals. "I believe we need each other to begin to forge a broad, inclusive ecumenical and evangelical theology that will deserve the attention and respect of both Christians and secularists in American society," he asserts.[57] He declares that a potential new middle ground is opening up. The question must be asked, however, why we should give our attention to a theological system that would deserve the attention and respect of both Christians and secularists. True secularists will not respect any theological system that seeks their respect.

We must remember Clark Pinnock's longstanding hope for evangelicals and liberals to come to consensus in the middle. Such an alliance between postconservative evangelicals and postliberals was represented in the 1995 Wheaton Theology Conference. From this conference came *The Nature of Confession*, a book that included such authors as postliberals George Lindbeck and George Hunsinger.[58] InterVarsity Press, which published the volume, has become a major vehicle for the postconservative evangelicals.

It is fully apparent that the middle position called for by both Olson and Pinnock now exists and is attracting many evangelicals. For years observers have identified a two-party system in American Protestantism: conservatives and liberals, or evangelicals and mainline Protestants.[59] This two-party system is now eclipsed by a three-party system that acknowledges this mediating position. Conservative evangelicalism, on one side, and liberal Protestantism, on the other, are now joined by this middle ground of postconservative evangelicals and postliberals coming together in an awkward coalition.

Our main concern should not be to demonstrate that those in this middle position do not measure up to the standards of evangelical identity. Though they do fall short, this is an outdated debate. We should instead try to seek to make clear that their system falls far short of biblical orthodoxy. Our concern must not be the perpetuation of a movement but the purity of the church.

In 1987, two years before the Evangelical Affirmations conference, Kenneth Kantzer wrote:

> Evangelicalism, as in the past, will present a cacophony of many voices. During the battles against liberalism, a common enemy held dissonant factions together. Yet this uneasy alliance seems unlikely to endure. Evangelicals will drift apart into two broad categories. The small group, more nebulous in doctrine and ethics, will seek rapprochement with the near-evangelicals so widely represented today in the top leadership of mainline denominations. The larger group, encompassing conservative evangelicals, both in and out of the mainline denominations, will join forces with the less truculent of the fundamentalists. On each side and in the middle, will fall significant groups that for one reason or another cannot quite stomach either group.[60]

Kantzer was precisely right and wrong. He was right that evangelicals would split into two different parties. It is not at all certain that he was right, however, in the numerical distinctions he made between the smaller and the larger party. It may well be that the reformists will outnumber the orthodox evangelicals.

Evangelical theologians such as Millard Erickson now acknowledge the emergence of this "middle position."[61] But again, concern for the perpetuation of a movement is a failed project. Instead, our concern must be for the truth of the gospel. Admittedly this is an argument that will be most unwelcome in many evangelical circles, if indeed "evangelicalism" still exists.

In terms of the model of set theory, a centered set without definable boundaries is doomed to fall by the death of a thousand qualifications. Simply look at some of the language of the postconservative evangelicals—the reformist evangelicals. The biblical narrative, they say, is "history-like." The biblical narrative is "realistic." God's sovereignty is "real," but it is not monarchical. Pinnock and others argue that God knows all things, except those things he cannot know. And so it goes.

A boundaried set without a center is also meaningless—and will fall by the death of spiritual collapse. Any genuine evangelicalism must be centered on the formal and material principles of evangelical faith—principles championed by the Reformers. But these very principles establish boundaries. They constitute not only a center but, rightly understood, they also establish boundaries. Faithfulness and integrity demand constant attention to the circumference as well as to the center. Otherwise, there is no set. There is no circle.

A word that can mean anything means nothing. If "evangelical identity" means drawing no boundaries, then we really have no center, no matter what we may claim. The fundamental issue is truth, and though the modernist may call us wrong and the postmodernist may call us naive, there is nowhere else for us to stand. There are lessons abundant. The failure of the postwar evangelical coalition was not rooted in its failure to draw from sufficiently diverse constituencies but in its failure to hold any confident or adequate understanding of evangelical identity.

The failure to draw the boundaries and to give attention to the circumference meant that the movement's center was itself lost. The same fate can befall the contemporary evangelical movement. We must respectfully respect and understand the logic of the postwar evangelical coalition and yet we must give primary attention to our confessional communities. We must ensure that our confessions are faithful to Scripture, which after all is the *norma normans non normata*.

This means that we can and should celebrate our common commitments to the formal and material principles of the Reformation: *sola scriptura* and *sola fide*. This means that as we represent diverse confessional communities, united by those two principles, we must hold each other accountable to them.

But it also means that we must honestly contend with each other concerning those doctrines on which we fail yet to agree—and seek to understand what God has revealed in his perfect Word and to make certain that our confessions are genuinely biblical. This is the great hope for the ongoing Reformation of the church by the Holy Spirit, through the Holy Scriptures, to the greater glory of God.

Notes

1. George Marsden, *Reforming Fundamentalism: Fuller Seminary and the New Evangelicalism* (Grand Rapids, Mich.: Eerdmans, 1987).
2. Carl F. H. Henry, *Conversations with Carl Henry: Christianity for Today* (Lewiston, N.Y.: Edwin Mellen Press, 1986), 24.
3. Carl F. H. Henry, *Confessions of a Theologian* (Waco, Tex.: Word, 1986), 384.
4. George Marsden, "The Evangelical Denomination," in George Marsden, ed., *Evangelicalism and Modern America* (Grand Rapids, Mich.: Eerdmans, 1984), vii-xix.
5. Carl F. H. Henry, *Evangelicals at the Brink of Crisis* (Waco, Tex.: Word, 1967), 111.
6. Ibid., 107-109. At that time in the 1960s, the leadership of the Southern Baptist Convention thought the National Association of Churches too conservative. Now the leadership of the SBC would see the NAE as too hopelessly theologically mixed.
7. For a discussion of the inerrancy controversy in the Southern Baptist Convention, see Robison B. James and David S. Dockery, *Beyond the Impasse? Scripture, Interpretation, and Theology in Baptist Life* (Nashville: Broadman, 1992); Nancy T. Ammerman, *Baptist Battles: Social Change and Religious Conflict in the Southern Baptist Convention* (New Brunswick, N.J.: Rutgers University Press, 1990); and L. Russ Bush and Tom J. Nettles, *Baptists and the Bible* (Nashville: Broadman and Holman, 1999).
8. Carl F. H. Henry, *God, Revelation and Authority*, 6 vols. (reprint, Wheaton, Ill.: Crossway, 1999).
9. William J. Abraham, *The Coming Great Revival: Recovering the Full Evangelical Tradition* (San Francisco: Harper and Row, 1984), 37.
10. For an analysis of the downgrade of *Christianity Today*, see David F. Wells,

No Place for Truth, or, Whatever Happened to Evangelical Theology? (Grand Rapids, Mich.: Eerdmans, 1993), 207-211.

11. James Davison Hunter, *American Evangelicalism: Conservative Religion and the Quandary of Modernity* (New Brunswick, N.J.: Rutgers University Press, 1983), and *Evangelicalism: The Coming Generation* (Chicago: University of Chicago Press, 1987).

12. Hunter, *Evangelicalism: The Coming Generation*, 19-156.

13. Martin Marty, "The Years of the Evangelicals," *Christian Century* (February 1989), 171-174.

14. Timothy L. Smith, "The Evangelical Kaleidoscope and the Call to Unity," *Christian Scholar's Review* 15 (1986): 125-140.

15. Robert K. Johnston, "American Evangelicalism: An Extended Family," in Donald W. Dayton and Robert K. Johnston, eds., *The Variety of American Evangelicalism* (Downers Grove, Ill.: InterVarsity, 1991), 252-272.

16. Nathan Hatch, "Response to Carl F. H. Henry," in *Evangelical Affirmations*, Kenneth S. Kantzer and Carl F. H. Henry, eds. (Grand Rapids, Mich.: Zondervan, 1990), 97-98.

17. Donald W. Dayton, "Some Doubts About the Usefulness of the Category 'Evangelical'," in *The Variety of American Evangelicalism*, 245-251.

18. Bernard Ramm, *After Fundamentalism: The Future of Evangelical Theology* (San Francisco: Harper and Row, 1983).

19. Letter to evangelical leaders from cochairmen Carl F. H. Henry and Kenneth S. Kantzer, announcing the May 14-17, 1989, "Convocation on Evangelical Affirmations" at Trinity Evangelical Divinity School, Deerfield, Illinois.

20. Carl F. H. Henry, *Evangelical Affirmations*, 17.

21. Kenneth S. Kantzer, "Afterword: Where Do We Go From Here?" in *Evangelical Affirmations*, 513.

22. Robert Brow, "Evangelical Megashift," *Christianity Today* (Feb. 19, 1990), 12-14.

23. Ibid., 12.

24. For an autobiographical sketch of his theological metamorphoses, see Clark H. Pinnock, "From Augustine to Arminius: A Pilgrimage in Theology," in Clark H. Pinnock, ed., *The Grace of God and the Will of Man* (Minneapolis: Bethany, 1995), 15-30.

25. Clark Pinnock, et al, *The Openness of God: A Biblical Challenge to the Traditional Understanding of God* (Downers Grove, Ill.: InterVarsity, 1994).

26. Ibid., 113.

27. Ibid., 107-109.

28. Clark H. Pinnock, "God Limits His Knowledge," in David Basinger and Randall Basinger, eds., *Predestination and Free Will* (Downers Grove, Ill.: InterVarsity, 1986), 146.

29. For a critique of the theological innovations of Pinnock and the other open-

ness theists, see R. Albert Mohler, Jr., "The Eclipse of God at Century's End: Evangelicals Attempt Theology Without Theism," *Southern Baptist Journal of Theology* 1, no. 1 (Spring 1997): 6-15.

30. Clark Pinnock, *A Wideness in God's Mercy: The Finality of Jesus Christ in a World of Religions* (Grand Rapids, Mich.: Zondervan, 1989).

31. John R. W. Stott, "The Logic of Hell: A Brief Rejoinder," *Evangelical Review of Theology* 18 (1994): 33-34.

32. For his earlier view, see Clark H. Pinnock, *Biblical Revelation: The Foundation of Christian Theology* (Chicago: Moody, 1971; reprint, Phillipsburg, N.J.: Presbyterian and Reformed, 1985); for his later view, see *The Scripture Principle* (San Francisco: Harper and Row, 1984).

33. Clark H. Pinnock, *Tracking the Maze: Finding Our Way Through Modern Theology from an Evangelical Perspective* (San Francisco: Harper and Row, 1990), 175.

34. Stanley J. Grenz, *Revisioning Evangelical Theology: A Fresh Agenda for the Twenty-first Century* (Downers Grove, Ill.: InterVarsity, 1993), and *Theology for the Community of God* (Nashville: Broadman and Holman, 1994).

35. George Lindbeck, *The Nature of Doctrine: Religion and Theology in a Postliberal Age* (Philadelphia: Westminster, 1984).

36. Grenz, *Revisioning Evangelical Theology*, 78.

37. Ibid., 79.

38. Ibid., 94.

39. Roger E. Olson, "The Future of Evangelical Theology," *Christianity Today* (Feb. 9, 1998), 40-48.

40. Ibid., 40.

41. Ibid., 42.

42. Ibid., 47.

43. Ibid.

44. Ibid.

45. Ibid.

46. Ibid.

47. Ibid., 48. "Much to the chagrin of most evangelical traditionalists," Olson writes, reformist evangelicals "find something of value in postmodern culture and philosophy and interpret it as an ally of Christian thought insofar as it rejects the modern project of elevating autonomous human reason above revelation and faith."

48. For a more detailed consideration of these issues, see R. Albert Mohler, Jr., "The Integrity of the Evangelical Tradition and the Challenge of the Postmodern Paradigm," in David S. Dockery, ed., *The Challenge of Postmodernism* (Wheaton, Ill.: Victor, 1995), 67-88.

49. Jean-Francois Lyotard, *The Postmodern Condition: A Report on Knowledge*,

trans. Geoff Bennington and Brian Massumi, vol. 10 of *Theory and History of Literature* (Minneapolis: University of Minnesota Press, 1984), xxiv.

50. Olson, "The Future of Evangelical Theology," 40.

51. Roger E. Olson, "Postconservative Evangelicals Greet the Postmodern Age," *Christian Century* (May 3, 1995), 480-483.

52. See Olson's analysis of the postliberal view of Scripture in his "Back to the Bible (Almost): Why Yale's Postliberal Theologians Deserve an Evangelical Hearing," *Christianity Today* (May 20, 1996), 31-34.

53. Olson, "Postconservative Evangelicals," 481.

54. Ibid., 482.

55. Ibid.

56. *Evangelical Affirmations*, 30.

57. Roger E. Olson, "Whales and Elephants: Both God's Creatures But Can They Meet?" *Pro Ecclesia* 4, no. 2 (Spring 1995): 169.

58. Timothy R. Phillips and Dennis L. Okholm, eds., *The Nature of Confession: Evangelicals and Postliberals in Conversation* (Downers Grove, Ill.: InterVarsity, 1996).

59. For a discussion of this two-party dynamic, see R. Albert Mohler, Jr., "A Call for Baptist Evangelicals and Evangelical Baptists: Communities of Faith and a Common Quest for Identity," in David S. Dockery, ed., *Southern Baptists and American Evangelicals: The Conversation Continues* (Nashville: Broadman and Holman, 1993), 224-239.

60. Kenneth Kantzer, "American Evangelicalism: What Does the Future Hold?" *United Evangelical Action* (May–June 1987), 7.

61. Millard J. Erickson, *The Evangelical Left: Encountering Postconservative Evangelical Theology* (Grand Rapids, Mich.: Baker, 1997), and *Postmodernizing the Faith: Evangelical Responses to the Challenge of Postmodernism* (Grand Rapids, Mich.: Baker, 1998).

PART THREE
OPPORTUNITIES

8

Is Reformation Theology
Making a Comeback?

David P. Scaer

1. Approaching the Question: Historical Recovery of the Reformation

Recent English translations of Lutheran Reformation sources have allowed a wider access to the sixteenth and seventeenth centuries. Presbyterians and Congregationalists have the advantage of English-language heritage in this respect. Until recently Reformation and post-Reformation works were largely unknown to conservative Lutheran church leaders who depended on secondhand sources for their knowledge of Reformation theology. Seminary students and pastors were at the mercy of denominational dogmatics books and denominational pronouncements. By coming into the Lutheran Church—Missouri Synod (LCMS) in the late 1950s, the late J. A. O. Preus[1] and Robert Preus[2] not only became church leaders but helped to recover Reformation sources. Lack of direct knowledge of these materials had left the theological underbelly of the LCMS open to infection and open assault by American Protestantism, as shown by the tolerance and promotion of, and enthusiasm for, church growth methods, Promise Keepers, and liturgical diversity. Some church services have become indistinguishable from the offerings of the Assemblies of God, except that on those days on which the Holy Communion is celebrated, the church bulletin may require belief in "the real presence," with the quotation marks adding to an already confused situation. A cornucopia of Reformation and post-Reformation sources is now pouring out its fruits. Whether anyone eats is another matter. Concordia Publishing House published the fifty-five-volume *Luther's Works* and four volumes of Martin Chemnitz's *Examination of the Council of Trent.* Independent presses are printing the works of other classical theologians, including Johann Gerhard.[3] The *ad fontes* of the Reformation movement is still to have its desired effect in Reformation recovery, although without these sources recovery would be impossible. In examining the sources, a self-consciously confessional church may face the embarrassment of discovering that some of its public positions may not have the support of Reformation sources. Recovery of the sources may present another set of problems, chiefly a transitory historical romanticism, which does not allow for a critical evaluation of these sources or the chief interpreters of them. In any event a comeback of a *sola scriptura* Reformation theology requires analyzing the current situation and ultimately addressing it with biblical resources.

Addressing the question, Is Reformation Theology Making a Comeback? allows for a variety of responses, each of which depends on what are considered the essential features of the sixteenth-century Reformation. This invites subjectivity.

For Lutherans, a recovery of the Reformation may have been rendered remote by the August 1997 détentes of the Evangelical Lutheran Church in America (ELCA) with the Vatican[4] and American Calvinist denominations and the non-confessional United Church of Christ.[5] For the ELCA to effect agreements with two church families whose origins are at the opposite ends of the Reformation spectrum, the sixteenth-century Reformation theology had to have lost its binding quality.[6] Those who have a serious commitment to the Reformation theology of the sixteenth-century confessions have been put on the defensive and forced into a siege mentality. A dark cloud hangs over the Reformation heritage.[7] When the fundamental Lutheran doctrines on justification, the sacraments, and christology have been officially compromised or surrendered, we can only be pessimistic about the survival of Reformation theology and see little hope for recovery.

A harbinger of bad things to come in regard to alliances with the Reformed was the placing of Lutheran, Reformed, and Union churches under the administrative umbrella of the Evangelical Church in Germany (1948); the adoption of the Leuenberg Concord (1973); and the Porvoo Declaration with the Anglicans (1996). Accommodation with Rome on justification was anticipated by the inability of the Lutheran World Federation (LWF) to articulate a common statement on this doctrine in 1963 in Helsinki. The seriousness of this compromise on the *sacramentum sacramentorum* (the Eucharist) and the *sola fide* (justification) cannot be overestimated. Hermann Sasse (1895–1976), who may be considered the most prominent confessional Lutheran theologian of the twentieth century, wrote, "The doctrines of Justification and the Real Presence are the two foci of the ellipse that symbolized the teaching and the life of the church of the Augsburg Confession. The two fronts of the Lutheran Reformation, Rome and Geneva, are addressed here."[8] Even as these distinctive Lutheran doctrines, which were defined in that church's confessions, were undergoing compromise, most of the Lutheran theological leadership had already moved away from the traditional Reformation doctrines of biblical inspiration and inerrancy, issues that later provided a basis of cooperation and doctrinal expression for Lutheran and Reformed conservatives.

Any survival and recovery of Reformation theology cannot be made to depend on a further compromise that identifies an essential core of agreement in order to save it. Such a proposal was offered about thirty years ago by Carl F. H. Henry, who said that conservatives ought not accentuate their differences in addressing the neo-orthodoxy of the 1960s. This kind of arrangement immediately puts Lutherans at a disadvantage, since they must concede what makes them Lutherans and the Reformed and Arminian church bodies lose nothing. Attempts to locate an essential doctrinal core will uncover the deep, unresolved differences between consciously confessional Lutherans and other conservative Christians on their views of God, the atonement, Christ, and the sacraments. An honest recovery of Reformation theology will require that, if evangelicals can cite Luther in their understandings of justification, biblical authority, and election, they must give him a hearing on other teachings, including the sacraments and christology, which provides the Bible with its unity.[9] Thus, if the Spirit provides unity in regard to origin, Christ provides unity in regard to substance. *Christum treibet* is what the Reformation is all about. Unless Lutherans can maintain their positions on these doctrines, they will soon be no more than an ecclesiastical antique, an idiosyncratic dot on the screen of history, a vanishing mist (James 4:14), the Shakers of the Reformation, whose artifacts are already now on display in a Wittenberg museum. Unacceptable is a recovery of Reformation theology which allows Luther the place of honor as the preface to the Reformation, a kind of introductory volume to sixteenth-century thought, while the greater splendor and interpretative authority is bestowed on and reserved for Zwingli, Calvin, Bullinger, and Knox and their Reformed faith. It has become common practice to place Calvin as the golden middle between Zwingli and Luther, a kind of synthesis between otherwise radical alternatives.[10] Confessional Lutheranism in America,[11] whatever remains of it, owes a debt to the evangelical revival, which provided the intellectual brainpower in responding to neo-orthodoxy and the historically destructive exegetical methods that arose after World War II.

Strangely, evangelicals are more aware of what is characteristically Lutheran than Lutherans are themselves, and are able to draw boundaries that restrict Lutheran views from permeating their circles. In their endeavors—e.g., their periodicals, publishing houses, conferences, and scholarly organizations—the Lutheran voice is limited to speaking only on those points where there is agreement with evangelicals.[12] Lutherans often naively acquiesce to these boundaries and unwittingly surrender their Reformation heritage, a sin of ignorance to be sure, but still as much of a sin as if it were the premeditated kind of the ELCA. An authentic recovery of Reformation theology requires that boundaries established by the sixteenth and seventeenth centuries first be recognized and, if unreconcilable then at least honored. Unless this is done, the first expression of Reformation theology will be lost, and we will have taken the same road as the ELCA, even if our motives are better. Sadly, Lutherans have already brought destruction upon themselves, without any external influence.

Lutheranism, like lemmings, has embarked on a route of ecclesial sui-
cide of monstrous proportions. Since the end of World War II, small
holes in the dike draining Lutheranism into Reformed and evangelical camps have flowed like rivulets into a mighty torrent. Even self-
styled conservative Lutherans are often not confessional in their
theology and practice. "Is reformation theology making a comeback?" If removing Marburg's burden is a contribution to the recovery of Reformation theology, then the answer is yes. If you mean, are
the Reformation doctrines of justification and the sacraments still in
place, then the answer is no.

2. CONFESSING AND CONFESSIONAL: TOWARD DEFINITION

Soon after the Reformation began, the Lutherans and the followers
of Zwingli and Calvin set forth their positions in confessions.
Confessing and confessional, as in "confessing" evangelicals and
"confessional" Lutherans, are part of Reformation heritage. At ordination, Roman Catholics give allegiance to pope and bishop but not
to confessions. The terms *confessing* and *confessional* share a common etymology. They are complementary but not interchangeable
ideas. One is necessary for understanding the other. "Confessing"
refers to the present activity of Christians to proclaim Christ as the
only way of salvation. "God forbid that I should glory, save in the
cross of our Lord Jesus Christ" (Gal. 6:14, KJV). It requires that a
clear biblical word be spoken both to a church with confused priorities and to a world resisting Christ which must be reached by his
gospel. "Confessional" means that what we confess finds its substance in the ancient creeds and Reformation confessions.
Confessions are not spontaneous creations of individual faith but
contain unchangeable doctrines which transcend time, space, language, and culture, and, at the same time, are defined at specific times
and places (1 Cor. 15:3-4). Peter's confession that Jesus is the Christ,
the Son of the living God, or the Apostles' Creed are not punctuated
with question marks. They are not conditional sentences. Distinctions
between essential and nonessential does not belong to the confessional vocabulary.

3. Elijah Has Already Come, and Will Come Again

a. Biblical Reformations

Reformation recovery has biblical precedents: the appearances of the judges from Joshua to Samuel; Elijah's reforms in overthrowing Baal worship; King Josiah's recovering the Book of the Law; and John the Baptist, who was sent by God to turn the hearts of the children to the fathers. Reformation involves historical restoration, going back to the fathers. Paul's admonishing Peter may be more revolution than reformation. Reformations come out of nowhere, but they belong to God's plan for his church. *Credo in unam sanctam catholicam et apostolicam ecclesiam* requires us to believe that God will act like he has acted in the past. "He's by our side upon the plain with his good gifts and Spirit" means that Jesus is no less with his church after his ascension than he was before (Mark 16:20). The real questions are whether God intends reformation now, and what kind of reformation he intends. Reformation was finally denied Israel, and after exile, Judah had to be content with incomplete restoration. The glory of the sixteenth-century Reformation has long faded for us.

b. Nineteenth-Century Recoveries

A prominent Reformation restoration unexpectedly took place after the devastations of the eighteenth-century Enlightenment, in whose wake little Christian life survived in Western Europe. Nineteenth-century German immigrants had a cultural Christianity whose finest feature was a latent pietism that had survived rationalism and had been reinforced by Immanuel Kant. He had surrendered empirical proofs to find the moral imperative within himself. All this was served up theologically by Friedrich Schleiermacher, who gave the world a Christianity without a transcendent God or the annoyance of empirical evidence. Modern Protestantism has not advanced beyond that pseudo-reformation.

This religiously unformed amalgam of European immigrants in America was coaxed into a confessional bloom by young pastors who had come upon the Reformation sources that surfaced for the 300th anniversaries of the Reformation in 1817 and the Augsburg

Confession in 1830. Schleiermacher's piety had a positive effect in creating an appreciation for things old. Never mind that his *Christliche Glaube* put contradictory aspects of Reformation confessions side by side. For him, religion had to do with piety and not mutually exclusive statements, something which the ELCA discovered for itself by letting the opposing views of the Reformed and Lutherans on the Lord's Supper represent earlier Judaic and later Hellenistic views respectively, both presumably embedded in the biblical texts. Despite these odds, the nineteenth-century restoration of Reformation theology in a confessionally hostile environment gives us hope that Reformation recovery is possible at any time.

c. Institutionalizing the Reformation

Surviving remnants of the nineteenth-century revivals on the Continent are the LCMS (1847) and the descendant church bodies of the Christian Reformed Church (1834). *Caveant Christiani.* Survival of the institutions historically rooted in the sixteenth century does not guarantee that Reformation principles remain operative—hardly a startling observation. The *una sancta* expresses itself through institutions each of which can be recognized as "church," but the *una sancta* cannot be permanently identified with particular organizations. Reformation, like the church itself, defies institutionalization. An original sin of church organizations is to equate uncritically current positions with those of the fathers and even the Scriptures. This is Rome's error, but she is not alone. Newer denominational positions are incorporated alongside older ones without benefit of annulment, a doctrinal polygamy in which one acquires new doctrinal formulations without divorcing previous ones. This provides opportunity and necessity for reformation. In spite of a rigid dogmatic facade, Rome provides cover for all. Papal infallibility is simply another way of saying that *our* organization cannot be wrong. Besides being an embarrassing obstacle in an ecumenically sensitive climate, it is so overly defined as to be inoperable. Luther years ago told us that councils can and do contradict themselves. So do popes. So does any church. No church is immune to searching for the truth in self-reflection, a theological narcissism. Its own history becomes its peculiar form of *Heilsgeschichte*. Reformation recovery is made all the more necessary but at the same time becomes more and more difficult. Institutions are more likely to be capable of self-admiration or, at least, self-preservation, than of self-critique.

Tragically, biblical and historical reformations are destined to find their conclusions in institutionalized failures. Perhaps this is God's will, so that believers do not look for the church's final consummation and restoration on earth. Joshua, the judges, David, Solomon, and the prophets all promised more than what they delivered. An earthly Israel can never be God's Zion.[13] Luther was disappointed in his own Reformation, and the seventeenth-century wars dulled whatever edges were left. The Enlightenment held that, if the differences between the Reformation parties were unimportant, then so were the differences between Christians and non-Christians. Today this is virtual dogma for most Christians, including Roman Catholics and some prominent evangelicals. Reformations are attempted, but projected goals remain at arm's length. The LCMS in the 1970s reaffirmed biblical inspiration and inerrancy and set the tone for Reformation recovery in other churches, but subsequent difficulties have arisen. Justification by grace through faith is fundamental to Reformation theology, but for constitutional reasons the Reformed Church in America has not been able to require that its pastors annually confess their acceptance of it. As revisionist as the Southern Baptist Convention is in returning to older roots, especially its recent resolution to affirm the biblical relationship between husbands and wives, its system does not allow a full exercise of discipline and it only recently (June 2000) effectively answered the presence of a growing number of women ministers in its midst. It has not resolved a contradiction between the polity of the autonomy of sovereign congregations, a system which allows its congregations to retain ordained women pastors, and the apostolic injunctions forbidding the practice. Other churches find themselves in the same dilemma. Reformation theology does not and cannot work by distinguishing essentials from nonessentials without compromising *sola scriptura*.

d. Not All Reformations Are Reformations

A history of Luther research shows that each subsequent age felt an obligation to find its positions in his. So we have Luther the Pietist, Luther the Rationalist, and with his views on James, Hebrews, and Revelation, Luther the higher critic.[14] Luther's doctrine of the universal priesthood of all believers is used to support the most radical forms of congregationalism, and the glory of this doctrine is seen in the founding of the United States. His idea of the Christian's immediate access to God is seen as merely an earlier version of the Declaration of Independence, that all men are created equal and have a right to believe whatever they want. (Perhaps the United States Congress should bestow honorary American citizenship on Luther, as it did on Winston Churchill!) In celebration of the 500th anniversary of his birth, the German Democratic Republic traced the Marxist system right back through the Anabaptists to Luther's doctrine of justification and the universal priesthood of all believers. Luther did not practice what he preached in this regard, but the Anabaptists practiced it for him. Luther, like the figure of Jesus, becomes the spokesman of the views of others. (Affirmative action should be invoked to give Calvin and Wesley equal treatment!)

4. Reformations Happen

Luther did not intend the Reformation—so much for church planning. It tumbled in on him. Five- and ten-year plans fail. The Soviet system proved that. The Reformation just happened, and Luther rode the tiger, which promised to devour him and almost did. Reformers live under the threat that the establishments they address have no other choice but to remove them from the religious scenery. Reformations threaten to replace administrative decisions with statements of faith. Modern church establishments offer not theologies but policies. Reformers have no earthly security. It is not coincidental that the appointed pericope for the Reformation is about wilderness voices—Elijah and John the Baptist. "The kingdom of heaven suffers violence, and the violent take it by force" (Matt. 11:12, NKJV). In the divine vocabulary, refor-

mation and martyrdom are virtual synonyms. Reformers are martyrs—
a kind of tautology. One Greek word, μάρτυς, carries the ideas of witness and martyr. "Elijah has come already, and they . . . did to him
whatever they wished" (Matt. 17:12, NKJV).

5. REFORMATIONS AS CHURCHLY HAPPENINGS

F. F. Bruce answered Bultmann's agnostic historical criticism by recovering the historical roots of Christianity and setting a foundation for
apologetics. He also attempted to recover reformation for himself, and
he was forever, so it seemed, going from one church to another.[15]
Reformation is an institutional business. Wheaton, Illinois, is a community with an independent "Bible-believing" church on every corner,
each supposedly claiming to be more conservative and biblical than
the other. Reformation is not the occasion for expression of individualism and its freedom, but for the recovery of biblical faith and the
acknowledgment that this truth has been expressed by the saints
before us and preserved in creeds and confessions. They are standards
to which even the weakest Christian can aspire and to which the most
uninformed must aspire. Confessions express the faith before the individual believes. What the church believes is not an amalgamation of
assorted individual beliefs blended into one dough, but that which was
given by the apostles and preserved in the church. *Catholic* belongs to
the definition of Reformation and its recovery. The historical
Reformation was not bent on establishing new churches in the style
of the Anabaptists, but on reforming the old one.[16] Luther was kicked
out—Rome's fatal error! What Rome considered to be the new church
looked astonishingly like the old one, but better. For all the trials the
Reformers experienced, including the absence of a trained clergy, the
Reformation product looked like what the Catholic Church should
have been but had not been for centuries. Church is where the gospel
is proclaimed and Christ is present in the sacramental mysteries.
Sermons and hymns became prominent, but altars, statues (especially
crucifixes), liturgies (even Latin masses), sacraments, and medieval
vestments remained in place. Reformation means returning the ancient
and catholic expressions of faith to their rightful place. Reformation

is the contemporary Pentecost, the perpetual Whitsuntide, the continued coming and presence of the Holy Spirit. *Veni Creator Spiritus.* The church filled with the Spirit prays that he would bring her to continual repentance, cleanse her of unbelief, ignite faith in those who do not know Christ, and rid the church of all false teaching. This prayer is answered because "the church of the living God [is] the pillar and ground of the truth" (1 Tim. 3:15, NKJV).

6. LOOKING FOR REFORMATION TODAY

Evangelicals, Lutherans, and Reformed have to come to terms with the fact some of their clergy, including some of its distinguished figures, are leaving for Rome or Constantinople. Reasons for these defections may be inscrutable, but a search for reformation may be among them, even if the defectors have not come clean on this. Jaroslav Pelikan, a scion of Lutheran pastors from Catholic Slovakia, a premier Luther scholar, and an editor of the American edition of Luther's work,[17] has turned his back on the Reformer and gone to Orthodoxy. He freed himself from the Reformation sources in which he was immersed. ELCA clergymen are quite open about sailing for other shores.[18] Richard John Neuhaus remains the most prominent of those who have swum the Tiber. Reading between the lines, the issue of the ordination of women was the last straw for that camel. As a Roman Catholic priest and influential advisor to pope and cardinal, he remains obsessed with his former Lutheranism, as the pages of *First Things* confirm. Often he states that Rome has satisfied Luther's demands for reformation even on such matters as justification. Or is it that Luther was a Catholic all the time? He puts a most positive twist on Rome's official positions, and an explicit Tridentine statement on justification by works has yet to fall from this lips.[19] Some of his statements on his hope of salvation breathe the air of his father's Lutheranism.[20]

A real factor in these conversions may be opposition to a modern gnosticism's resemblance to the ancient kind. In choosing Constantinople (Moscow) or Rome, these converts have judged the early church's protest to have a greater relevancy for them than that of the sixteenth century. Facing a feministic-fueled gnosticism, they have opted for churches where the Apostles' Creed is confessed with literal intent, and where real sacraments are offered. One female ELCA pastor went to Rome, perhaps in search of the earlier apostolic reformation which saw God only as Father, Son, and Holy Spirit and not as Mother,[21] a faith which the feminism of the ELCA denied her.[22] Baptism into triune metaphors is of little value. Better to die among Catholics than in the apostasy of Protestant sects riddled with feminized gnosticism.

All this brings us to the acknowledgment that reformations are not necessarily all of one kind. Athanasius, in defining the Trinity, was as much a reformer as was Luther in defining justification. One shoe does not fit all. Reformation today may first have to take its cue from the protest against gnosticism and from the faith of Athanasius. A properly defined doctrine of God precedes justification.

Arguably evangelicals, Lutherans, and Calvinists who have chosen Rome and perhaps Orthodoxy may have understood that assent to the ancient creeds allows continued assent to the doctrine of justification, a plausible view if the sixteenth century had not happened.[23] But it did happen, and its definitions of God's saving relationship to sinners can no more be ignored than the creeds' and councils' definitions of the Trinity and the person of Christ. Rome tolerates a Reformation formulation of justification[24] and encourages Lutherans to bring their doctrine into their church.[25] This is possible because justification has no function in Rome's theology. Rome's doctrine of justification (i.e., that grace is given to the sinner to transform his life) is not a doctrine of justification but of sanctification.[26] Justification, for Rome, is a possible human achievement and not a prior divine reality. Atonement is juxtapositioned to sanctification without an intervening doctrine of justification. Justification consists in God giving grace in the sacraments, and the human response to God made possible by that grace. The idea of locating justification in the individual and not in God appeared among some Reformation Lutherans and was condemned.[27] It appeared again in Arminianism. Justification happens when the individual believes. Subjective justification without a prior justification in Christ, whether it be Roman or Arminian style, is no justification at all. The absence of a meaningful doctrine of justification gives Rome an advantage in negotiating with Lutherans, the

Reformed, and evangelicals, because she has no doctrine of justification to put on the table and risks nothing. On the other hand, by acquiescing to Rome's definition, Lutherans, the Reformed, and evangelicals lose the heart of their programs.

7. BIBLICAL HISTORICITY, CREED, APOLOGETICS, AND JUSTIFICATION: *MODERN REFORMATION*

With the contemporary historical agnosticism so prevalent, a fitting parallel for a twenty-first-century Reformation may be the first- and second-century world, when some did "not confess Jesus Christ as coming in the flesh. This is a deceiver and an antichrist" (2 John 7, NKJV). Without the central tenet of the Apostles' Creed, that is, that the μονογενής ("only begotten") has taken on flesh in the historical figure of Jesus of Nazareth, the best-articulated doctrine of justification has no meaning. Modern gnosticism requires that we place apologetics on the first line of defense for the sake of justification. Apologetics does more than prove the correctness of the Christian message for evangelistic purposes; it affirms *incarnatus est de Spiritu Sancto ex Maria Virgine* ("He was incarnate by the Holy Spirit of the Virgin Mary."). The history of Jesus of Nazareth, especially its display in the Resurrection, becomes essential to Christian belief (1 Cor. 15:5-8, 13).[28] Resurrection also provides for "a justification which relates to not only the past but also the present and the future,"[29] and so is the basis of the *"new resurrected life,"*[30] that is, it has value for sanctification (Rom. 8:4). The meaning of the Resurrection, however, is not exhausted by apologetics, evangelistic purpose, and the sanctified life, but *Christ's resurrection is the historical event whereby forensic justification has occurred once and for all times.* Paul attaches atonement to Christ's death, but justification occurs in Christ's resurrection: He "was put to death for our trespasses and raised for our justification" (Rom. 4:25, RSV). The Resurrection is the moment in which God justified sinners. Atonement and justification, like Christ's death and resurrection, form an inseparable constellation. God's righteousness compelled him to raise Jesus from dead. Our justification belongs to the same divine necessity which brought Jesus back from the dead. In one act God vindicates Jesus; that is, he finds him to be just, and by *justifying* or *vindicating* Jesus, he justifies us in him—one act with two sides. Christ's resurrection is more than saying Christianity is the true religion and hence is worthy of belief; it is itself our justification, our acceptance by God. The core of Reformation theology is God pronouncing us righteous in Christ's resurrection. Rome confesses historical resurrection, *et resurrexit*, without justification and leaves sinners to wrestle with *gratia infusa* (infused grace). Bultmann offers a radical reformation principle of a *sola fide* justification, but without real incarnation and historical resurrection, and gives us existentialism, which is at best a gnostic sanctification. In the resurrection of Jesus we not only have the evidence of our justification—it *is* our justification.

8. REFORMATION: *SOLA GRATIA*

Whether Reformation theology is making a comeback depends on one's perspective of what such a Reformation should involve. I have indicated personal despair, but signs of hope appear in the strangest places. In the first three petitions of the Lord's Prayer we pray for a reformation which is nothing more than holding to God's Word and trusting in Christ alone for all good things. Christianity's survival and Reformation's recovery depend on God alone. Lutheran Reformation hymns breathe a defeatist air for which only God can provide relief. If the Reformer's "A Mighty Fortress" breathes fire, his "O Lord, Look Down From Heaven and Behold" and "Lord, Keep Us Steadfast in Thy Word" reveal the sorrowing soul of Christ's church looking for relief from sin, false doctrine, lethargy, and the presence of "the false sons within her pale." Reformation confessional theology is destined to win battles, but never wars, except the final one, when God shall put everything under Christ's feet. When all is lost, God and God alone comes to the aid of his beleaguered church. Psalm 115:1 (NIV): "Not to us, O LORD, not to us, but to your name be the glory."

Notes

1. In addition to translating Philip Melanchthon's *Loci Communes* (St. Louis: Concordia, 1992) and Martin Chemnitz's *Two Natures in Christ,*

Justification, and *Loci Theologici,* he is the author of *The Second Martin: The Life and Theology of Martin Chemnitz* (St. Louis: Concordia, 1994).

2. Only two volumes appeared in his *The Theology of Post-Reformation Lutheranism.*

3. Repristination Press (3555 Lover Drive, Decatur, Illinois 62526) lists writings by such Post-Reformation Lutheran Orthodox theologians as David Chytraeus, Johann Gerhard, and David Hollaz.

4. *Joint Declaration on the Doctrine of Justification* was prepared between 1995 and 1997 by Roman Catholic and Lutheran theologians. Acting for the Vatican was the Pontifical Council for Promoting Christian Unity. The Lutheran World Federation (LWF) represented its 124 member churches and on June 16, 1998, its council approved the *Declaration.* Final approval for the Vatican requires action by its Sacred Congregation for the Doctrine of the Faith, headed by Cardinal Ratzinger. This approval was given and officially recognized on October 31, 1999. Some LWF churches have not recognized the document.

5. *A Formula of Agreement* with the Presbyterian Church (USA), the Reformed Church in America, and the United Church of Christ was adopted at the same convention as was the *Joint Declaration.*

6. Responses to both ELCA actions were made by the Department of Systematic Theology of Concordia Theological Seminary, Fort Wayne, Indiana. "Joint Lutheran/Roman Catholic Declaration on Justification: A Response," *Concordia Theological Quarterly* 62, no. 2 (April 1998): 83-106; and "A Formula of Agreement: A Theological Assessment," ibid., 107-124. *Christianity Today* reports that 165 German Protestant (evangelical) theologians are opposed to the *Declaration* and have urged rejection (June 15, 1998, 12).

7. The following news release explains a recent development: "Adelaide, Australia/Geneva, 4 June 1998 (ALC/LWI)—The Lutheran Church of Australia (LCA) has approved the Lutheran-Roman Catholic Joint Declaration on the Doctrine of Justification. Welcoming the declaration enthusiastically, LCA President Lance G. Steicke said: 'We appreciate the great ecumenical importance of this Declaration. It is the first tangible outcome of dialogue between the two churches on a global level.' The LCA is an associate member of the Lutheran World Federation (LWF)." The LCA is a partner church of the LCMS.

8. Hermann Sasse, "Liturgy and Lutheranism," in J. Khola and Ronald Feuerhahn, eds., *Scripture and Church: Selected Essays of Hermann Sasse,* Concordia Monograph Series (Saint Louis: Concordia, 1995), 43.

9. Attention to Luther's position on the Scriptures may be the key to Reformation recovery. Mark D. Thompson offers the following: "Martin Luther's approach to Holy Scripture remains controversial. Though most recognize his significance in the history of biblical interpretation, no genuine consensus has yet emerged concerning the basic elements of his approach. Attempts to betray him as the forefather of biblical criticism, an archetypical

fundamentalist, and even a proto-existentialist, all attract trenchant criticism. The interests of the twentieth century repeatedly intrude and distort many reconstructions. In the commotion, Luther's own voice is often lost." "Authority and Interpretive Method in Luther's Approach to Scripture," *Tyndale Bulletin* 48, no. 2 (November 1997): 373. This article is a summary of his, "A Sure Ground on Which to Stand: The Relation of Authority and Interpretive Method in Luther's Approach to Scripture," (unpublished D.Phil. thesis, Oxford University, 1997).

10. For example, Michael Horton's review of *Calvin's First Catechism: A Commentary,* by I. John Hesselink, *Christianity Today* (June 15, 1998), 57: "Poised against Zwingli's symbolism and the Lutheran doctrine of ubiquity, Calvin insisted that in the Supper believers receive nothing less than the body and blood of Christ, and yet not by the ascended Savior's physical presence at the altar, but the union with Christ in heaven which is effected by the Holy Spirit."

11. Confessional and Reformation theology, Lutheran and Reformed, are for the sake of convenience used as virtual synonyms.

12. The clue to the real fissure between Lutheran and Reformed (evangelical) theologies may be found in acknowledging that Luther saw the Bible christologically and that Calvin was a "theologian of the Holy Spirit" (Horton, ibid.). Rather than first addressing the sacraments, the issue where the differences are apparent, it might be better to discuss the relationship of the Holy Spirit to Christ, beginning with the significance of the *filioque* and Christ's giving of the Spirit for biblical authority and the sacraments.

13. One wonders what was intended in publishing the earliest history of the LCMS under the title of *Zion on the Mississippi.*

14. See Thompson's comment on Luther in footnote 9, above.

15. See my review of *Retrospect: Remembrance of Things Past,* by F. F. Bruce, in *Concordia Theological Quarterly* 45 (October 1981): 321.

16. This issue is addressed by Timothy George, "What I'd Like to Tell the Pope About the Church," *Christianity Today* (June 15, 1998), 42.

17. *Luther's Works,* 55 vols., Jaroslav Pelikan and Helmut Lehmann, eds. (St. Louis and Philadelphia: Concordia Publishing House and Fortress Press, 1955–1972).

18. See, for example, *Forum Letter* 27, no. 2 (February 1998): 2-3.

19. See Richard John Neuhaus, "Newman, Luther, and the Unity of Christians," *Pro Ecclesia* 6, no. 3 (Summer 1997): 277-288.

20. "But in seeking entry to that heavenly kingdom, I will plead Christ and Christ alone." Richard John Neuhaus, quoted in *Forum Letter* 25, no. 5 (May 1996): 1.

21. See Kathryn E. Greene-McCreight, "When I Say God, I Mean Father, Son and Holy Spirit: On the Ecumenical Baptism Formula," *Pro Ecclesia* 6, no. 3 (Summer 1997): 289-308. Suggested alternatives for the divine name include

Creator, Redeemer, Sustainer; Fountain, Offspring, Wellspring; Abba, Servant, Paraclete; Father, Son, Holy Spirit: One God, Mother of Us All.

22. *Forum Letter* 27, no. 5 (May 1998): 4-6.

23. Concerning the agreement with Rome, Robert D. Preus writes, "All these basic truths were the common belief of Lutherans and Roman Catholics in the sixteenth century and were assumed in their confessions. And this seems to be the case also today among Lutherans and Roman Catholics, at least among those who take their doctrine and confession seriously." *Justification and Rome* (Saint Louis: Concordia, 1997), 33.

24. So Hans Küng, *Justification* (Philadelphia: Westminster, 1981), 223-224: "All men are justified in Jesus Christ and only the *faithful* are justified in Jesus Christ. . . . In the death and resurrection of Jesus Christ, God's gracious saving judgment on sinful mankind is promulgated. . . . Here God pronounces the grace and life-giving judgment which cause the one just man to be sin and in exchange makes all sinners free in him." Lutherans endorse this recovery of Reformation theology among Roman Catholics.

25. So Neuhaus: "It is important for Lutherans who see it as their duty to enter into full communion with the Church [sic!] to know that they need not leave behind the truth they cherish in the Lutheran view of justification." *Pro Ecclesia* 6, no. 3, 288.

26. In the *Catechism of the Catholic Church*, justification takes up a bit more than two pages (481-483) and nine paragraphs (1987-1995). Justification is defined as what the grace of the Holy Spirit can do in us, and not what God has accomplished in Christ. (Liguori, Missouri: Liguori, 1994). More telling is the index, where justification is said to be "made possible by God's grace" (778).

27. Osiander taught that man was saved by the indwelling of Christ's divine nature, an aberration not only in justification but in christology, which was condemned by the Formula of Concord III.

28. See the theme for *Modern Reformation* 7, no. 2 (March–April 1998), "Exploring Mars Hill: Common Ground in Apologetics," especially Michael Horton, "Can We Still Believe in the Resurrection?" 5-14.

29. *Modern Reformation* 7, no. 3 (May–June 1998): 28-30. This description is taken from the Table of Contents (1).

30. Ibid., 29, emphasis his.

9

Full Circle: "Confessing" Mainliners

Paul F. M. Zahl

Let us pray:

Blessed Lord, which hast caused all holy scriptures to be written for our learning; Grant that we may in such wise hear them, read, mark, learn, and inwardly digest them, that by patience and comfort of Thy holy Word, we may embrace, and ever hold fast, the blessed hope of everlasting life, which Thou hast given us in our Saviour Jesus Christ. Amen.

—*Collect for the Second Sunday in Advent*
(Book of Common Prayer)

"CONFESSING"

The subject of my chapter, concerning confessing mainliners, confronts us immediately with two defining words, *confessing* and *mainliner.* I take the expression *confessing* to refer to our confession of Jesus Christ in a lively faith, as in Philippians 2:5-8 (RSV):

Have this mind among yourselves, which is yours in Christ Jesus, who, though he was in the form of God, did not count equality with God a thing to be grasped, but emptied himself, taking the form of a servant, being born in the likeness of men. And being found in human form he humbled himself and became obedient unto death, even death on a cross.

We see our confession as that of the risen Lord Jesus who died on the Cross. This is the "word of the cross" (1 Cor. 1:18) to those who are perishing. It is the essence of our confession as Christian people.

"MAINLINER"

The word *mainliner* draws one to the important passage in chapter 2 of St. Paul's letter to the Ephesians, where the apostle describes the "mainline" church in its rooted and enduring nature, in particular verses 11-22 and, most importantly, verses 19-22 (RSV):

> So then you are no longer strangers and sojourners, but you are fellow citizens with the saints and members of the household of God, built upon the foundation of the apostles and prophets, Christ Jesus himself being the cornerstone, in whom the whole structure is joined together and grows into a holy temple in the Lord; in whom you also are built into it for a dwelling place of God in the Spirit.

IS IT POSSIBLE TO BE A CONFESSING MAINLINER?

"Mainline" means to be rooted and built into the central, abiding root. The question now becomes: Can one *be* such a person? Can one be a confessing Christian who makes the good confession of faith in Christ Jesus, while at the same time being related and established within a mainline Christian denomination? Are the two, "confessing" and "mainliner," exclusive, or are they parallel, or are they in fact possible to hold together as one? The question is first: Can one be a confessing mainliner? If the answer is yes, the second question arises from the first: How can one *live* as a confessing mainliner? What does it mean today, in the trenches, to be both confessing and mainline?

Let me speak for a moment from my experience, the experience of a confessing Episcopalian. Having grown up more or less within the mainstream Episcopal Church, it is accurate to say that Christianity, in its first saving experience, took me *out* of that church and involved me in an almost relentless criticism of the church in which I had been

reared. That is to say, when I embraced Christianity in a heartfelt manner in my early twenties, I immediately found myself asking, as so
many have in our generation, why did we not hear the message of the
saving, redeeming love of Christ, the grace of God in the gospel, from
the church and parishes in which we had been reared?

This is a classic, familiar criticism which almost everyone who has
had a "born-again" or conversion experience finds herself or himself
asking. Why did I not hear these things? Where was the gospel in the
church? The fact that the gospel may well have been preached in the
church, the fact that godly men and women may well have helped to
shape and form one over the years, is not a recollection that occurs to
most of us in the first blush of conversion. Our tendency is to be stren-
uously, even passionately self-righteous. Nonetheless, the criticism
remains, both personally and in the larger historical sense, active and
dynamic—this tension between being a fully conscious Christian and the
experience of Christian nurture in the church prior to that experience.

For myself, I returned to the church, you might say, from within
my Christianity, or *from* Christianity returned *to* the church, not as a
retreat from a culturally unfamiliar free-church evangelicalism, but as
a return to roots and a return to a vision that one could in fact be a
fully conscious Christian and a member of the visible church. For
myself, I can thank early exposure and assimilation within the evangelical party in the Church of England, into which after only a few
months of conscious Christian experience I was drawn and invited. In
the bosom of that tradition, my theological training and further formation and Christian sustenance occurred, from A to Z.

I returned to the mainline church as a confessing Christian by the
providence of this association with a band of brothers and sisters who
themselves seemed quite remarkably and non-fissiparously to combine
fervent Christian faith with loyalty, albeit somewhat detached, to the
visible Church of England or Anglican Church. Such a combination of
allegiance to Christ and functioning with relative satisfaction within the
mainline church is not a common experience in the American Episcopal
Church. But my wife and I did have the great boon of seeing such a
combination embodied among evangelicals in the Church of England.

So, from the church to Christianity, then back into the church, gladly and even gratefully, given the new tradition we had been given, yet always with what Eric Peterson referred to in the 1920s as the "eschatological proviso." This is a great phrase to note: the always penultimate character of the mainline church in light of the kingdom and in light of the great *eschaton* of Jesus Christ our Lord. To be a confessing Episcopalian: One's own *biography* bears on this question. There are many who cannot see the possibility of being a confessing Christian and a mainstream Presbyterian or Lutheran or Methodist or Congregationalist or Episcopalian. My own ability to answer the question in the affirmative stems directly from personal history in the early and middle 1970s.

How to Be a Confessing Mainliner

We come to the second great question. If one *can* be a confessing mainliner, *how* can one exist and continue to exist as one? On what grounds is it possible to hold the two themes together? Here I can only offer the rudiments of such a unity between confessing Christianity and denominational Christianity within the format that I know myself. And this will refer to the charter documents and integrating foci of the Anglican tradition. But I would suspect that you, as a Presbyterian or Lutheran or Methodist or whatever your particular nurture has been, can find within your tradition certain pillars or potential foci of a position upon which to stand and a rock on which to be grounded.

For Anglican Christians, the character of the mainline church as also a confessing, lively Christian church has four fundamental points of recognition and encouragement. These four points we could consider the Protestant tradition within the Episcopal and larger Anglican life and stream. These four pillars, foci, bulwarks, whatever you may choose to denominate them, are vital for achieving a position of confessing Christianity within the mainline.

1. The Prayer Book Tradition

The first pillar is the prayer book tradition associated with the Cranmerian Protestantism of Anglicanism during the later reign of

King Henry VIII and during the full reign of King Edward VI, coming to its settled form under Elizabeth I. Here we have as the fundamental basis document the prayer book of 1549, reformed even more thoroughly in 1552 and brought to its final and established form for roughly three centuries in the year 1662. The Cranmerian tradition of prayer and liturgy as found in the historic Anglican prayer book, still the official prayer book of the Church of England, is a pervasively scriptural and evangelical founding document of the tradition. We can add to it the homilies under King Edward and the Articles of Religion finalized in 1563, the Thirty-Nine Articles under Elizabeth. In addition to the prayer book, we have strong, shorter documents of indispensable confessional character, which provide many of us with a place to stand both as confessing Christians and as mainline Christians, despite the winds and shocks of fashion and the *Zeitgeist*.

2. The Freedom Tradition

The second pillar that gives to this one denomination (among many) a sense of lasting identity for confessional purposes is the freedom or toleration tradition. The Anglican Church carries within its history the seed of Protestant enlightenment, that is to say, a broadly politically tolerant view of intellectual investigation rooted in strong links with Dutch Calvinism in the middle and later seventeenth century. This toleration or freedom tradition, to which I myself can appeal as a distinctively and *positively* liberal note within Reformed orthodoxy, can be dated to the accession of King William of Orange to the throne of England in 1688 and the Act of Toleration of 1689.

3. The Integrated Pastoral Tradition

The third note or pillar of mainline confessing Christianity is the pastoral tradition within the Church of England. This pastoral, or theological-practical *integrative* tradition, seeks the cure of souls as being one of the great marks, heralds, and signatures of the church. This particular tradition takes many forms. I myself choose the date 1966, the publication date of Dr. Frank Lake's epic work of integrative pastoral theology entitled *Clinical Theology*,[1] as the rubric over the integrative pastoral tradition within Anglicanism. Dr. Lake's watershed book gives us reason to see the pastoral task and the theological task of explicating the Cross and justification by faith as *one*—as tasks that can dwell in unity and not as tasks to be alienated and separated from each other. I am not speaking of the great awakening of pastoral counseling ideas in this country in the 1970s, by which biblical theology itself was drummed out of the mainstream of mainline Protestant pastoral care; I am speaking of an integrated impulse which goes as far back as the Vicar of Wakefield and the Parson in Chaucer's *Canterbury Tales*, and which finds a fabulously evocative expression in the publication of *Clinical Theology* in 1966.

4. The Missionary Tradition

There is a fourth pillar or bulwark of the Anglican tradition in which many confessing Christians find a shield and hiding place: In the missionary tradition of the Episcopal tradition and especially of the Church of England, we see the impelling evangelistic urge to bring the gospel to the nations, evinced most classically in the founding, under the leadership of Charles Simeon and several others, of the Church Missionary Society in Cambridge, England, in the early nineteenth century. On the American Episcopal scene, the consecration in 1811 of the Rt. Rev. Alexander V. Griswold, is the symbolic ignition point for the missionary tradition. This moment becomes a kind of turning point in which missionary zeal and even the rite of ordination seem to coalesce and we have the great evangelical expansion of this tradition in America and throughout the British Empire, in the middle years of the nineteenth century.

COALESCENCE WITHIN THE OTHER TRADITIONS

A Lutheran might see moments of interface between the confessional tradition and the mainline tradition in the pietistic movement within Germany, which culminated for our purposes in the creative highwater mark of the chorale tradition and especially in the cantatas of J. S. Bach. A Presbyterian might discern the same unity of confessionalism and church standing in the Reformed church interiors of the northern United Provinces (the Netherlands), which display the most remarkable blending of massive grandeur and Reformed church simplicity. The painter Peter Saenredam integrated the mainline with the confessional character of Christian believing. In my own case, speaking as an Anglican, the God-centeredness of the prayer book tradition and the English choral tradition and the tradition of the settled parish system all represent and help to find their deeper gravity within the fourfold markers of mainline confessional identity of which I speak.

The reader needs to apply these principles to his or her own tradition. Can you have a sense, out of the tradition from which you spring, of being a confessing Christian who *also* identifies with a particular mainstream tradition? This is not the view that was common in many circles of confessing Christians in England after World War II; then, the common view seemed to be that, for confessing Christians, it was a good thing to be part of the mainline Church of England simply because it was *the best boat to fish from*. That is an argument from utility, an argument of convenience, which would not prove satisfactory in any long-term intellectual sense and would finally prove ephemeral and disappointing.

We should wish neither to argue our way from confessionalism to mainline Christianity along the lines of an argument born of expedience (the best boat to fish from), nor from the standpoint of the discovery of the *church idea,* the ecclesiological option that we have now suddenly or most brilliantly come upon, the pearl of great price which is the doctrine of the church. Neither approach is in keeping with mainstream Reformation basics, the four *particula exclusiva* of the Reformation. It smells of desperation to discover the church idea suddenly or out of starvation. It was never the fifth exclusive particle!

I hope it is clear from at least this writer's standpoint that it is possible to be a confessing Protestant Christian in the tradition of the second chapter of Philippians, confessing the faith of Christ who rose and yet was even submitted to death on the Cross, within at least one mainstream tradition, in this case the Anglican tradition. I invite you to con-

sider this question in the light of your own tradition, charter documents, and denominational history. I ask you to discover if there is in
fact a place for you to stand within that tradition.

FOUR CAUTIONS

As confessing mainliners we should consider, nevertheless, *four cau-
tions* in the way of remaining in this hopeful position of integration.
Despite the possibility of confessing Christ in his scriptural magnitude
within the flawed and blinkered church *per mixtum,* there are
nonetheless at least four shoals on which we need to shine some light
if we are to avoid them.

1. Cultural/Aesthetic Factors

The first shoal needs to be clearly seen and understood so that we do
not find ourselves on a Titanic of ecclesiological false hopes. Many confessing Christians who are attracted to the vision of the mainline
church find themselves "on the Canterbury trail"—or for that matter
on the Wittenberg trail, the Geneva trail, or the road to Dordrecht. It
is important to see that the ecclesiology question is a shoal upon which
many are likely to be wrecked. I invite you not to go down that road.
For example, you might be attracted to the Anglican tradition and yet
retain your principles as a confessing Christian, such that your tilt
toward Canterbury is a purely cultural or aesthetic thing. It is easy to
dismiss much of the cultural baggage of Protestant free-church life in
the United States as being *tacky.* The hymn-sandwich approach to worship, the hit-or-miss of an entirely *ad-hoc* approach to putting together
Sunday services, the self-righteousness that riddles the free churches and
has ever been a besetting sin of evangelicalism culturally, and any number of the attributes of evangelicalism that *The Wittenberg Door* used
to parody. The cultural baggage and surface attributes of American
free-church evangelicalism can be a total turn-off.

On the other hand, the beauty of an Anglican evensong, the calm
dignity of a well-conducted cathedral service, the intrinsic depth of the
Book of Common Prayer, not to mention its rhetorical majesty: All

these things could be decoys along the way to an overemphasis on *church* as such. What we find with those on the Canterbury trail is that their desire to find an alternative to traditional evangelicalism is captivated, even snared, by cultural/aesthetic factors rather than by lasting, abiding, and even biblical reasoning. There is a tendency in those who take the ecclesiological option on cultural-aesthetic grounds to become superficial. Ask yourself, therefore, what you are really looking for. Ask what you are really missing. Is this a cultural question or is it a theological and deeply rooted biblical question?

2. Authority

A second caution or caveat in the rush to an ecclesiological solution for the historic and concrete existence of confessing Christians in the here and now is the problem of authority. Many who are seeking a stronger and more decisive voice from the church will find in the mainline, at least in *theory*, the possibility of authoritative leadership—thus, for example, the attraction for those on the Canterbury trail of the three-fold order of ministry and the potential for decisive leadership in an episcopal polity. One antidote to congregational and highly diffused authority structures *could* be located within the kind of governance that characterized the historic churches of the Reformation. If, however, you are hankering after a place of hierarchical or vertical authority in the church, you will not be satisfied for very long in any one of the mainstream Protestant churches.

Generally speaking, the Canterbury trail, insofar as it is a quest for authority, leads to Rome! In some cases the Anglican communion has been a way-station on the road to Greek Orthodoxy or the "Antiochian Orthodox Church" or some other branch of Eastern Christianity. This way out has limited appeal for any with a non-ethnic understanding of Christianity. Generally speaking, most of us, if we do not have the genes to make the transition, will find the ethnic churches of the East unsatisfying over the long haul. If, on the other hand, we are seeking a clear banner-of-truth trumpet sound, we will very soon be drawn through the funnel of the mainstream Reformation churches to Roman authority.

3. Romanticism

A third shoal upon which the integrative tendency of the confessing mainliner can be wrecked is the area of romanticism. It is easy for me, for example, to speak of four-fold Anglican Protestant identity. This four-fold construct is a place to stand as a confessing Anglican Christian. It is, on the other hand, to some extent only a *construct*. I have to confess that the Protestant Anglicanism of which I speak with warmth and joy exists somewhat in the mind. It is an *idea,* because Anglicanism as it really is, in most sectors of the world, may in fact be very different from the picture I have sketched out. The Thirty-Nine Articles are an unexplored tract for many, maybe most, in the Anglican Church. The toleration or freedom tradition of 1689 is in practice almost completely forgotten—not to mention the notion of a Protestant confessing Enlightenment! The integrative pastoral tradition? Yes, that is more generally experienced and understood. The Anglican missionary tradition, on the other hand—the tradition associated with Bishop Griswold, Charles Simeon, and their innumerable spiritual descendants—is totally unknown by many of us in the Episcopal Church.

I speak for a tradition which in many ways died, for all practical purposes, in 1873, with the departure from the Episcopal Church of the Reformed Episcopalians. I caution myself and all others who seek to carry through the integrative impulse against a form of adolescent romanticism. The contrast between confessional Anglicanism as I discern it and Anglicanism as it really is, is at times terrifying. We can draw much too close to hero worship!

4. The Spong Factor

A fourth shoal on which we can founder can be called the Bishop Spong factor. It is really a factor as old as Christianity.

Is it possible to live within a church mixed to the extent that Bishop John Shelby Spong's form of inquiry can coexist officially within the mainstream? This is an enormous difficulty presented by the mainline church. Those who favor a pure church or a purer church or even a church with modest guidelines in faith and practice are stumped by Bishop Spong's rubbery ability to evade censure. This is a problem for all Anglicans, but the same problem exists in the other mainstream churches as well.

(Parenthetically, Bishop Spong's voice *was* silenced at the Lambeth Conference of July/August 1998. Bishop Spong was caught by his own words, which implied contempt for African and other Southern Hemisphere bishops. He referred to them as being only one generation away from the witch doctors! Spong drew upon his head such an outcry from the East African bishops in particular, such a demand for apology and such a devastating critique of his own condescension, that his voice was gratefully stifled for the entire course of the conference.)

Here we need to focus on our own relationship to negative and unorthodox doctrine. I myself believe that Spong's most obvious weakness is the ethics of his style of argumentation. His contemptuous and *ad hominem* attack on all who disagree with him creates an impression of sub-Christian attitudes and sub-Christian manner. In staying within the mainline, the confessing Christian has always to ask himself or herself, am I acting in the spirit of the Beatitudes? Is my humility anything like the humility of Christ? Am I meek in my prophetic role of witness and confession? This is a vital factor in the continuing ability of confessing persons to retain an investment within the mainline churches.

A Footnote on Reformed Orthodoxy

A final interpretive thought concerning the confessing mainline: It is buoying to be able to claim the Reformed tradition in its orthodox seventeenth-century solidity within our respective traditions. It is a good and right part of our legacy that in Presbyterian polity and in Anglican polity we can look without embarrassment—and at the same time with a contemporary sense of loss—at the Reformed dimension within the theological testament of our forebears. Within my own tradition I can refer specifically to the Lambeth Articles of 1595, which were an early and vital Calvinist statement of faith sponsored by the Church of England bishops and endorsed at Lambeth Palace under Archbishop Whitgift. Queen Elizabeth I refused to sign them into law—mainly because she had not been consulted before they were approved by the bishops—but they nevertheless remain the high-water mark of Reformed inheritance in this particular mainstream denomination.

THE POSSIBILITY OF REMAINING

To conclude, it is possible to be confessing *and* mainline. It is possible because Scripture has joined together what none of us can finally in our flesh pull asunder, despite all the heresies and implicit fractures in the earliest Christian churches. St. Paul was a confessing mainline Christian. And those to whom he spoke wished to be so. As long as that tradition is in the bedrock of the earliest Christian foundation documents, we are required constantly to ask ourselves the question of whether we can keep together that which human nature and our precisionism, and indeed our very normal tilt toward self-righteousness, would seek to split. I invite you, within the tradition from which each has been hewn, to consider positively the possibility of remaining in the mainstream, on good foundations and confessing that Jesus Christ is Lord to the glory of God the Father.

The concluding prayer comes from the Collect for the Tuesday in Easter Week (Book of Common Prayer, 1549). This prayer, from Cranmer's prayer book, reflects that perfect unity of Reformation theology and classic Christian piety which this chapter aspires to nurture:

> Almighty Father, which hast given thine only son to die for our sins and to rise again for our justification, grant us so to put away the leaven of malice and wickedness that we may always serve thee in sureness of living and truth; through Jesus Christ our Lord. Amen.

Notes

1. Frank Lake, *Clinical Theology* (London: Darton, Longman and Todd, 1966).

10

Yale Postliberalism:
Back to the Bible?

Michael S. Horton

One of the revelations derived from spending two years at Yale Divinity School was that there is no such thing as the "Yale School." One wouldn't know that from all of the press it has received in recent years. The halls of evangelical theology are humming with various efforts at appropriating the insights of the "Yale School."[1] Although Yale's current theological faculty is more diverse than a nickname might suggest, it is possible to discern a number of common features in the work of formative members of this community. Furthermore, this contemporary school is at least too important to overlook and may even be a catalyst for thinking through our own hopes of reintegrating exegesis (analysis) and systematics (synthesis).

As is well known by now, Yale postliberalism is a species of narrative theology—and perhaps its most prominent expression at present. In addition to literary trends (especially structuralism and New Criticism, the latter of which was centered in Yale's literature department), this version of narrative theology is especially indebted to Karl Barth. While one should not fail to recognize the distinct contributions of its own representatives, this approach championed by Hans Frei, Brevard Childs, George Lindbeck, and their influential students Kathryn Tanner, William Placher, Stanley Hauerwas, and George Hunsinger, grows out of Barth's method and orientation. However, Yale had its own indigenous sources, such as H. Richard Niebuhr, whose *The Meaning of Revelation*[2] distinguished between an "inner" and "outer" history, emphasizing this meaning as "the Story of Our Lives." Already many of the major lines of narrative theology were suggested. At the same time, G. Ernest Wright's *God Who Acts*[3] announced a new program, away from the ahistorical approaches which had dominated modern theology, emphasizing revelation as a history of divine acts. Oscar Cullmann raised a similar banner, and by mid-century theology was locked in a battle over word-revelation versus act-revelation.

Meanwhile, Niebuhr and his younger colleagues were working out the implications of a postcritical hermeneutic while some time later Erich Auerbach's *Mimesis*[4] brought still greater focus to the integration of biblical and literary studies. Not surprisingly, it was Yale's biblical theologian, Brevard Childs, who launched the first salvo in his work *Biblical Theology in Crisis*,[5] and in subsequent works his emphasis on canonical unity became a key tenet of this narrative project. Yale graduate Stanley Hauerwas contributed *Vision and Virtue*[6] and, with David Burrell and Richard Bondi, *Truthfulness and Tragedy*,[7] in which narrative was linked to ethics in richly suggestive ways. But in 1974 Yale University Press published Hans Frei's magnum opus, *The Eclipse of Biblical Narrative*,[8] to which we shall return.

But it was especially in the 1980s that narrative theology took its general shape. Robert Alter's *The Art of Biblical Narrative*[9] stressed the dominance of the narrative genre in biblical interpretation, and in that same year Alasdair MacIntyre's *After Virtue*[10] offered a persuasive argument for the dependence of ethics on narrative. Other noteworthy contributions followed, including Michael Goldberg's *Theology and Narrative*[11] and Ronald Thiemann's *Revelation and Theology: The Gospel as Narrated Promise*.[12] But no contribution has been more seminal for the so-called Yale school since the publication of Frei's classic than George Lindbeck's *The Nature of Doctrine*.[13] If Frei set forth the analysis of biblical theology's demise, then Lindbeck contributed to the school a distinct theological method.[14]

Meanwhile, narrative approaches have become increasingly popular in evangelical circles and have contributed in some measure to greater interaction and overlap between evangelical and mainline scholars. Gabriel Fackre's *The Christian Story*[15] is one early example of this overlap and represents one of the few actual exercises in theology, beyond method, among evangelical writers. At a conference which I attended at Wheaton College in April 1995, representatives of Yale postliberalism engaged in lively discussion with evangelical scholars.[16] And in the estimation of a fair number of the latter, this trend represents a renaissance of biblical Christianity.

Here, then, I propose to do three things: First, to describe the basic outline of this school; second, to analyze its strengths and weaknesses; and third, to briefly suggest a model which might incorporate its strengths while avoiding its weaknesses.

DESCRIPTION

Upon one thing current systematicians can agree, and that is, in David Tracy's words, "*The* problem of the contemporary systematic theologian, as has often been remarked, is actually *to do* systematic theology."[17] Although their advocates feel obliged to apologize for apologetics, Yale theologians believe that one of the real problems in constructive theology today is that we cannot seem to get beyond prolegomena. Frei observes, "Someone has rightly said, 'A person either has character or he invents a method.' I believe that and have been trying for years to trade method for character, since at heart I really don't believe in independent methodological study of theology (I think the theory is dependent on the practice), but so far I haven't found that I'm a seller to myself as a purchaser."[18]

As I have hinted above, Barth's influence and inspiration guides the Yale school's own adaptations of and variations on his method. Especially significant is Barth's notion of "the strange, new world of the Bible."[19] Nevertheless, it would be reductionistic to dismiss this school as merely a different verse of the same hymn.

In his criticism of Bultmann, his contemporary Julius Schniewind reflected the direction that becomes explicit in Frei's approach when he writes, "The right imagery is to be won from the narrative of the gospels."[20] In *The Eclipse of Biblical Narrative*, Frei argues that, until the Enlightenment, Christians had read the Bible as a unity. Following the *sensus literalis*, the church understood the text in terms of promise and fulfillment, a theory of "figuration" guiding its hermeneutic. Despite the multiple-sense hermeneutic, the literal sense dominated even in the Middle Ages, Frei contends, although the Reformation restored to it considerable clarity and normativity. But the first cracks in the wall appeared with the emergence of pietism in the seventeenth century, especially through the millenarian extravagancies of Bengel and others. Meanwhile, the orthodox (partly in reaction) increasingly treated the Bible as a cabinet of proof-texts to be dispensed as prescriptions against heresy. Finally, the Enlightenment drove a wedge between the world of the text and the "real" world of history, giving rise to the higher-critical enterprise. Consequently, the meaning of the text was to be lodged in something above or behind the text itself. The *real* meaning was to be discovered not in the narrative but in another ostensibly truer reality to which the narrative pointed or which it in some way illustrated.

While eighteenth-century theology was still focused on Jesus as revealer and revelation (though chiefly in terms of ethics), the nineteenth century turned to the inner state of the soul as the subject of revelation. Hegel preserved the professional respectability of believing in the Incarnation and Resurrection, but these were no more taken literally by the nineteenth-century theologians than they were by Hegel himself. So, finally, D. F. Strauss entered the picture and demanded to know the relation between the Jesus of history and the Christ of faith. The historical method is intrinsically incapable of yielding a unique God-Man, says Frei, and his model cannot be understood at all apart from this assertion. But critics, from Strauss to Troeltsch to Van Harvey, have answered that one cannot grant the historical person while denying, in principle, historical access to that person. Frei is closer to Barth than to Strauss's descendants and their critics on this point: "I am persuaded that historical inquiry is a useful and necessary procedure," Frei admits, "but that theological reading is the reading of the *text*, and not the reading of a source, which is how historians read it."[21] For that reason, the nearest disciplinary relative to theology "is not history at all," but "a certain kind of social anthropology," especially that of Clifford Geertz, with a close kinship as well to literary studies. Anticipating Lindbeck, Frei writes,

[Christianity] is not a network of beliefs, it is not a system, first of all. It may be an intellectual system also, but not in the first place. Further, it is not first of all an experienced something, an experienced shape, an essence. Rather, it is first of all a complex, various, loosely held, and yet really discernable community with varying features—a religious community of which, for example, a sacred text is one feature that is typical of a religion. And the sacred text usually (and certainly in Christianity), in the tradition of interpretation within the religion, comes to focus around a sacred story.[22]

What would an appropriation of this sort of theology look like? For Frei, it would look a lot like the *sensus literalis* of the historic Christian practice. But what does he mean by the *sensus literalis*? First, borrowing from Jewish scholar Raphael Loewe and Charles Wood, he defines it as "precisely that meaning which finds the greatest degree of agreement in the use of the text in the religious community. . . . So the first sense of the literal reading stems from the use of the text in the Church. The second rule concerning the literal sense is that it is the fit enactment of the intention to say what comes to be in the text."[23]

The literal sense is not literalism. Nor does Frei wish to confuse this sense with any theory of biblical inspiration. It is just such grand endeavors, says Frei, that have undermined or distracted us from the plain reading of the text, treating it as a source for an extrabiblical theory rather than simply reading it and then reading ourselves and our world through its lens. Theology for Frei is most succinctly (and frequently) described as "Christian self-description." It is not religion (a universal phenomenon of human experience) that is in view, but a particular community of discourse. Therefore, theology must be *Christian* self-description. A metatheory of religious consciousness will not account for the distinct narratives, doctrines, rituals, and practices that surface through the grammar of faith. "Theology, in other words, is the grammar of the religion, understood as a faith and as an ordered community life."[24]

This metaphor of a "grammar," borrowed from the social sciences in its appropriation from linguistics, is so important to Frei at least in part because it expresses this communal-contextual nature of religious discourse.[25] As with all grammars, Christian theology is shaped by a text and by rules for reading that text, rules that are indigenous to and are exclusively determined by the text itself. The specific doctrines that seek to interpret that text faithfully are the grammar's "rules." And here we come to a central thesis of the cultural-linguistic method in theology:

> First, there is what we might call first-order theology—that is, Christian witness, including the confession of specific beliefs (for instance, the creeds) that seem on the face of them to be talking about acknowledging a state of affairs that holds true whether one believes it or not. But second, there is what we have just called the logic, or grammar, of the faith, which may well have bearing on the first-order statements. And third, there is a kind of quasi-philosophical or philosophical activity involved even in this kind of theologizing, which consists of trying to tell others, perhaps outsiders, how these rules compare and contrast with their kinds of ruled discourse.[26]

Accordingly, we must live with the ambiguity of belonging to a religion that is a particular cultural-linguistic community with its own rules and yet makes universal truth claims. Better the ambiguity than to give in to the temptation to turn Christianity into "a metaphysical construct or an ontological vision."[27] A key question Frei asks us is this: "Is theology, as reflection on the ruled use of the Christian community's language, completely internal to that community?"[28] For Frei, the Bible, the sacraments, the creeds, and the life-patterns are not significations of a larger something called religion, but are themselves the constitutive parts of that particular religion called Christianity. Reminiscent of the social historian's untiring critique of intellectual history, Frei's concern is that the particular context is too often swallowed whole in universalizing, totalizing metanarratives.

In short, while centuries of Christians had been absorbed by the world of Scripture, theology was now (according to Frei's account of modern theology) increasingly committed to the task of absorbing the world of Scripture into the world of modernity. The Bible's story was made to be *about* some other, more universal and accessible story. But the Bible's defenders were unwitting coconspirators, says Frei, in that their apologetics tended to accept this Enlightenment premise by trying to render the Bible acceptable on the grounds of autonomous, universal reason and experience. Like their critics, the apologists were caving in to the pressure to make the biblical narrative *about* something else, something behind or above the text. To all of this Frei replies that the point of the narrative *is* the narrative. This is the real world: Let it absorb you and stop trying to make it "relevant" or "applicable" to the modern age. Resist the urge to locate the meaning of Scripture somewhere outside of Scripture. For the orthodox, he argues, the real meaning of the text was timeless propositions; for Schleiermacher, feeling. In recent theology, the indigenous framework of biblical narrative has been replaced with such frameworks as "radical hope, radical faith, radical obedience, or radically authentic being," which leads to "ethicizing, existentializing, [and] privatizing" the biblical story.[29]

Inspired perhaps by Niebuhr's "Christ and Culture" typology, the Yale school has a fondness for describing its program in contrast to various schema. Frei's discussion of "types" takes place against the backdrop of *Wissenschaftslehre*, "the inquiry into the universal, rational principles that allow us to organize any and all specific fields of inquiry into internally and mutually coherent, intelligible totalities," or, "an inquiry into the transcendental principles justifying all systematic method and explanation."[30] As a university discipline in which the natural sciences were now queen, theology had to adopt methods and criteria that were alien to its own character. It was therefore inevitable that Christian theology would be reduced to psychology or some other form of scientific analysis which would consider such theology nothing more than a variation on the theme of universal religious experience—in other words, comparative religion. How can academic theology be done for and within the community of ecclesial commitment, the community whose narrative it is and whose own rules govern the reading and practice of its founding text? Barth's

Kirchliche Dogmatische, with an emphasis on *Kirchliche*, is therefore, according to Frei, the pattern for doing theology.[31]

According to Frei, the options in theological method today may be grouped under four or five distinct "types." Let us briefly consider them.

Type One (Kaufman)

Kant, of course, believed that the mind was active in the business of thinking. Unlike the empiricist, who thought his mind was simply receiving the sensory data from the world and immediately knowing this or that, Kant was convinced that the mind actually organized the data of perception into a rational whole, imposing order on what would otherwise be random sensory data. Frei appeals to Kant's *Religion within the Limits of Reason Alone* as an example of the influences on Harvard's Gordon Kaufman. "Kant tells us that what the author intended to say is far less important than what a reasonable mind can make of what he or she wrote—the reasonable constructs the writing provides."[32] Thus, before one has laid eyes upon the biblical text, he or she already knows what is true and false, right and wrong, and comes ready to appropriate the text as something more akin to aphorisms than to normative Scripture. Frei writes of Kant,

> For him, every persona that he discovered in the Bible was a mark or stage along a single-storied succession, none of which took place in time; instead, each is a stage in the self-understanding and self-improvement of the moral reasoner. The biblical story as a whole, and every part of it, is an allegory. There is Adam, who is really the moral reasoner as freely disobedient to his own rational freedom. There is the incarnate Christ, who is the archetype of humanity well-pleasing to God, ineradicable in the moral reasoner's mind.[33]

Type Two (Tracy)

"Authority" is disparaged by Kant and Kaufman, and Tracy also chooses a substitute: "sacredness." "Authority," writes Frei, "does not strike a numinous spark in the phenomenological breast because phenomenology is a reflexive examination of the self as consciousness."[34] Ever since Kant, the modern self demands autonomy, so that freedom is not necessarily to live without *any* constraints but to live under *self-imposed* constraints. Externally imposed limits, according to this Kantian paradigm, are intrinsically evil. But sacredness, linked to similarly non-threatening words such as "meaning," "dimensions," and "essences," is a much more acceptable category. The story of Jesus is not actually about Jesus at all but is an occasion for a greater story, "existential possibility," a new "mode-of-being-in-the-world." In other words, it is still the self rather than God who is the center of the story.[35]

Type Three (Schleiermacher)

"One must," says Schleiermacher, "avoid the impression that a doctrine must belong to Christianity because it is contained in Scripture, whereas in point of fact it is only contained in Scripture because it belongs to Christianity."[36] According to Frei, Schleiermacher himself reduces theology to statements about the self. "It is really the turn to the subject with a vengeance," Frei concludes.[37] It is *Christus in nobis*, not *Christus extra nos*, that Schleiermacher championed.[38] This, of course, affects Schleiermacher's view of the atonement: "No substitutionary view!" What the atonement actually effects, according to Frei's interpretation of Schleiermacher, is a change in us, the possibility of change in our self-consciousness. As Frei points out, this cannot be a very significant matter even for Schleiermacher, since already "it is the very essence of human being. . . . You can see that even if it were to be demonstrated that Jesus was not crucified, it wouldn't matter to Schleiermacher's outlook, for the crucial thing about his death was only the attitude manifested in it, significantly indeed but not indispensably. . . ."[39] For Schleiermacher, there was a historical method and a faith method, distinct but in need of being correlated.

Type Four (Barth)

According to Frei, in Barth's system Jesus is given not only soteriological and ecclesial but also epistemological supremacy. Only "in the life to come we will know how the rules are based on the very nature of things and therefore how they all fit together."[40] While applauding his consistency, Frei observes that Barth

> cannot specify the manner or mode in which the textual state-ments are historical, while nonetheless asserting that they are. . . . He will often and rightly say that textually the resur-rection happened to, is a predicate of, Jesus, not to the disciples, and he will go on to say that there is no reason to think some-thing nonhistorical just because it is in principle not accessible to scientific historical inquiry. In what sense, then, is the resur-rection, unlike the crucifixion, historical? To consign the resurrection to the category of myth is a typical species of mod-ern laziness or a typically lazy modernism.[41]

And yet, Frei warns against historical literalism by suggesting that the supposed contradictions concerning the Resurrection nevertheless leave the Gospels adequate "under an analogical scheme." At this point, Frei appears to skirt the issue considerably just as one hopes he will tease out his point and turn his assertion into a more useful argument:

> In the meantime, even if correlates are not available, a resurrec-tion of Jesus remains *a* or *the* crucial ingredient in Christian dis-course, understood, like every religious community's discourse, as a distinctive and irreducible language form. . . . At some point, though not too quickly, philosophical agnosticism has to set in in the interest of full-blooded Christian theology.[42]

Colin Gunton wisely reminds us that such anti-foundationalist challenges "may appear to be attempts to render their contents immune from outside criticism and so become forms of intellectual sectarianism." Gunton adds,

> In other words, they may appear to evade the challenges of the universal and objective, and to run the risk of the rank sub-jectivism and relativism into which their extreme representa-

tives have fallen. Theologically speaking, they evade the intellectual challenge involved in the use of the word God. If that word refers in part to the universal source of being, meaning and truth, then those who would use it must be prepared to take some responsibility for intellectual enterprises which impinge upon theirs from "outside." . . . [For] although Barth is by no means subject to a temptation to play down the universal implications of his use of the word, he is most in danger of appearing to make unsupported assertions precisely where he evades the challenge of the links between theological and other epistemology.[43]

But it is just these "links" which, to Frei's mind, require too great a sacrifice in terms of accommodating to the *Wissenschaftsliche* model of the research university. For him, "the typology cuts right across the ordinary lines of liberal and conservative," claiming that Tracy and Carl Henry are more alike methodologically than either would wish to admit. Both Tracy and Henry require philosophical foundations for theology. But Frei insists once more that theology is chiefly practical rather than theoretical, renewing the question raised by Protestant scholasticism. At the end of the day, Frei's major concern, *pace* Tracy, is to see us accept the notion that Christian language is not—and never can become—"neutral or informational language."[44] Just at this point Frei cites Geertz to the effect that religious symbols "synthesize a people's ethos," providing a world-picture that admirably and strikingly redescribes the world in convincing terms.[45]

RULES OF THE ROAD: THE NATURE OF DOCTRINE

This leads us to George Lindbeck's proposal in *The Nature of Doctrine*. We recall Frei's thesis statement that "Christianity is not a network of beliefs, it is not a system first of all." Nor, says Frei, is it an experience first of all. It involves these, but it is chiefly a religious community with all that goes with that, including a sacred story.[46] Lindbeck expands on this frontier with considerable skill. First, he states up front that his postliberal project is not simply a return to premodern theology. In fact, Lindbeck is also more self-consciously determined than Frei to distance himself from preliberal orthodoxy: "Whatever else might be said about it, the recommended mode is clearly in conflict both with traditionalist propositional orthodoxy and with currently regnant forms of liberalism"[47] Beyond both orthodox and liberal strategies, "A third, a postliberal, way of conceiving religion and religious doctrine is called for."[48]

Lindbeck's work can be fully appreciated only against the background of his nearly half-century commitment to ecumenism as a theologian in the Evangelical Lutheran Church in America (ELCA) and the World Lutheran Federation. His driving passion, ecclesial unity, seems hopelessly trapped within anathemas and counter-anathemas, as well as conciliar and confessional distinctives. "If, for example, doctrines are said to be 'irreformable,' as was said by Vatican I, what understanding of doctrine would make such a view intelligible without, however, excluding the contrary position?"[49] No question, to my mind, is more like a thesis statement for his work than this.

In the tradition of the Yale school, Lindbeck describes three principal "types" of theological method. First is the "cognitive-propositionalist" type, influenced by analytic philosophy, which "stresses the ways in which church doctrines function as informative propositions or truth claims about objective realities."[50] Second is the "experiential-expressive" type, which "interprets doctrines as noninformative and nondiscursive symbols of inner feelings, attitudes, or existential orientations," and this type is characteristic of liberal theologies. It is this tradition, mediated from Schleiermacher through Rudolf Otto and Mircea Eliade, that has been "at the heart of the romantic, idealistic, and phenomenological-existentialist streams of thought that have dominated the humanistic side of Western culture ever since Kant's revolutionary Copernican 'turn to the subject.'"[51] The bottom line is that, in Lindbeck's analysis, neither the "cognitive-propositionalist" nor the "experiential-expressivist" can offer a methodological model that could achieve "doctrinal reconciliation without capitulation."[52]

Lindbeck's alternative is the "cultural-linguistic" model. While propositionalists have tended to view religion as a type of science or philosophy, Lindbeck, like Frei, seeks an analogue in the social sciences, especially cultural anthropology. A beneficiary of the "hermeneutical turn," in this approach Lindbeck suggests that,

> Religions resemble languages together with their correlative forms of life and are thus similar to cultures. . . . The function of church doctrines that becomes most prominent in this perspective is their use, not as expressive symbols or as truth claims, but as communally authoritative rules of discourse, attitude, and action. . . . A regulative approach has no difficulty explaining the possibility of reconciliation without capitulation. Rules, unlike propositions or expressive symbols, retain an invariant meaning under changing conditions of compatibility and conflict.[53]

Lindbeck elucidates this point with an illustration that is quite significant for comprehending his model:

> For example, the rules "Drive on the left" and "Drive on the right" are unequivocal in meaning and unequivocally opposed, yet both may be binding: one in Britain and the other in the United States, or one when traffic is normal, and the other when a collision must be avoided. Thus oppositions between rules can in some instances be resolved, not by altering one or both of them, but by specifying when or where they apply, or by stipulating which of the competing directives takes precedence.[54]

One gains a clear impression of Lindbeck's entire proposal from this illustration. We may replace his example (transubstantiation) with our own. The Reformation doctrine of justification and the Tridentine doctrine of justification are both "unequivocal in meaning and unequivocally opposed, yet both, according to Lindbeck, may be binding: one in Wittenberg and Geneva and the other in Rome, or one when church relations are normal, and the other when a collision must be avoided." It is thus, according to Lindbeck, not a question of Protestants giving a little here and Rome giving a little there, meeting in the middle, "but specifying when or where they [the rules] apply, or by stipulating which of the competing directives takes precedence."[55] This practice will become clearer as Lindbeck proceeds.

It is nothing new to suggest that doctrines function as *regula fidei*: The idea goes all the way back to the early church, Lindbeck acknowledges. The regulative function of language in community formation is also prominent in Wittgenstein, of course, whose influence Lindbeck acknowledges.[56] Wittgenstein's view of philosophical discourse seems to parallel Lindbeck's theological method when Wittgenstein writes that, "philosophy may in no way interfere with the actual use of language; it can in the end only describe it. For it cannot give it any foundation either. It leaves everything as it is."[57] "What is innovative about the present proposal," Lindbeck suggests, "is that this becomes the only job that doctrines do in their role as church teachings."[58] For Lindbeck, "Doctrines regulate truth claims by excluding some and permitting others, but the logic of their communally authoritative use hinders or prevents them from specifying positively what is to be affirmed."[59] William Placher offers an example:

> Consider the assertion, "We are saved by grace alone." The propositionalist will take this as a *factual* claim about the mechanism of salvation. The experiential-expressivist will understand it as the *symbolic expression of an experience* of the power of God in salvation. On Lindbeck's view, the meaning of the doctrine can be expressed in a *rule* like, "Christians should always speak and act about their salvation in a way that expresses gratitude to God, not pride in their own accomplishment."[60]

Thus, becoming religious, according to Lindbeck, is a lot like "achieving competence in the totally nonoptional grammatical patterns and lexical resources of a foreign tongue." In some interesting ways, this parallels the nineteenth-century debate between traditional Reformed and Presbyterian theologians and the revivalists, the former emphasizing covenantal nurture while the latter called for radical conversions. The modern spirit, evident in the latter, calls such grammatical acquisition "indoctrination," a restriction of the self's autonomy. It is much easier in our day for religious interests to take the experiential-expressive form of individual quests for personal meaning. This is true even among theological conservatives, as is illustrated by the stress placed on conversion experiences by the heirs of pietism and revivalism. The structures of modernity press individuals to meet God first in the depths of their souls and then, perhaps, if they find something personally congenial, to become part of a tradition or join a church. This is one reason why religion in these contexts, whether liberal or conservative, is seen chiefly as a private affair rather than as a communal practice.[61] Lindbeck observes that this pattern "was already well-established in American Protestantism in the nineteenth century. . . . Religions are seen as multiple suppliers of different forms of a single commodity needed for transcendent self-expression and self-realization."[62] Thus, although the experience of religion may be quite private and intuitive, it is usually (in this experiential-expressive model) regarded as universal. But on the cultural-linguistic model, one can "no more be religious in general than one can speak language in general."[63] Thus, Lindbeck accepts the fact that his model will yield ecumenical fruit within a particular religion, but will not unite world religions.[64]

For Lindbeck, one of the most crucial passages from Geertz is taken from his chapter, "Religion as a Cultural System," in *The Interpretation of Cultures*.[65] There Geertz seeks "an analysis of the system of meaning embodied in the symbols which make up the religion proper."[66] As Geertz himself noted, the cultural-linguistic approach is often suspected as possessing a marked idealist-subjectivist tendency. Lindbeck, in fact, admits, "it functions somewhat like a Kantian *a priori*, although in this case the *a priori* is a set of acquired skills that could be different."[67] As Kant believed that we form concepts as a way of screening reality, so in the cultural-linguistic paradigm it would appear that the role of concepts is transferred to semiotic systems. Reality is what it "is" because of the language and rules we use to describe it, and that cannot be separated from our particular communities of discourse. We will explore this linguistic idealism more fully below. Lindbeck says, "It is not primarily an array of beliefs about the true and the good (though it may involve these) or a symbolism expressive of basic attitudes, feelings, or sentiments (although these will be generated). Rather, it is similar to an idiom that makes possible the description of realities, the formulation of beliefs, and the experiencing of inner attitudes, feelings, and sentiments."[68]

This, of course, follows Wittgenstein's argument concerning the priority of language as a "form of life." In fact, closely related to Wittgenstein's notion are the familiar phrases of such phenomenological philosophers as Husserl ("life world") and Heidegger ("mode-of-being-in-the-world"), and such linguistic philosophers as Ricoeur ("inhabiting a world"), Gadamer ("historically effected consciousness"), and others. In fact, this idea may be traced to Dilthey's *Lebensgefühl.* Michael G. Harvey's description of Wittgenstein's notion of theology as grammar sounds identical to Lindbeck's theory:

> Theological and religious utterances are examples of propositions which do not have the grammatical role of making factual claims about how things really are or of comparing with reality. They provide us with theological and religious pictures. However, the importance of these pictures does not lie in what they are "about" or "of", but what uses they have in a religious life. Their decisive importance does not consist in making metaphysical claims about the universe, but in the role they play in forming a religious consciousness and mode of living.[69]

Thus, according to Lindbeck, the relation of religion and experience is "not unilateral but dialectical."[70] So, despite his general emphasis, Lindbeck does believe that the relationship is reciprocal, that it is more of a two-way street than one might at first recognize from his earlier comments. Nevertheless, linguistic competence is generally prior to and a condition of religious experience:

> To become a Christian involves learning the story of Israel and of Jesus well enough to interpret and experience oneself and one's world in its terms. A religion is above all an external word, a *verbum externum,* that molds and shapes the self and its world, rather than an expression or thematization of a preexisting self or preconceptual experience. The *verbum internum* (traditionally equated by Christians with the action of the Holy

Spirit) is also crucially important, but it would be understood in a theological use of the model as a capacity for hearing and accepting the true religion, the true external word, rather than (as experiential-expressivism would have it) as a common experience diversely articulated in different religions.[71]

It is at this point that Lindbeck distances himself from idealism (as well as from liberalism), contrasting his position (which he identifies as Aristotelian) with that of Tillich, shaped as Tillich was by Schelling and Hegel. But he has no intention of rebounding into the arms of orthodoxy. While a cognitivist-propositionalist (and, he adds, voluntarist) approach regards becoming a Christian as a decision to believe propositions and follow imperatives, Lindbeck's model sees this as a process of becoming "culturally or linguistically competent," acquiring a certain set of skills by practice, much as one becomes a competent member of a culture or tribe by actually *engaging in* the practice of speaking the language, participating in its symbolic and ritual expressions, and living out the implications in the community. Doctrines, as grammatical rules, will be invoked by the more competent members of the community, but the actual process of becoming a Christian, says Lindbeck, will look more like acquiring skills than accepting propositions: "The primary knowledge is not about the religion, nor that the religion teaches such and such, but rather how to be religious in such and such ways. Sometimes explicitly formulated statements of the beliefs or behavioral norms of a religion may be helpful in the learning process, but by no means always. Ritual, prayer, and example are normally much more important."[72]

Such comments lead one to wonder whether, on this point, this model really is fundamentally distinct from the experiential-expressivist position, however. Is it not the case that modern theologians ever since Schleiermacher have insisted that Christianity is not to be confused with its dogmas? Was it not Troeltsch who stressed the community, and was it not the *Religionsgeschichte Schule* that championed historicism in religious studies? Is the cultural-linguistic model too much in debt to historicism? In fact, does it not simply replace the relativism of historical contexts with that of cultural-linguistic systems? These are pressing questions which will be discussed below.

Instead of denying propositionalism *simpliciter* (which he is too often accused of doing), Lindbeck wants to argue for a constitutive whole as being more meaningful and definitive for Christianity than particular doctrines. While the cognitivist thinks of this or that particular doctrine as being either true or false, Lindbeck says that it is the Christian language-game or semiotic system as a whole which is either true or false. The parts are only "true" or "false" intrasystematically. Obviously, according to Lindbeck, a coherence theory of truth has priority over a correspondence theory. It is not particular assertions or dogmas, but the whole, which has ontological reference. This "single gigantic proposition" is likened to a map.[73] There are meaningful maps of two types: relevant and irrelevant. And there are meaningless maps (categorically false). Hinduism is an example of the categorically false, while only within Christianity can "maps" of the first type (relevant/irrelevant) appear. While Christianity may be variously flawed internally, its general status as a true proposition is established by whether it gets us to our destination. This links us to the earlier discussion of becoming a Christian as a matter of *practice* rather than chiefly of the *acceptance* of beliefs and practices. We are reminded of Wittgenstein's assertion that, "when we first begin to believe anything, what we believe is not a single proposition, it is a whole system of propositions."[74] The doctrine of the Trinity does not assert something about ontological reality but about what Christians mean when they speak of God.

So Christianity is the one true "gigantic proposition," and other religions are thoroughly incommensurable with it, just as German is incommensurable with Japanese.[75] Thus, a non-Christian religion is not false but meaningless. At first this sounds more pejorative than even the orthodox option, but that is only because of the unfortunate side-issue of the salvation of adherents of other religions. Since he rejects the notion that explicit faith in Christ is necessary for salvation, Lindbeck does not have trouble saying that non-Christian religions are meaningless.[76] Lindbeck concedes that his model at first blush raises questions. For instance, if there is "one true faith," what is the status of those who deny it? How do we retain the Christian commitment to *solo Christo* while avoiding the "exclusivist" view that at least ordinarily there is no salvation apart from faith in Christ? That is the dilemma Lindbeck poses. Cognitive-propositionalists who have tried to solve this dilemma have generally turned to general revelation and have reduced the number of propositions to as few as possible, while experiential-expressivists today often find Rahner's "anonymous Christian" attractive. But for Lindbeck, neither of these approaches seems to work; he explains this point with uncharacteristic vagueness: "Thus the only currently available alternative for those of a cultural-linguistic inclination is a prospective theory. It has been proposed that non-Christians can share in the future of salvation even though they, unlike those with living Christian faith, have not yet begun to do so. According to this view, saving faith cannot be wholly anonymous, wholly implicit, but must be in some measure explicit: it comes, as Paul put it, *ex auditu,* from hearing (Rom. 10:17)."[77]

Remarkably, Lindbeck argues that the New Testament pictures Gentiles as "not heading toward either heaven or hell," but as merely "trapped in the past, in the darkness of the old aeon."[78] This is not the place to explore it, but one wonders how the words of Jesus and the apostles can be reconciled with this interpretation (although it is reminiscent of Heidegger and Bultmann). No wonder Lindbeck concludes that, "The decision between these two views [Rahner's and his own] depends, it seems, not on exegesis, but on the systematic historical framework within which one interprets the biblical data."[79] Here is an example of the method in operation. The sensitive dialectic which the older theologians tried to achieve between the analytic and synthetic (or exegetical and systematic) movements in theology breaks down and the system (here, the cultural-linguistic structure) determines the results of exegesis unidirectionally. This should be something of a scandal (not to mention, an irony) for a method that regards Protestant orthodoxy as a grand metaphysical scheme which fails to pay attention to the text. Astonishingly, Lindbeck asserts that the Christian tradition is just as ostensibly opaque on this question as Scripture. The early Christians "do not seem to have worried about the ultimate fate of the overwhelming majority of non-Christians among whom they lived."[80]

Thus, Lindbeck distinguishes again between the "intrasystematic" and "ontological" truth status of a claim. This basically parallels the distinction between coherence and correspondence. "The first is the truth of coherence; the second, that truth of correspondence to reality which, according to epistemological realists, is attributable to first-order propositions." Intrasystematic truth has to do with the notion of a religion as "one gigantic proposition" or "map." "The crusader's battle cry, '*Christus est Dominus*,' for example, is false when used to authorize cleaving the skull of the infidel even though the same words in other contexts may be a true utterance."[81] Meaning is *constituted* and not merely *described* or *expressed* through language.[82] Jay Wesley Richards has criticized Lindbeck's model on just this point:

> Consider Lindbeck's claim that the crusader crying "*Christus est Dominus*" while "cleaving the skull of the infidel" does not make the claim meaningless, but *false*. This would seem to make it difficult for someone to be a hypocrite (at least for long), since this term usually designates someone who assents to the truth of a certain belief, but then contradicts that belief with some action. . . . Surely there is a better way of negotiating the consistency of theory and praxis than to degrade the notion of truth in this way. Perhaps what the crusader *meant* by this statement is false, since it claims something that is not true, namely that Christ is "Lord" in the same way that Genghis Khan is "Lord." . . . [The crusader] would be a *hypocrite*, and we have a perfectly good word for that, without fiddling with the notion of *truth*. Unfortunately, Lindbeck does not put the matter this way, since it would require a stronger distinction between *meaning* and *use* than he is willing to make.[83]

Richards believes that Lindbeck conflates truth with verification, justification or certainty: "This is doubly surprising given the anti-positivist tenor of his proposal. . . . He claims that since we cannot *confirm* how a theological statement can 'correspond' to divine reality, it is *informationally vacuous* (67, emphasis added). How does this follow?

Surely it is possible to know what someone is saying even in circumstances (which are legion) in which we are unable to confirm its truth or 'correspondence.'"[84] Although Richards does not refer to him, Frege's distinction between "true" and "taking-to-be-true," which the philosopher saw conflated in psychologism, finds a parallel in Lindbeck's proposal.

The ecumenical significance of Lindbeck's rule-theory is obvious: What is abiding is the story; what is adaptable are the "propositionally formulated truths."[85] A postliberal theology will focus once again on the "immanent meanings" of texts. Great literature shapes us, even when we do not seek external references in psychology, history, or science. "For those who are steeped in [the scriptures], no world is more real than the ones they create. A scriptural world is thus able to absorb the universe. It supplies the interpretive framework within which believers seek to live their lives and understand reality. This happens quite apart from formal theories."[86] Instead of going to the Bible in order to find their stories, believers, Lindbeck insists, "make the story of the Bible their story." Instead of making biblical motifs symbolic or figurative of some supposedly higher truth in the world or in experience, we should make nonscriptural "realities" figurative or symbolic of the ultimately true world of the biblical text: "The cross is not to be viewed as a figurative representation of suffering nor the messianic kingdom as a symbol for hope in the future; rather, suffering should be cruciform, and hopes for the future messianic."[87]

Of course, the traffic can work the other way around: "This is what happened, so the Christian mainstream concluded, in the case of Gnosticism. Here Hellenism became the interpreter rather than the interpreted."[88] Lindbeck shares Frei's lament concerning the eclipse of biblical narrative "under the combined onslaughts of rationalistic, pietistic, and historical-critical developments." "Scripture," he notes, "ceased to function as the lens through which theologians viewed the world and instead became primarily an object of study whose religiously significant or literal meaning was located outside itself."[89] Lindbeck also echoes his colleague's concerns when he writes, "The meaning must not be esoteric: not something behind, beneath, or in front of the text; not something that the text reveals, discloses, implies,

or suggests to those with extraneous metaphysical, historical, or experiential interests. It must rather be what the text says in terms of the
communal language of which the text is in instantiation."[90]

In other words, "The primary focus is not on God's being in itself,
for that is not what the text is about, but on how life is to be lived and
reality construed in the light of God's character as this is depicted in
the stories of Israel and of Jesus."[91] I am not aware of a single orthodox Protestant theologian who would deny this point, but Lindbeck
extrapolates this to include Frei's well-known distinction: "The Bible
is often 'history-like' even when it is not 'likely history.' It can therefore be taken seriously in the first respect as a delineator of the character of divine and human agents, even when its history or science is
challenged. As parables such as that of the prodigal son remind us, the
rendering of God's character is not in every instance logically dependent on the facticity of the story."[92]

But in point of fact, all that parables remind us of is that *in parables* the rendering is not dependent on the facticity of the story.
However, is it not the case that a narrative which does in fact have a
historical rather than history-like character must be treated seriously
on its own terms within this genre? Francis Watson's criticisms seem
entirely appropriate on this point.[93] And this, we submit, brings us
ineluctably to the summit of extralinguistic reference. Lindbeck's
assertion that "the literary genre of John is clearly not that of veridical history" reveals an astonishing degree of unwillingness of postliberalism to practice what it preaches. Would the *sensus literalis* justify
this assertion? Surely, at the very least, the *consensus fidelium* has
always read the Gospel of John as veridical history. Paul did not say
that, if Jesus is not raised, the narrative becomes entirely incoherent,
but rather that (if Jesus is not raised) we have been duped and we are
still in our sins. The existential and historical concerns are not dis-
tractions from the narrative but belong to their internal integrity. The
claim to historical accuracy is not imposed from without, but is part
of the narrative structure itself, as Luke's preface indicates:

> Many have undertaken to draw up an account of the things that
> have been fulfilled among us, just as they were handed down to

us by those who from the first were eyewitnesses and servants of the word. Therefore, since I myself have carefully investigated everything from the beginning, it seemed good also to me to write an orderly account for you, most excellent Theophilus, so that you may know the certainty of the things you have been taught (Luke 1:1-4, NIV).

CONCLUDING ANALYSIS

At the level of epistemology, it would appear that Yale's version of postliberalism fails to advance beyond post-Kantian thought. Despite doses of James and Wittgenstein, the paradigm is essentially idealist. Of course, this is not a damning criticism in itself, but it does make one suspect that we still have not seen a significant model that challenges historicism, mere coherentism. Nor does it advance a theological project that actually resolves the antithetical thinking of modernity (Historie-Geschichte, fact-value, sense-reference, phenomenal-noumenal, etc.) without collapsing one into the other in a false synthesis. For reasons beyond the scope of this article, I am certain that Wittgenstein did not intend his brilliant references to the "language game" to be interpreted and applied as broadly as it has been. I do not even think it is correct to assume that Professor Lindbeck accurately appropriates him in the service of incommensurable cultural-linguistic systems.[94] Donald Davidson has demonstrated the conceptual incoherence of such a perspective.[95] There cannot even be genuine disagreement unless there is some shared space of agreement. Lindbeck's rule-theory serves as a useful analogy for an aspect of theological method, but by rendering it something like a univocal explanation, the cultural-linguistic model seems epistemologically vulnerable. By conflating the truth with one's taking-to-be-true (which Frege identified as psychologism), this model perpetuates a confusion of the *fides quae creditur* and *fides qua creditur* that is part and parcel of modern theology.

Jeffrey Hensley makes a convincing case for regarding Lindbeck as a conceptual rather than a metaphysical antirealist,[96] and that is an important qualification. Nevertheless, Alister McGrath is surely right when he says that evangelical theology requires not only a coherence theory but also a correspondence theory of truth for its method.[97] "In effect, the priority of Scripture is defended on grounds that appear to be cultural, historical or contractual. . . . For the evangelical, truth claims cannot be evaded at this juncture. Scripture has authority not because of what the Christian community has chosen to make of it, but because of what it is and what it conveys. . . . Evangelicalism has difficulty with any approach, whether originating with Bultmann or Frei, that apparently weighs history so lightly."[98] At no point does Yale's postliberalism reveal its debt to Karl Barth more directly.

At the level of hermeneutics, the postliberal jury is still out with respect to the status, much less the reliability, of Scripture. Do these texts derive their normative authority from the community or is God the primary cause of their authority, however the latter might be thematized? Although the goal has clearly been to return to Scripture in some sense, such postliberal thought, by indefinitely postponing the issue of reference, shows no signs of being able to restore the rent fabric. Reuniting history and narrative, critical and exegetical operations, is not a likely outcome of Yale's postliberal project. While the Resurrection of Jesus Christ is affirmed as central, there is a reluctance to defend the doctrine beyond a coherentist (take-it-or-leave-it) position: Lindbeck writes, "I want to emphasize that I am well aware of, but not terribly distressed by, the fact that my refusal to speak speculatively or evidentially about the resurrection of Christ, while nevertheless affirming it as an indispensable Christian claim, may involve me in some difficult logical tangles. Even so, I believe this is a better way than the contrary path (taken, for example, by Wolfhart Pannenberg) and a religiously significant way at that."[99]

In fact, if those more influenced by Hegel (such as Pannenberg) represent the still-flickering embers of the Aufklarung, the Yale school does not seem to get beyond the fideism that has dominated the other (Kierkegaardian) side of modern theology's swinging pendulum. While there is evidence that could count against the Resurrection, Frei maintained that "there is no historical evidence that counts in favor of the claim that Jesus was resurrected," since there is nothing to which it could be compared. "This is a good thing, because faith is not based on factual evidence."[100] But whatever happened to Frei's criticism that, "To consign the resurrection to the category of myth is a typical species of modern laziness or a typically lazy modernism"? While Frei refuses to consign the Resurrection to myth, how can he charge others with laziness in this respect when he is unwilling to explain the relationship between the narrative (coherence) and history (correspondence)? And yet, this ostensibly fideistic shrug is mitigated somewhat by such suggestive remarks as the following: "But at one point a judgment of faith concerning the inspiration of the descriptive contents and a judgment of faith affirming their central factual claim would have to coincide."[101] It is disappointing that the Yale school has not yet carried out the burden of that recognition.

At the level of theological method, postliberalism resists the relativist temptation, but one may be justified in wondering why. It would appear that one is a Christian simply because he or she happened to be born and nurtured in a particular cultural-linguistic community, with conversion reduced to the attainment of linguistic competence. Granting the imbalance of conversionistic paradigms often associated with evangelical revivalism, this postliberal explanation is open to the charge of historical determinism.

Further, Lindbeck's analysis of first-order and second-order status sounds somewhat reminiscent of modern theology's running polemic against the normative status of "mere formulations" of the truth rather than the truth itself (variously defined). We are told by Frei and Lindbeck that postliberal theology will focus once again on the "immanent meanings" of texts. "For those who are steeped in [the scriptures], no world is more real than the ones they create. A scriptural world is thus able to absorb the universe. It supplies the interpretive framework within which believers seek to live their lives and understand reality. This happens quite apart from formal theories."[102] This will appeal to many evangelicals who have never had much interest in formal theories anyway (although such a dismissive attitude toward dogmatic formulae is not Lindbeck's intention). Furthermore, what is the "immanent meaning" of, for instance, Romans 4 (or any other *locus classicus* for the doctrine of justification) if it is not that God imputes the perfect righteousness of Jesus Christ to the believing sinner *as* sinner? If the text explicitly says that God "justifies the wicked," is that a mere formulation (second-order) or an "immanent meaning" (first-order)? Or what of the doctrine of the Trinity, which is formulated in metaphysical language? Is it for that reason less regulative? A naive reading of Scripture has led many throughout history to deny that this doctrine corresponds to the immanent meaning of the text. But what is an "immanent meaning"? As we have seen, given Lindbeck's coherentism, any particular meaning is determined by its relation to the whole system. But can a part (say, for instance, a text which one has previously overlooked) cause disturbance and even reconstruction for the whole?

In actual practice, Lindbeck's method seems arbitrary at times. As noted earlier, Placher defends Lindbeck's insistence that "the meaning of the doctrine ['salvation by grace'] can be expressed in a rule like, 'Christians should always speak and act about their salvation in a way that expresses gratitude to God, not pride in their own accomplishment.'"[103] But is that really more "immanent" a meaning than "God justifies the wicked by imputing Christ's righteousness," when this is precisely what the text declares in various places? Perhaps the second-order formulation is actually the looser and more opaque rule, while the first-order ascription is the tighter and more controversial (even potentially divisive). Lindbeck's rule-theory seems vulnerable to arbitrary constructions of that which is absolutely necessary for Christian identity as opposed to that which is merely a historically conditioned formulation. This does not represent a great advance methodologically beyond modern theology.

But despite these concerns, this collective enterprise has generated enormous possibilities for theological reflection at the dawn of the new century. First, it has played a significant hand in calling biblical studies and theology into conversation. If exegesis and system are to be reunited in theology, this had to happen. That the priority of biblical narrative and canonical unity is conceivable in contemporary theology is due in no small measure to this school. Furthermore, it has provided a helpful correction to naive epistemological and hermeneutical tendencies that do frequently surface in evangelical theology. The insistence on attending to the text rather than that which is below, above, or behind the text, is refreshing after two centuries of a historical criticism that is able to recognize the relativity and historical situatedness of every perspective but its own.

Despite the lingering shadow of Kant, there has been an important break with modernist autonomy by postliberals, indicative of a more general anti-foundationalist criticism. Like Barth, Frei and Lindbeck draw on Calvin's analogy of spectacles.[104] Sharing some striking affinities with Dutch Calvinism (Kuyper, Bavinck, Van Til), Yale's postliberalism begins with the biblical world (or, to borrow from Gadamer, the horizon of the text), rather than with human experience. In fact, the critique of the experiential-expressivism which is so representative of modern Christianity, whether conservative or liberal, is generally as accurate as it is bracing. However (and this will come as no surprise), we cannot praise the critique of "cognitive-propositionalists" so highly. We do not have the space here to become more specific; it is enough to say that while there is, no doubt, something out there in popular evangelicalism and fundamentalism which surely corresponds to Lindbeck's analysis, this caricature (especially in the absence of even the slightest documentation of examples) displays a surprising lack of awareness of the more sophisticated systems of the Protestant scholastics and their better successors. It is here where the weakness of typological or schematic formulations runs roughshod over particular data.

As an analogy, theology as "grammar," "narrative," and "cultural-linguistic" or "semiotic" system is richly suggestive and underscores the importance of a unified system of faith and practice. It takes seriously the normative status of truth claims while providing an account of changing formulations. If we are still justifiably unsatisfied with this account, we will at least have to answer many of these same questions. Theology is badly divided as a discipline—not only between various ecclesial traditions but between biblical, historical, and systematic theology, and ethics. Students of the Yale school have fleshed out narrative theology within various disciplines: Frei and Childs in biblical theology; Lindbeck and Kelsey in systematics; Placher in apologetics (or anti-apologetics?); and Hauerwas in ethics. It is in this last sphere where the theory meets practice with such resonance that, even if one regarded the theory as hopelessly flawed, its sheer usefulness (in the absence of significant alternatives) is persuasive to many. Orthodox theologies will not overcome this balkanization by repristinating their systems (which in many instances are actually nineteenth- and twentieth-century manuals from the last theologians who actually knew the systems). They will have to face the challenges to their method as well as to the substance itself. While Yale postliberalism falls short of providing a model that postmodern orthodoxies might appropriate whole, it surely points us in the direction of the right questions. And more than we might suspect, it even gives us some of the right answers.

Let me briefly suggest what some of those right answers might include. First, the emphasis on the centrality of Christ, determined by intratextual factors (most notably, figural interpretation), is far more concrete than Barth's "christocentrism," due in part to the fact that it lacks Barth's paranoia about textual (or any) mediation of Jesus Christ. From the perspective of a postmodern orthodoxy, this can only represent a step forward. Far from advancing relativism, this brand of narrative theology refuses to view the reader as a constructivist who makes what he will of a plastic text. It is more the case that the reader is acted upon rather than active in this process. If anything, this reaction against treating Scripture as a wax nose is too reductionistic about immanent meanings and the literal sense. The leading representatives of this school are explicit in their contention that Luther and Calvin point in the right hermeneutical direction, and that their christocentric reading of Scripture is the best hope for overcoming the eclipse of biblical narrative.

Furthermore, Yale postliberalism shares Barth's determination to preserve a Chalcedonian christology, which is no small thing to suggest in modern theology. Frei's appropriation of speech-action theory with respect to intentionality for describing Christ's enactment (and not just manifestation) of his messianic identity is superb.[105] The bodily resurrection of Jesus Christ is necessary and central for Christian faith and practice, according to the school's leading representatives (especially Frei).

Finally, Lindbeck, pressing the implications of Frei's work, has reasserted an important point that confessional Lutherans and Calvinists have frequently made in the face of typically American forms of Protestantism. I am referring to Lindbeck's point that the liturgical and ritualistic activities of the church are not "mere external decorations," but actually *embody* the core beliefs of the community. They do not merely illustrate, amplify, or symbolize the church's identity, but participate in *constituting* it. This needs to be stressed particularly in our day, when a barren rationalism (i.e., cognitive-propositionalism) and a subjective pietism (i.e., experiential-expressionism) have become strange bedfellows. At least in practice, an implicit docetism, shared often by evangelical pietists and liberals alike, ignores the visible church and its visible structures, including the visible means of grace, in favor of disembodied beliefs and experiences. And I do have some sympathy with the suggestion that this doceticism in Christian practice has as its corollary (and perhaps as its illicit premise) a more general "docetism" which sees language and ecclesiastical forms as the accident rather than the substance of religion. Furthermore, religious conversion is often understood in both conservative and liberal circles in radically individualistic and experiential ways, in contrast to the emphasis on communal norming that is identified with traditional or confessional churches and often criticized by evangelicals (sometimes with justification) as "formalistic." Lindbeck's model is good therapy for distorted versions of Christian identity and comes closer to describing what actually happens in the life of a typical Christian, whether concrete forms-of-life are acknowledged or not.

Even where we might judge this program deficient, I still maintain that it is suggestive. It is not simply that there are areas of agreement and that where the postliberal proposal falls short, we carry the ball to victory. I am convinced that, as orthodox believers who want to revive the practice of doing theology in our own circles, we actually have a lot to learn from the Yale school. There are areas even in terms of theological method where we are deficient or are content to pick up where Turretin or Quenstedt left off, as if the last three centuries never happened. And here, I think, Yale's brand of postliberalism offers profound wisdom for finding our way through rather than around the shoals of modernity. Its acceptance of Scripture as the starting point for theology, which is perhaps due more to anti-foundationalism than to any precise definition of biblical authority, represents sufficient overlap with the concerns of those contributing to this volume. And I think that a fair number of us would be interested in taking George Hunsinger up on his invitation to continue the discussion. Favorably citing the direction of Richard Gaffin on many of these points, Hunsinger writes, "If I am not wholly mistaken about the continuum that seems to run from the likes of Calvin through the likes of Kuyper and Bavinck to the likes of Frei and Lindbeck, then it would not seem amiss to suggest that a similar possibility exists also for evangelicals and postliberals today."[106]

Notes

1. A very thoughtful interaction between evangelicals and postliberals took place in a conference at Wheaton College in April 1995. The results were published as *The Nature of Confession*, Timothy R. Phillips and Dennis L. Okholm, eds. (Downers Grove, Ill.: InterVarsity, 1996). Cf. the article by Roger E. Olson in the May 20, 1996, issue of *Christianity Today*, titled, "Back to the Bible (Almost): Why Yale's Postliberal Theologians Deserve an Evangelical Hearing."

2. H. Richard Niebuhr, *The Meaning of Revelation* (New York: Macmillan, 1941).

3. G. Ernest Wright, *God Who Acts* (Chicago: Regnery, 1952)

4. Erich Auerbach, *Mimesis* (Princeton, N.J.: Princeton University Press, 1968).

5. Brevard S. Childs, *Biblical Theology in Crisis* (Philadelphia: Westminster, 1970).

6. Stanley Hauerwas, *Vision and Virtue* (Notre Dame, Ind.: Fides, 1974).

7. Stanley Hauerwas, David B. Burrell, and Richard Bondi, *Truthfulness and Tragedy* (Notre Dame, Ind.: University of Notre Dame Press, 1977).

8. Hans W. Frei, *The Eclipse of Biblical Narrative* (New Haven, Conn.: Yale University Press, 1974).

9. Robert Alter, *The Art of Biblical Narrative* (New York: Basic Books, 1981).

10. Alasdair C. MacIntyre, *After Virtue* (Notre Dame, Ind.: University of Notre Dame Press, 1981).

11. Michael Goldberg, *Theology and Narrative* (Philadelphia: Trinity, 1981).

12. Ronald F. Thiemann, *Revelation and Theology: The Gospel as Narrated Promise* (Notre Dame, Ind.: University of Notre Dame Press, 1985)

13. George A. Lindbeck, *The Nature of Doctrine: Religion and Theology in a Postliberal Age* (Philadelphia: Westminster, 1984).

14. The faculty at Yale Divinity School, including some who were present during Frei's tenure, would protest the suggestion that there is "a distinct theologi-

cal method" which it follows. David Kelsey, for instance, has shown why he doesn't think that such typologies work anyway (*The Uses of Scripture in Recent Theology* [Philadelphia: Fortress, 1975]). But, as with the whole notion of the "Yale School," there are sufficient elements shared by representatives to constitute a common "method."

15. Gabriel Fackre, *The Christian Story* (Grand Rapids, Mich.: Eerdmans, 1978).

16. It is perhaps another sign of our parochialism that, despite the fact that nearly every member of the Yale circle is quite vocally committed to a particular ecclesiastical tradition (chiefly Lutheran and Reformed), interaction with conservatives has been almost entirely limited to evangelicals rather than to confessional Protestants.

17. David Tracy, *Blessed Rage for Order* (New York: Seabury, 1975), 238.

18. Hans Frei, *Types of Christian Theology* (New Haven, Conn.: Yale University Press, 1992), 19.

19. This is the title for chapter 2 of Karl Barth, *The Word of God and the Word of Man*, trans. Douglas Horton (New York: Harper, 1957).

20. Julius Schniewind, in Hans Werner Bartsch, ed., *Kerygma and Myth: A Theological Debate* (London: SPCK, 1953), 87.

21. Hans Frei, *The Eclipse of Biblical Narrative* (New Haven: Yale University Press, 1974), 12.

22. Ibid.

23. Hans Frei, *Types of Christian Theology*, edited by George Hunsinger and William C. Placher (New Haven: Yale University Press, 1992), 15.

24. Ibid., 20.

25. For deeper insight into the sources of the cultural-linguistic application, see Clifford Geertz, *The Interpretation of Cultures* (New York: HarperCollins, 1973), especially chapters 1, 4-7, and *Local Knowledge* (New York: HarperCollins, 1983), especially chapters 2, 4, 7, and 8.

26. Frei, *Types*, 21.

27. Ibid.

28. Ibid.

29. Frei, *Eclipse*, 230.

30. Frei, *Types*, 98.

31. I am told by a colleague of Frei's that, when the aging professor was living out his last days, this colleague asked him why he never wrote a systematic theology. Frei responded that it had already been written, referring to the *Church Dogmatics*.

32. Frei, *Types*, 58.

33. Ibid., 59.

34. Ibid., 60.

35. Ibid., 62.

36. Ibid., 65.

37. ibid., 70

38. Ibid., 74.

39. Ibid., 75-77.

40. Ibid., 90.

41. Ibid., 90-91.

42. Ibid., 91.

43. Colin Gunton, *The One, the Three, and the Many: God, Creation, and the Culture of Modernity* (Cambridge, England: Cambridge University Press, 1993), 134.

44. Frei, *Types*, 26.

45. Ibid., 26-27.

46. Frei, *Eclipse*, 12.

47. Lindbeck, *Nature of Doctrine*, 10.

48. Ibid.

49. Ibid., 9.

50. Ibid., 16.

51. Ibid., 21.

52. Ibid., 16.

53. Ibid., 18.

54. Ibid.

55. Ibid., 19.

56. Cf. Ludwig Wittgenstein, *Philosophical Investigations* (New York: Macmillan, 1973), par. 190-205.

57. Wittgenstein, *Philosophical Investigations*, par. 124.

58. Lindbeck, *Nature of Doctrine*, 19.

59. Ibid.

60. William Placher, "Postliberal Theology," in David F. Ford, ed., *The Modern Theologians*, vol. 2 (Oxford: Basil Blackwell, 1989), 120, emphasis his.

61. Lindbeck, *Nature of Doctrine*, 22.

62. Ibid.

63. Ibid., 23.

64. Ibid.

65. See note 25, above.

66. Geertz, *Interpretation of Cultures*, 125.

67. Lindbeck, *Nature of Doctrine*, 33.

68. Ibid.

69. Michael Harvey, "Wittgenstein's Notion of 'Theology of Grammar,'" *Religious Studies Journal* 25, no. 1 (March 1989): 93.

70. Lindbeck, *Nature of Doctrine,* 33.

71. Ibid., 34.

72. Ibid., 35.

73. Ibid., 52.

74. Wittgenstein, *Philosophical Investigations,* par. 141-142.

75. Of course, even this analogy may be defeated by the observation that languages are not entirely incommensurable. Perhaps at this point Professor Lindbeck would reply that, while syntactical rules may be coincidental across languages, grammars are not—and, after all, grammar (not syntax) is the analogy.

76. Lindbeck, *Nature of Doctrine,* 54.

77. Ibid., 57.

78. Ibid., 58.

79. Ibid.

80. Ibid.

81. Ibid. For the similarities to Wittgenstein here, see *Philosophical Investigations,* par. 29.

82. The priority of language to experience and thought may be accepted without adopting Lindbeck's reduction of the latter to the former.

83. Jay Wesley Richards, *Religious Studies Journal* 33, no. 3 (September 1997): 43-44, emphasis his.

84. Ibid., 44.

85. Lindbeck, *Nature of Doctrine,* 58

86. Ibid., 117. For a similar notion of a "classic," see Frank Kermode, *The Classic Literary Images of Permanence and Change* (Cambridge, Mass.: Harvard University Press, 1983).

87. Ibid., 118.

88. Ibid.

89. Ibid., 119.

90. Ibid., 120.

91. Ibid., 121.

92. Ibid., 122.

93. Francis Watson, *Text and Truth: Redefining Biblical Theology* (Edinburgh: T. and T. Clark, 1997), chapter 1. Also see page 274 (n. 41) for a concise critique of Lindbeck's analysis of the phenomenon of religion.

94. It would even seem that Lindbeck's use of "language games" is explicitly rejected by Wittgenstein's proscription of "private language." Cf. Saul A. Kripke, *Wittgenstein on Rules and Private Language* (Cambridge, Mass.: Harvard University Press, 1982).

95. Donald Davidson, "On the Very Idea of a Conceptual Scheme," *Proceedings and Addresses of the American Philosophical Association* 47 (1973–74): 5-20.

96. Jeffrey Hensley, "Are Postliberals Necessarily Antirealists?" in *The Nature of Confession*, 69-80.

97. Alister McGrath, "An Evangelical Evaluation of Postliberalism," in ibid., 38

98. Ibid., 43.

99. Lindbeck, *Nature of Doctrine*, 59.

100. Frei, *Types*, 45.

101. Ibid., 44.

102. Lindbeck, *Nature of Doctrine*, 117.

103. William Placher, "Postliberal Theology," 120.

104. George Lindbeck, *Nature of Doctrine*, 90 (n. 23).

105. Hans Frei, *The Identity of Jesus Christ* (Eugene, Ore.: Wipf and Stock, 1997), part 4 (131-155).

106. George Hunsinger, "What Can Evangelicals and Postliberals Learn from Each Other?" in *The Nature of Confession*, 134-150.

11

Reintegrating Biblical Theology
and Dogmatics

Paul R. Raabe

A s we approach the third millennium, Christendom just within this country is fragmented and fractured into countless different theological positions. The only way forward toward a creedal and confessional unity, it seems to me, needs to begin with theologians talking with each other.

Right now, to a great extent, the disciplines of biblical scholarship and dogmatics are separate and unrelated. I fear that some dogmaticians could not exegete their way out of a paper bag, and I know that some biblical scholars could not even spell Arianism. Yet, the two disciplines desperately need each other. Therefore I wish to press the case for reintegrating biblical theology and dogmatics, for leading biblical exegetes and dogmaticians into the same room and forcing them to talk theology together. I would like to offer eight suggestions for your consideration. The first four suggestions have to do with how dogmatics needs the input of biblical scholarship; the last four discuss how biblical scholarship needs dogmatics.

How Dogmatics Needs Biblical Scholarship

Dogmatics Needs to Be Held Accountable to the Biblical Texts as Understood Historically and Contextually

This means, first of all, that systematic theologians, at least those who do dogmatics within and for the church, must at least *include* the Bible in their systematics. It astounds me how many theologians try to concoct a whole new theology without any attention to the Bible at all, let alone serious biblical exegesis; just throw into the stew some Tillich, a bit of feminism here and ecology there, add in gay liberation, and mix it with some postmodernism. I have often wondered what the rules are for this kind of theologizing.

But even within more conservative, confessional circles one can see theologizing by a process of free association: some theology of the Cross here, some law-gospel distinction there, and so on. Whenever I catch my students theologizing up in the sky this way, by creatively putting together some orthodox ideas, I ask them, "Is there any biblical text or book that even comes close to matrixing these ideas together in your way?" The response is usually silence. It is difficult at least for me as an exegete to evaluate a given theological position if "there is no text in this class," as Stanley Fish would say. This does not mean simply quoting Bible passages in a biblicistic sort of way, but it does mean having some kind of scriptural warrant for the position, some biblical text or group of texts that we can all study and discuss.

Moreover, when systematicians do reference the Scriptures, they need to do it competently. For example, exegesis has demonstrated that "Abba" is not baby talk for "Daddy," but this misunderstanding continues.[1] The old dogmatic position that took the Hebrew plural form for "God" (*'elohim*) as a proof for the Trinity in the Old Testament is linguistically unwarranted. And there are many other examples. This is one reason why dogmaticians need to work with exegetes.

Dogmatics Should Provide Some Kind of Biblical Explanation for Its Categories and Jargon

No one insists that we have to use only biblical words in theology. But do the dogmatic terms convey biblical meaning? Why use the term "natures" or the phrase "communication of attributes" when speaking of Christ's humanity and divinity? Why employ the term "persons" or "hypostases" in reference to the Father and the Son and the Holy Spirit? I realize that this language goes way back in the history of the church, but is there any biblical justification for these terms or categories?

Moreover, dogmatics needs to give some kind of biblical rationale for the dogmatic loci or doctrinal articles that it uses. How did you or earlier dogmaticians even come up with these loci and not some other loci? What is a "doctrine," and how do readers of the Bible recognize it when they see it? The sentence, "Nimrod was a mighty hunter" is not a doctrine, but the sentence, "You are the Christ, the Son of the living God" is. Does a systematics even deal with a key biblical text or theme, such as the kingdom of God or the covenant or the wrath of God? Where in the systematics do you discuss it, and why do you place it in this dogmatic basket instead of that one? I am not suggesting that systematicians need to reinvent the systematic wheel— although sometimes that is a healthy thing to do—but I am suggesting that they present some kind of biblical rationale for their categories. This will enable exegetes to enter the discussion more easily, and by asking these kinds of questions the exegetes can keep the systematicians honest.

In Addition to Describing the Content of the Scriptures and the Church's Faith, Dogmatics Has the Task of Examining and Explaining Its Overall Matrix in a Biblical Way

How do the various theological truths organically relate to each other? Why relate them in this way and not in that way? I would submit that many of the doctrinal differences among the various Christian traditions stem from using different matrices and frameworks. Each tradition will use biblical pieces, but it will put them together differently.

Dogmatics also should give more attention to the question of when a given theme even belongs to the discussion of a particular topic. Take the topic of prayer, for example. In the psalms it is clear that the psalmists were trying to persuade God, to move God's heart with their petitions and arguments. Whenever I try to belabor this obvious exegetical point in class, students who have taken the course on the doctrine of God will inevitably throw in a red herring: "How does this square with the omniscience of God?" They do not realize that their question, if taken to its logical conclusion, would inevitably render the whole idea of prayer pointless. So I try to explain that that consideration should be left out of this discussion. The psalmist is addressing God as a personal being who hears prayer and allows himself to be persuaded with the result that God will change his course of action and intervene. So which theological considerations belong to the discussion of a given topic and which ones do not apply?

Or consider the topic of Christ's death. Paul will sometimes speak of Christ dying for us and sometimes of *our* dying with Christ.[2] The first way of speaking emphasizes that Christ's death happened *extra nos,* apart from our participation. "While we were yet sinners Christ died for us" (Rom. 5:8, RSV). But the second way of speaking stresses our participation in Christ's death; by being baptized into Christ's death we died with him, we were crucified with him, we were buried with him, we were raised with him (Rom. 6:4). So when does Paul articulate the gospel the first way and when the second way? It seems to me that the first pattern deals with human guilt and the sinner's justification, whereas the second pattern concerns our relationship to the power of sin. Thus we are righteous before God by virtue of Christ's *extra nos* death and resurrection, but we are dead to the power of sin and alive to God by virtue of our baptismal dying and rising with Christ. If we just mix the two together without differentiation, we will distort the inner logic of the Pauline gospel. At any rate, questions that concern the relationship among the different pieces are made to order for dogmaticians.

Dogmatics Should Seek More Intentionally to Incorporate the Old Testament into Its Discipline

The first three-fourths of the Bible cannot simply be marginalized or treated as mere background. After all, contra Marcion, the God of ancient Israel, the Creator of heaven and earth is, in the words of Paul, "the God and Father of our Lord Jesus Christ." So how can Christian dogmatics incorporate the Old Testament more? This seems to me to be one of the great theological questions that needs attention. Here I wish to spend some time on this issue and to suggest just a few ways in which the Old Testament is important for Christian dogmatics and Christian theology in general.[3]

Consider first of all the doctrine of God. Do we begin with a Greek philosophical notion of God as the unmoved mover and then on that basis demote the Old Testament's God-language to merely "anthropomorphic" language? I would argue that if we took the Old Testament's God-language seriously and not just as metaphorical, we could see it as "incarnational" language. This is the God who locates himself with Israel in space and time and from that position "remembers" the past and "promises" the future. He makes himself accessible to Israel in certain ways, such as at Zion. He delivers with his strong arm; he hears with his ears and sees with his eyes and speaks with his mouth. This is the God who reveals himself already in the Old Testament in a way that anticipates the Incarnation.

Second, the Old Testament keeps our feet on the ground. Everywhere it presupposes and affirms the goodness of God's creation. The ancient Israelites were a down-to-earth people, for the most part, agriculturalists and owners of sheep and goats. They rejoiced in their concrete and physical life. Their hope was not to become deified or divinized but to live in fellowship with YHWH in a fully human way, the way the Creator had made them and intended them to be. To live under your own vine and fig tree, to enjoy the fruits of your own fields, to drink the wine from your own vineyard—that was the good life. "It doesn't get any better than this."

No one steeped in the earthy Old Testament, when taken at face value, would be tempted toward gnosticism, platonic dualism, docetism, asceticism, or spiritualism—alternatives that are as prevalent today as they ever were. The Old Testament keeps our Christian life facing outward toward the concrete needs of the neighbor in the external world, rather than turning inward toward the inner world of the soul. It invites us to rejoice in our flesh-and-blood creatureliness, in the way God has created us. In fact, the first article of the Apostles' Creed and Nicene Creed to a great extent depends upon the Old Testament. It was no coincidence that Marcion, under the influence of gnosticism, wanted nothing to do with the Old Testament, since he wanted nothing to do with the "maker of heaven and earth." Against Marcion, the early church fathers rightly emphasized that it was the Creator who redeemed, and that what he redeemed was his own creation and not something alien to him. The work of the new creation presupposes the work of the Creator.

Third, the Old Testament is necessary for the understanding, preservation, and proclamation of the gospel itself. Without a good understanding of the Old Testament, one can hardly understand the apostolic witness, since it so often presupposes and assumes the witness of the Scriptures of ancient Israel. The Old Testament establishes the "lexicon" of the apostolic testimony to the person and work of Jesus of Nazareth in that the very terminology of the gospel is rooted in the Torah, Prophets, and Writings: Messiah, Son of David, Second Adam, suffering servant, prophet, priest after the order of Melchizedek, King, Lamb of God, sacrifice, atonement, justification, kingdom of God, covenant, and so on. I would venture to say that every book in the New Testament is strongly influenced by the language and categories of the Old Testament, including Luke-Acts and the letters written to Gentiles.

The church claims that Jesus is the fulfillment, but the fulfillment of what? Of every sort of human dream or ideal or philosophy? Is Jesus the fulfillment of New Age spirituality or American egalitarianism and individualism? Without seeing how the gospel is rooted in the Scriptures of ancient Israel, one can easily treat it as a wax nose to be shaped by self-determined needs or by the ideologies and fads that prevail in a given culture. It is not surprising that the Jesus Seminar constructs Jesus as an itinerant Cynic philosopher or an egalitarian social reformer, since the Seminar's excessive preoccupation with the criterion of dissimilarity in effect divorces the historical Jesus from the Torah, Prophets, and Writings. For example, the Seminar posits a (Marcionite) historical Jesus who never cited the Scriptures!

We need the witness of the Old Testament lest we have a fulfillment without an older promise, or a Christ-event that stands isolated from any preceding plan of God. Such a view characterized Marcion, as Jaroslav Pelikan states: "This continuity Marcion denied, in the name of the newness of the gospel of Christ. Any continuity or sequence (*ordo*) was unnecessary, for the coming of Christ had been sudden and immediate."[4] Even the letter to the Hebrews, which stresses perhaps more than anywhere else the discontinuities between the old covenant and the new covenant, also presupposes continuity between the two. If we were to drive a hard wedge between the two, we would end up with something like "old" *apples* and "new" *oranges*. Against such a dichotomy the church needs to continue to stress the soteriological and evangelical unity of the two parts of the Christian Bible. For the church's faith rests in the Good News that comes from the God of ancient Israel, the Good News about the fulfillment of the ancient promises and history by Jesus the Messiah, the Son of God.

Fourth, the Old Testament is necessary for understanding ecclesiology, particularly the place where Gentiles live in God's plan. Gentiles do not form their own independent people of God, parallel to Israel. On the contrary, they are foreign branches from a wild olive tree that have been grafted into the cultivated olive tree, the Israel of God (Rom. 11). By being incorporated into Christ, who is Abraham's seed reduced to one, they are descendants of Abraham and fellow heirs of the ancient promise (Gal. 3). Formerly they were "alienated from the commonwealth of Israel, and strangers to the covenants of promise, having no hope and without God in the world," but in Christ Jesus they were "brought near" by his blood (Eph. 2:12, 13, RSV).

God never gave promises directly to Gentiles as Gentiles. The only place of salvation has always been located in Israel, and the Gentiles, if they would be saved, must be brought under the promises made to Israel by the God of Israel. Only YHWH, the God of Israel, deserves to be worshiped as "God," and only in Zion is there salvation. These particular claims of the B.C. biblical writers were as scandalous in their context of religious pluralism as the claims of the apostles are today. The scandal of particularity was not first introduced during the first century A.D. The only hope for Hispanics or Chinese or Germans or Americans is to come to Zion and worship the God of Israel, not to build their own Gentile religion or Gentile temple. It says something about our identity that ancient Israel's psalms hold such a prominent place in the church's liturgy, for they provide the church with a God-pleasing "language" for prayer and praise to the God of Israel through Christ Jesus.

Fifth, the Old Testament provides the historical and eschatological framework for Christian theology. It sets our faith and life into the context of a history that moves toward a *telos,* instead of the context of cyclical mythology. There is a future-oriented thrust throughout the story of Israel. The prophets make this explicit in their announcements of the coming day when God will set all things right. But we see it already implicitly in the narratives, which trace the wanderings of the patriarchs or the march of Israel from Egypt to Sinai, from Sinai to the promised land, and from exile back to Zion.

Through our baptism into Jesus the Christ, we Gentiles have been incorporated into *his* Israelite history, and thereby we have a share in *Israel's* history. And we still have a not-yet existence, a foot in B.C. time as it were, as we wait in hope for the consummation, the eschatological kingdom of God, the glorious coming of the Christ who has been revealed to us not by flesh and blood but by his Father. In short, the Old Testament helps prevent the Christian story from leaving the historical world of space and time and flying off into the realm of platonic ideas or turning inward to the private and individualistic world of the subjective psyche.

Finally, the Old Testament contains certain accents that might be obscured or overlooked by Christian theology if we were to use only the New Testament. One thinks of wisdom literature, for example, and its invitation to acquire wisdom in the fear of the Lord, to inquire into the enigmas of life and the art of living, to investigate with human reason and observation the whole created order—from the ways of humans to the ways of ants. The narratives that show the faithful serving in the governments of this age, such as those about Joseph, Esther, and Daniel, encourage Christians in their vocation as citizens in the earthly city. Or consider the way that *faith* delights in the good and righteous law of God, as expressed, for example, by Psalms 19 and 119. While we affirm with Paul the accusing and condemning role of the Law against sinners, we also need to hear this positive side, which, by the way, is not absent from Paul himself (cf. Rom. 7:12, 22; 13:8-10). Furthermore, how many suffering Christians down through the ages have not received great benefit from praying along with the psalms of lament in the name of the One who suffered, died, and was raised from the dead? In countless ways, Christian faith and life would be greatly diminished if we were to de-emphasize or neglect the Old Testament in the theological and dogmatic task.

Now I wish to address the other side of the coin: how biblical scholarship needs dogmatics.

How Biblical Scholarship Needs Dogmatics

The Unexamined Assumptions of Biblical Scholarship Need to Be Challenged by Dogmatics

Ever since the Enlightenment, much of biblical scholarship has endeavored to "free" the Bible from the "shackles" of church dogma. This assumes that church dogma has fundamentally misread and distorted the original meaning of the Bible. Therefore the goal has been to sift through the layers of church tradition to arrive at the historical Jesus or the historical meaning of the biblical authors. To do this, the interpreter must study the Scriptures from a totally objective and disinterested position.

If postmodern critiques of Enlightenment modernism have accomplished anything, they have powerfully called into question the idea of any purely objective science. There is no such thing as a totally objective and disinterested reader, since every reader lives in a community and is shaped by that community's presuppositions, values, and methods. Every step of the way, dogmaticians should challenge exegetical assumptions and methods. They should call into question the dominant genetic fallacy, that if one knows the origin and development of a phenomenon then one truly understands that phenomenon. They should repeatedly ask biblical scholarship: "Has orthodox dogma really misread the Scriptures as you claim? How do we know that the historical Jesus was so different from the depiction given in the Gospels? What are your criteria for separating out the strata in the biblical material, and what is the basis for those criteria?" Dogmatics should challenge biblical scholarship just as much as the reverse.

Dogmatics Can Benefit Biblical Scholarship by Raising the Deeper
Theological Questions Necessary for Understanding the Theological
Framework and Implications of a Given Biblical Text

When Peter confesses Jesus as "the Son of the living God," it is exeget-
ically not enough just to say, "Here Peter calls Jesus the Son of God."
What do those words mean? The word "God" here does not refer to
the Trinity or to the divine essence, but to God the Father. And what
does the word "Son" mean, given that Jesus displays his deity in
Matthew and at the end includes the word "the Son" as the second
member of the Triadic name in the Great Commission? If Jesus is not
only man, then the word "Son" must mean more than merely adopted
as son. But if the Son *is* God and does not merely *represent* God, how
can that be true without having two gods? Dogmatics answers: What
equates the Son with the Father lies in the term "God," but what distinguishes the Son from the Father pertains to the terms "Son" and
"Father." The creeds and the early ecumenical councils simply sought
to clarify with precision the biblical faith. Dogmatics has the value of
forcing biblical scholarship to deal with these kinds of "mega" questions, and biblical scholars would be fools if they were simply to ignore
what the traditional dogma says.

In fact, it is impossible to read the Scriptures with any degree of
theological awareness without seeking the kind of definition and clarification given in dogmatics. The only question is whether the reader
of the Bible will *knowingly* and *competently* reckon with the "dogmatic" concerns. The best way to do that without having to reinvent
the wheel is by studying the creeds and church dogma.

Dogmatics Marks Out for Biblical Exegetes the Theological
Wrong Turns and Dead Ends to Avoid

So many of the theologies attempted by biblical scholars today have
been proposed before and found to be heretical. Why unwittingly
repeat the mistakes of the past? With respect to some biblical scholarship on christology, for example, one still sees adoptionism being
promoted. The evolutionary view that posits first the *man* Jesus of
history and then later the church treating him as *God* is simply

Nestorianism set into a chronological framework. Nestorianism was tried before and found to be ruinous for the saving gospel. Another example is the substitute trinitarian formula of "Creator, Redeemer, and Sanctifier." In addition to other problems, this formula ends up dividing the *opera ad extra* of God (i.e., God's works in the world, distinct from those within the essential Godhead) and thus dividing the deity.

The Ancient Orthodox Dogma Supplies the Church's Biblical Scholarship with a Hermeneutical Guide for Reading Scripture in a Theologically Orthodox Way

Among other things, a church is a community of readers and interpreters of the Scriptures. Since every reader as part of a community reads within some kind of hermeneutical circle, whether self-consciously or unwittingly—and it is better to be intentional and self-conscious about it—how does the church read the biblical texts? For the churches committed to the creedal faith, the hermeneutical circle involves that same creedal faith. (To say that Scripture interprets Scripture is essentially the same position, since the creedal faith summarizes the scriptural faith.)

On the one hand, the church's biblical scholarship should respect each text's integrity and try not to read it against its context or force it to say something one wants it to say. The hermeneutical circle is no excuse for interpretive somersaults. On the other hand, as all readers are inevitably shaped and formed by something—for it is impossible to approach any text *tabula rasa*—biblical scholars working within and for the church should be informed by her dogma as they read the Scriptures. As Robert Jenson states, "The final reason that one cannot interpret the Bible independently of the church and its dogma is that without these there is no such book."[5]

As a hermeneutical guide, the dogma functions like a map—as Charles Arand pointed out in chapter 1 of this book. It does not replace the reading of the Scriptures, just as a map does not replace taking the trip. Its purpose rather is to send us back into the Scriptures with more reader competence. It points out the highlights to enjoy and the dangers to fear. It reveals how the various spots are related to each other, how to matrix the pieces together. This has always been a key function of the "rule of faith." Bits of information need some type of overall narrative or framework in order to make sense of them. Irenaeus, for example, likens one who interprets apart from the rule of faith to one who reassembles the pieces of a beautiful mosaic of a king into the image of an ugly dog.[6] The rule of faith does not replace the Bible, but it provides the overall picture necessary for making sense of a given piece.

One of the goals of the Enlightenment was to "free" the Bible from the "shackles" of church dogma. But when it separated the Bible from the creeds, it simply ended up substituting a different interpretive framework. It is time to reexamine that entire enterprise and move in the opposite direction. It is time to reintegrate biblical theology and dogmatics.

Notes

1. For example, see Jürgen Moltmann, *The Way of Jesus Christ: Christology in Messianic Dimensions,* trans. Margaret Kohl (London: SCM, 1990), 142-145.

2. On the distinction, see Paul R. Raabe, "Who Died on the Cross? A Study in Romans and Galatians," *Concordia Journal* 23 (1997): 201-212.

3. Some of this material appears in my article, "Why the B.C. Scriptures Are Necessary for the A.D. Church," *Lutheran Forum* (Pentecost 1998 issue): 11-15. For a stimulating discussion of this question, see Hans-Georg Fritzsche, *Lehrbuch der Dogmatik I: Prinzipienlehre* (Göttingen: Vandenhoeck and Ruprecht, 1964), 122-134. Some of his suggestions are developed here.

4. Jaroslav Pelikan, *The Christian Tradition,* vol. 1 (Chicago and London: University of Chicago Press, 1971), 78.

5. Robert W. Jenson, *Systematic Theology Volume 1: The Triune God* (New York and Oxford: Oxford University Press, 1997), 59.

6. *Against Heresies,* 1.8.1; cf. 1.9.1-4.

12

Redemption and Resurrection: An Exercise in Biblical-Systematic Theology

Richard B. Gaffin, Jr.

C hrist's resurrection, inseparably connected with his death, is at the heart of the gospel (e.g., Rom. 10:9; 1 Cor. 15:3-5). Central to the hope ministered by the gospel is the Christian's resurrection (e.g., Rom. 8:23; 1 Cor. 15). A reality so evidently dominant presents a variety of aspects for reflection. As my title suggests, I propose here to consider particularly its relationship to our salvation by taking a so-called biblical-theological approach.

I.

1. I should probably make clear how I understand "biblical theology." Briefly, I have in view not so much one particular discipline or area of study among others, as I do methodological considerations indispensable for sound biblical interpretation. Specifically, in terms of the principle of context, the text, whatever its relative size, is always to be read in its redemptive- or salvation-historical context, understanding the text's subject matter within the horizon of the unfolding history of salvation—that, I take it, is the distinguishing concern of biblical-theological exegesis (= redemptive-historical interpretation).

Such an approach stems from recognizing that Scripture as a whole, with its various human authors and diverse literary genres, has its integrity as the God-breathed record of the actual revelation process in back of Scripture, the Bible's own origin being an essential part of that process. This history of (verbal) revelation, in turn, is tethered, as a strand within, to the larger history of the accomplishment of redemption (deed revelation); that history begins already in the Garden, subsequent to the Fall (Gen. 3:15), and reaches its consummation in the fullness of time (Gal. 4:4), in the incarnate Christ and his work.

The clearest, most explicit biblical warrant for this fundamental theological construct is provided by the opening words of Hebrews 1:1-2a: God, having spoken in the past to the fathers through the prophets at many times and in various ways, has spoken to us in these last days by his Son. This umbrella statement, intended to provide an overall perspective on the teaching of the entire document, is fairly applied, by extension, to the Bible as a whole. Note how it captures three interrelated factors: a) revelation as a historical process; b) the diversity involved in that process (including, we might observe, multiple modes and literary genres—as well as, too, whatever legitimate methodologies have emerged, particularly in the modern era, for dealing with them); and c) the incarnate Christ as the integrating omega-point (cf. 2:2-4; 3:1-6, esp. 5-6), the nothing-less-than-last days, eschatological endpoint of the process.[1]

The biblical-theological treatment of the Resurrection offered here is primarily with a view to the expressed focus of this volume: the revitalization of systematic theology. That, in brief, I understand to be the presentation, under appropriate topics (loci), of the unified teaching of the Bible as a whole, an overall statement of what is either expressly set down in Scripture or by good and necessary consequence may be deduced from Scripture (Westminster Confession of Faith, 1:6). Systematics (or church dogmatics), then, is radically nonspeculative, in that its viability depends on biblical exegesis. Because of that, in my view, nothing will more serve to revitalize systematics than exegesis that is redemptive-historically sensitive, biblical-theologically regulated.

2. Our reflections on the Resurrection here need to be set against a broad historical background. As a generalization—no doubt subject

to qualification but still fair as a generalization—we may say that in the history of doctrine, especially in soteriology, Christ's resurrection has been relatively eclipsed. In Eastern Orthodoxy, if I rightly understand, the accent has been on his incarnation (with a view to salvation understood as theosis or deification). In Western Christianity (both Roman Catholic and Protestant), especially since Anselm (eleventh century) and the ensuing debate triggered, say, by the views of Abelard, attention has been focused heavily and at times almost exclusively on Christ's death and its significance. The overriding concern, especially since the Reformation, has been to keep clear that the Cross is not simply an ennobling and challenging example but a real atonement—a substitutionary, expiatory sacrifice that reconciles God to sinners and propitiates his judicial wrath. In short, the salvation accomplished by Christ and the Atonement have been virtually synonymous.

My point here, you will understand, is not to challenge the validity or even the necessity of this development, far less the conclusions reached. But in this dominating preoccupation with the death of Christ, the doctrinal or soteriological significance of his resurrection has been largely overlooked. Not that the Resurrection has been deemed unimportant, but all too frequently it has been considered exclusively as a stimulus and support for Christian faith (which it undoubtedly is) and in terms of its apologetic value, as the crowning evidence for Christ's deity and the truth of Christianity in general.

(Especially since the Enlightenment and with the emergence of the historical-critical method, this apologetic value has been rendered more and more problematic as increasingly the historicity of the Resurrection has been questioned or denied. On that large issue I simply assert here that for the New Testament the gospel plainly stands or falls with the reality of the Resurrection understood, despite all that is unique and unprecedented about it, as lying on the same plane of historical occurrence as Christ's death [1 Cor. 15:14, 17].)

3. Turning now to the New Testament, such an oversight or lack of emphasis on the doctrinal meaning of the Resurrection proves particularly impoverishing. That is especially true for Paul. His writings, which constitute such a substantial subunit within the larger organism of New Testament revelation, evidence, with their fully occasional

character taken into account, a coherent and pervasive concern with how Christ's resurrection is integral to our salvation, or, as we might also put it, a concern with the specific saving efficacy or redemptive efficiency of his resurrection. I proceed now to sketch the basic dimensions of what we may fairly call Paul's resurrection theology, and then to reflect on several aspects in more detail.[2]

II.

1. The longest single continuous treatment of the Resurrection in Paul is 1 Corinthians 15. There, in verse 20 (cf. v. 23), he affirms that Christ in his resurrection is the firstfruits of those who are fallen asleep. We begin our survey here because this declaration expresses a key thought, one that governs not only much of the argument from verse 12 to the end of the chapter but, in large measure, Paul's teaching as a whole on resurrection.

This description of the resurrected Christ as firstfruits is more than an indication of bare temporal priority or even preeminence. Rather, commensurate with its Old Testament cultic background (e.g., Ex. 23:19; Lev. 23:9ff.), the metaphor conveys the idea of organic connection or unity; the firstfruits is the initial quantity brought into view only as it is a part of and so inseparable from the whole; in *that* sense it represents the whole.

The resurrection of Christ and of believers cannot be separated, then, because, to extend the metaphor as Paul surely intends, Christ is the firstfruits of the resurrection-harvest that includes believers (note, as 15:23 shows, that this harvest is an entirely soteriological reality; the resurrection of unbelievers, taught by Paul elsewhere, e.g., in Acts 24:15, is outside his purview here). Christ's resurrection is the guarantee of the future bodily resurrection of believers not simply as a bare sign but as "the actual beginning of th[e] general epochal event."[3] The two resurrections, though separated in time, are not so much separate events as two episodes of the same event, the beginning and end of the *one and same* harvest.

This unbreakable unity between the two resurrections is a controlling presupposition in the hypothetical argumentation of the immediately preceding section (vv. 12-19), so much so that a denial of the future resurrection of the believer entails a denial of Christ's resurrection (vv. 13, 15, 16). Essentially the same idea of solidarity in resurrection is also expressed elsewhere in the description of Christ as the firstborn from among the dead (Col. 1:18).

In view, further, is Christ's resurrection as an innately eschatological event. In fact, as much as any, it is the key inaugurating event of eschatology, the dawn of the new creation (2 Cor. 5:17; Gal. 6:15), the arrival of the age to come (Rom. 12:2; Gal. 1:4). It is not an isolated event in the past, but, in having occurred in the past, it belongs to the future consummation and from that future has entered history. In Christ's resurrection the resurrection-harvest at the end of history is already visible. Pressed, if present, say, at a modern-day prophecy conference, as to when the event of bodily resurrection for believers will take place, the first thing the apostle would likely want to say is, it has already begun!

2. The emphasis on Christ as the firstfruits of resurrection points up that, for Paul, the primary significance of Christ's resurrection lies in what he and believers have in common, not in the profound difference between them; the accent falls not on his true deity but on his genuine humanity. The Resurrection, as we will presently note in more detail, is not so much an especially evident display or powerful proof of Christ's divine nature as it is the powerful transformation of his human nature.

This emphasis is confirmed in an implicit but pervasive fashion by Paul's numerous references, without elaboration, to the simple fact of the Resurrection.[4] These undeveloped statements display a consistent, unmistakable pattern: 1) God in his specific identity as the Father raises Jesus from the dead (Gal. 1:1); 2) Jesus is passive in his resurrection. This viewpoint is held without exception, so far as I can see. Nowhere does Paul teach that Christ was active in or contributed to his resurrection, much less that he raised himself; Jesus did not rise but was raised from the dead. The stress everywhere is on the creative power and action of the Father, of which Christ is the recipient.

To see a conflict here with statements such as that of Jesus in John 10:18 ("I have authority to lay [my life] down and authority to take it up again," NIV) is both superficial and unnecessary. The Chalcedon formulation proves helpful here: The two natures coexist hypostatically (in one person), without either confusion or separation; Jesus expresses what is true of his person in terms of his deity, Paul expresses what is no less true in terms of his humanity.

3. To fill out this basic sketch, one other element needs to be noted. The passages so far considered express the bond between Christ's resurrection and the future, bodily resurrection of believers. But Paul also speaks of the Christian's resurrection in the past tense; believers have already been raised with Christ (e.g., Eph. 2:5-6; Col. 2:12-13; 3:1). This past resurrection, it needs to be recognized, is so not only in the sense that Christ represented the church in his resurrection. Rather, it is an experience in the actual life-history of each believer. That is apparent from Ephesians 2, where the Resurrection in view 1) terminates on being dead in your transgressions and sins (vv. 1, 5), and 2) effects a radical, 180-degree reversal in walk or actual conduct—from walking in the deadness of sin (v. 1) to walking in the good works of new-creation existence in Christ (v. 10). It bears emphasizing that to speak of this experiential transformation as resurrection is not merely metaphorical; Paul intends such language no less realistically or literally (and, we might add, no less irrevocably) than what he says about the hope of bodily resurrection.

4. To sum up this overview of Paul's resurrection theology: An unbreakable bond or unity exists between Christ and Christians in the experience of resurrection. That bond is such that the latter (the resurrection of Christians) has two components—one that has already taken place, at the inception of Christian life when the sinner is united to Christ by faith; and one that is still future, at Christ's return. From this it will be readily apparent how Paul's teaching on the fundamental event of resurrection reflects the overall already/not-yet structure of eschatological fulfillment in the period between Christ's resurrection and his return.

If we raise the question of distinguishing the two episodes of the believer's resurrection, various proposals suggest themselves: secret/open; nonbodily/bodily; internal/external.[5] Paul himself offers the distinction between the outer man and the inner man (2 Cor. 4:16), which we should understand not as two discrete entities but as two aspects of the whole person. So far as believers are "outer man," that is, in terms of the body, they are yet to be raised. So far as they are "inner man," they are already raised and, he adds, the subject of daily renewal.

III.

This pattern of teaching is open to being explored further along two interrelated but distinct lines: what concerns Christ (christology), and what concerns Christians/the church (soteriology and ecclesiology). The reflections that follow are necessarily selective.[6]

1. So far as the Christ is concerned, most striking is the relationship between Christ and the Holy Spirit resulting from the Resurrection. Here the key, single most important passage is also in 1 Corinthians 15, where Paul says of Christ that the last Adam became the life-giving Spirit (v. 45). The observations that follow will have to be brief; an effort at more careful exegesis is found in several endnotes.

1) The noun πνεῦμα (spirit) in 1 Corinthians 15:45 is definite[7] and refers to the person of the Holy Spirit.[8] This is the view taken, across a fairly broad front, by a substantial majority of contemporary commentators and other interpreters who address the issue.[9] In English translation, Spirit should be capitalized;[10] Paul knows of no other "life-giving" πνεῦμα than the Holy Spirit (2 Cor. 3:6; cf. Rom. 8:11).[11]

2) "The life-giving Spirit," it should not be missed, is not a timeless description of Christ—who he has always been. Rather, he "became" ἐγένετο such. The time-point of this "becoming" is surely his resurrection or, more broadly, his exaltation.[12] As "firstfruits" of the resurrection-harvest (vv. 20, 23) he is "life-giving Spirit" (v. 45); as "the life-giving Spirit" he is "the firstfruits."

As resurrected, the last Adam has ascended; as "the second man," he is now, by virtue of ascension, "from heaven" (v. 47),[13] "the man from heaven" (v. 48). All told, the last Adam, who has become "the life-giving Spirit," is specifically the *exalted* Christ.

3) In the immediate context (vv. 42-49), "life-giving" contemplates

Christ's future action, when he will resurrect the mortal bodies of believers (cf. v. 22). Within the broader context of Paul's teaching, however, his *present* activity, as well, is surely in view. As we have already noted, the resurrection of the Christian, in union with Christ, is not only future but has already taken place (e.g., Gal. 2:20; Col. 2:12-13; 3:1-4).

2. Here, more pointedly than anywhere else in Paul (or, for that matter, anywhere else in the New Testament), the significance of the Resurrection (and Ascension) for the relationship between Christ and the Spirit comes to light. In context, two closely related realities are in view: 1) Christ's own climactic transformation *by* the Spirit; and 2), along with that transformation, his unique and unprecedented reception *of* the Spirit.

1) Paul affirms what has not always been adequately elaborated in the church's christology: the momentous, epochal significance of the exaltation for Christ *personally;* he has, as the firstfruits, what he did not have previously, a spiritual body.[14] In his resurrection, something really *happened* to Jesus; by that experience he was and remains a changed man, in the truest and deepest, even eschatological sense.

As Paul puts it elsewhere (on the most likely reading of Rom. 1:3-4), by the declarative energy of the Holy Spirit in his resurrection, God's eternal (v. 3a) and now incarnate (v. 3b) Son has become what he was not previously, the Son of God with power (v. 4). Relatively speaking, according to 2 Corinthians 13:4, while Christ was crucified in (a state of) weakness, he now lives by God's power; his is now, by virtue of the Resurrection and Ascension, a glorified human nature.

Here, as so often in Paul, christology and soteriology are inextricable. Christ does not receive his glorified humanity merely for himself but for the sake of the church. In the language of Romans 8:29, the Resurrection constitutes him the image to which believers are predestined to be conformed, so that he, the *Son,* might be firstborn among many *brothers;* specifically, the exalted Christ is that image into which Christians are even now already being transformed (2 Cor. 3:18) and which they will one day bear bodily in their future resurrection at his return (1 Cor. 15:49).

2) This resurrection-transformation of Christ by the Spirit also results in a climactic intimacy, a bond between them that surpasses

what previously existed, a relationship involving, in fact, a new and permanent equation or oneness that Paul captures by saying that Christ became the life-giving Spirit.[15] This is not to deny that previously Christ and the Spirit were at work together among God's people.[16] But now, dating from his resurrection and ascension, their joint action is given its stable and consummate basis in the history of redemption; that culminating synergy is the crowning consequence of the work of the incarnate Christ actually and definitively accomplished in history.

First Corinthians 15:45 is, in effect, a one-sentence commentary on the primary meaning of Pentecost: Christ is the receiver-giver of the Spirit. What Peter delineates in his Pentecost sermon as inseparable once-for-all events—resurrection, ascension, reception of the Spirit, outpouring of the Spirit (Acts 2:32-33)—Paul telescopes by saying that the last Adam became the life-giving Spirit.[17]

3. It bears emphasizing that this oneness or unity of Christ and the Spirit, though certainly sweeping, is at the same time circumscribed in a specific respect; it concerns their *activity*, the activity of giving resurrection (= eschatological) life. In *this* sense it may be dubbed "functional" or "eschatological," or, to use an older theological category, "economic" (rather than "ontological"[18]).

In other words, the scope, the salvation-historical focus of Paul's statement, needs to be kept in view. Essential-eternal, ontological-trinitarian relationships are quite outside his purview here. His concern is not with who Christ is (timelessly), as the eternal Son, but with who he "became," what has happened to him in history, and, specifically, in his identity—Paul could hardly have been more emphatic—as "the last *Adam*," "the second *man*" (v. 47), that is, in terms of his true humanity.

Consequently, it is completely gratuitous to find here and elsewhere in Paul, as the historical-critical tradition has long and characteristically maintained, a "functional" christology in the sense that it denies the personal difference between Christ and the Spirit and so is in conflict with later church formulation of trinitarian doctrine. In no way is Paul here even obscuring, much less denying, the distinction between the second and third persons of the Trinity. The personal, parallel distinction between God (the Father), Christ as Lord, and the (Holy) Spirit—underlying subsequent doctrinal formulation—is clear enough elsewhere in Paul (e.g., 1 Cor. 12:4-6; 2 Cor. 13:14; Eph. 4:4-6).[19] His trinitarian conception of God is not at issue but is properly made a presupposition in the interpretation of 1 Corinthians 15:45.

4. The last clause in 1 Corinthians 15:45 not only connects closely, as already noted, with Romans 1:4 but also with the subsequent statement at the beginning of 2 Corinthians 3:17: "the Lord is the Spirit." There, the "Lord" (ὁ κύριος) likely refers to Christ, and an equation between him and the Spirit is affirmed.[20] Here, too, essential, trinitarian identities and relationships are not being denied or blurred, but simply remain outside Paul's purview. His focus, clear from the immediate context (see esp. v. 18), is the conjoint activity of the Spirit and Christ as *glorified*. The "is" (ἐστιν) of 2 Corinthians 3:17, we may say, is based on the "became" of 1 Corinthians 15:45. The exaltation experienced by the incarnate Christ results in a (working) relationship with the Holy Spirit of new and unprecedented intimacy. They are one here, specifically, in giving (eschatological) "freedom" (3:17b), the close correlative of the resurrection life, in view in 1 Corinthians 15. That correlation is particularly unmistakable in the phrasing of Romans 8:2: ". . . the *Spirit* of *life* in *Christ Jesus* has set me *free* . . ."

IV.

1. First Corinthians 15:45, Paul's most pivotal pronouncement on the relationship between the exalted Christ and the Spirit, is consequently the cornerstone of his teaching on the Christian life and the work of the Holy Spirit. Life in the Spirit has its specific quality as the shared life of the resurrected Christ, in union with him. There is no activity of the Spirit within the believer that is not also the activity of Christ; Christ at work in the church is the Spirit at work.

Romans 8:9-10 is particularly instructive here. There, in short compass, four expressions are virtually interchangeable: "you . . . in the Spirit" (9a); "the Spirit . . . in you" (9b); "belong to [Christ]" (9d, equivalent to the frequent "in Christ"); and "Christ . . . in you" (10a).

These four expressions hardly describe different experiences, distinct from each other, but have in view the same reality in its full, rich dimensions. The presence of the Spirit is the presence of Christ; there is no relationship with Christ that is not also fellowship with the Spirit; to belong to Christ is to be possessed by the Spirit.

This truth about the believer's experience, it bears emphasizing, is so not because of some more or less arbitrary divine arrangement, but preeminently because of what is true *prior* to our experience, in the experience of Christ, because of (in virtue of his death and resurrection) who the Spirit now is ("the Spirit of Christ," v. 9c), and who Christ has become ("the life-giving Spirit."[21] So, elsewhere (in the prayer for the church in Eph. 3:16-17), for "you . . . to be strengthened . . . through His Spirit in the inner man" is nothing other than for "Christ [to] dwell in your hearts through faith (NASB)."

2. The Spirit at work in the church, then, is Christ at work in nothing less than eschatological (because resurrection) power. In fact, the New Testament has no more important or more basic perspective on being a Christian than this: The Christian life is resurrection-life. As we have already noted, it is part of the resurrection-harvest that begins with Christ's own resurrection (1 Cor. 15:20); the believer's place or share in that harvest is now—not only in the future but already in the present. The radical edge of Paul's outlook on the Christian life comes to light in the observation that, at the core of their being (the "inner man," 2 Cor. 4:16; or what he also calls the heart, Rom. 2:29; 6:17; Eph. 1:18), Christians will never be more resurrected than they already are! Christian existence across its full range is a manifestation and outworking of the resurrection life and power of Christ, the life-giving Spirit (Rom. 6:2ff.; Eph. 2:5-6; Col. 2:12-13; 3:1-4).

These considerations need to be stressed in view of the tendency in much historical Christian thinking to de-eschatologize the gospel and its implications, especially where the work of the Holy Spirit is concerned. His present activity, characteristically, is viewed in a mystical or timeless way, as what God is doing in the inner life of the Christian, detached from eschatological realities. The result, too often, has been largely privatized, individualistic, even self-centered understandings of the Spirit's work. The church ought constantly to make clear in its proclamation and teaching that, in the New Testament, "eternal life" is *eschatological* life, specifically resurrection life. It is "eternal," not because it is above or beyond history—"timeless" in some ahistorical sense—but because it has been revealed, in Christ, at the end of history and, by the power of the Spirit, comes to us out of that consummation.

3. It seems fair to suggest that at issue here is a still-to-be-completed side of the Reformation. The Reformation, we should not forget, was a (re)discovery, at least implicitly, of the eschatological heart of the gospel; the *sola gratia* principle is eschatological in essence. Justification by faith, as the Reformers came to understand and experience it, is an anticipation of final judgment. It means that a favorable verdict at the last judgment is not an anxious, uncertain hope (where they felt themselves to be left by Rome), but a present possession, the confident and stable basis of the Christian life. Romans 8:1 ("There is therefore now no condemnation for those who are in Christ Jesus," NASB), which they clung to, is a decidedly eschatological pronouncement.

But while the Reformation and its children have grasped, at least intuitively, the eschatological thrust of the gospel for justification, that is not nearly the case for sanctification and the work of the Spirit. Undeniable is a tendency, at least in practice, to separate or even polarize justification and sanctification.[22] Justification, on the one hand, is seen as what God does, once for all and perfectly; sanctification, on the other hand, is what the believer does, imperfectly. Sanctification is viewed as the response of the believer, an expression of gratitude from our side for salvation defined in terms of justification and the forgiveness of sins—usually with an emphasis on the inadequate and even impoverished quality of the gratitude expressed.

The intention of such an emphasis is no doubt to safeguard the totally gratuitous character of justification. But church history has made all too evident that the apparently inevitable outcome of such an emphasis is the rise of moralism, the reintroduction into the Christian life of a refined works-principle, more or less divorced from the faith that justifies and eventually leaving no room for that faith. What is resolutely rejected at the front door of justification comes in through the back door of sanctification and takes over the whole house.

Certainly we must be on guard against all notions of sinless perfection. Forms of "entire" sanctification or "higher," "victorious" life, supposedly achieved by a distinct act of faith subsequent to justification, operate with domesticated, voluntaristic notions of sin that invariably de-eschatologize the gospel and in their own way, despite their intention, end up promoting moralism. Certainly we must not forget that "in this life even the holiest have only a small beginning" (Heidelberg Catechism, answer 114).

But—and this is the point—that beginning, however small, is an *eschatological* beginning. It stands under the apostolic promise that "He who began a good work in you will perfect it until the day of Christ Jesus" (Phil. 1:6, NASB). Sanctification, no less than justification, is *God's* work. In the New Testament there is no more basic perspective on sanctification and renewal than that expressed in Romans 6: It is a continual "living to God" (v. 11) of those who are "alive from the dead" (v. 13). Elsewhere, it is a matter of the "good works" of the eschatological new creation, for which the church has already been "created in Christ Jesus" (Eph. 2:10). In their sanctification, believers begin at the "top," because they begin with Christ; in him they are those who are "perfect" (1 Cor. 2:6) and "spiritual" (v. 15), even when they have to be admonished as "carnal" (3:1, 3).[23]

An important and fruitful challenge for the teaching ministry of the church today is to give adequate attention to the eschatological nature of sanctification and the present work of the Holy Spirit (ensuring at the same time, by the way, that justification is clarified within the already/not yet structure of New Testament eschatology).

4. But, it might now be asked, hasn't the resurgent Pentecostal spirituality of recent decades seen and, in large measure, recaptured the eschatological aspect of the Spirit's working and so compensated for the traditional neglect and shortcomings just noted?

One brief observation concerning this multifaceted question will have to suffice.[24] A current widespread misperception notwithstanding, the New Testament does not teach that spiritual gifts, especially miraculous gifts such as prophecy, tongues, and healing, belong to realized eschatology. For instance, a concern of 1 Corinthians 13:8-13 is to point out that prophecy and tongues are temporary in the life of the church. Whether or not at some point prior to the Parousia (I leave that an open question here), Paul is clear that they will *cease* and *pass away* (v. 8). But that cannot possibly be said of what is *eschatological*. Such realities, by their very nature, *endure*.[25] Phenomena such as prophecy and tongues, where they occur, are no more than provisional, less-than-eschatological epiphenomena.[26] I suggest that this reading of the passage helps with the perennial problem exegesis has wrestled with in verse 13: How can faith and hope be said to continue after the Parousia, in the light, say, of 2 Corinthians 5:7 (for the present, in contrast to our resurrection-future, we "walk by faith, not by sight") and Romans 8:24 ("hope that is seen is not hope," NASB)? That question misses the point. The "abiding" in view is not future but concerns the present, eschatological worth of faith and hope (as well as love), in the midst of the non-enduring, sub-eschatological quality of our present knowledge, including whatever word gifts bring that knowledge.

All told, the New Testament makes a categorical distinction between the gift (singular) and the gifts (plural) of the Spirit, between the eschatological gift, Christ, the indwelling, life-giving Spirit himself, in which all believers share (e.g., 1 Cor. 12:13), and those sub-eschatological giftings, none of which, by divine design, is intended for or received by every believer (1 Cor. 12:28-30, for one, makes that clear enough).

The truly enduring work of the Spirit is the resurrection-renewal already experienced by every believer. And that renewal manifests itself in what Paul calls fruit—like faith, hope, love, joy, and peace (to mention just some, Gal. 5:22-23), with, we should not miss, the virtually unlimited potential for their concrete expression, both in the corporate witness as well as in the personal lives of the people of God. This fruit—preeminently love, not the gifts—embodies the eschatological "firstfruits" and "deposit" of the Spirit (to use Paul's metaphors). However imperfectly displayed for the present, such fruit is eschatological at its core. Not in particular gifts, however important such gifts undoubtedly are for the health of the church, but in these fruits we experience the eschatological touch of the Spirit in our lives today. This is a point, I hope, on which charismatics and noncharismatics, whatever their remaining differences, will eventually agree.

5. A question may now come from another quarter: Will not stressing the resurrection quality of the Christian life and the eschatological nature of the Spirit's work minister an easy triumphalism, a false sense of attainment? Trivializing options such as "possibility thinking" and "prosperity theology" in various forms are by no means an imaginary danger, as our own times make all too clear.

The New Testament itself is alert to this danger—the perennial danger for the church of an overly realized eschatology. In the interim between Christ's resurrection and return, believers are "alive from the dead," but they are that only "in your mortal body" (Rom. 6:12-13); Christians experience "the powers of the age to come" (Heb. 6:5), but only as "the present evil age" (Gal. 1:4) is prolonged, only within the transient "form of this world" (1 Cor. 7:31) (all references NASB).

What such interim existence entails is captured perhaps most instructively and challengingly, even if at first glance a paradox, in several passages in Paul. Though, strictly speaking, autobiographical and having uniquely apostolic dimensions, they intend the suffering he experienced as a paradigm for all believers.

Philippians 3:10 is a particularly compelling instance. As part of Paul's aspiration to gain Christ and be found in him (vv. 8-9), he expresses the desire to "know [Christ] and the power of His resurrection, and the fellowship of His sufferings, being conformed to His death" (NASB). In this declaration, I take it, the two "ands" are not coordinating but explanatory. Knowing Christ, the power of his resurrection, and the fellowship of his suffering are not sequential or alternating in the believer's experience, as if memorable and exhilarating times of resurrection power are offset by down days of suffering. Rather, Paul is intent on articulating the *single,* much more than merely cognitive, experience of knowing Christ, what he has just called "the surpassing greatness of knowing Christ Jesus my Lord" (v. 8, NIV). To know Christ, then, is to know his resurrection power *as* a sharing in his sufferings—an experience, all told, that Paul glosses as being conformed to his death. The imprint left in our lives by Christ's resurrection power is, in a word, the Cross.

Similarly, 2 Corinthians 4:10-11 speaks of always carrying around in the body the dying of Jesus, so that the life of Jesus may be manifested in our body, and, again, of always being given up to death for Jesus' sake, so that the life of Jesus may be manifested in our mortal flesh. Here the two counterposed notions of the active dying of Jesus and of his resurrection life do not describe somehow separate sectors of experience. Rather, the life of Jesus, Paul is saying, is revealed in our mortal flesh, and nowhere else; the (mortal) body is the locus of the life of the exalted Jesus. Christian suffering, described as the dying of Jesus, molds the manifestation of his resurrection-life in believers.

This "Cross-conformity" of the church is, as much as anything about its life in this world-age, the signature of inaugurated eschatology. Believers suffer, not in spite of or even alongside the fact that they share in Christ's resurrection, but just because they are raised up and seated with him in heaven (Eph. 2:5-6). According to Peter (1 Pet. 4:14), it is just as Christians suffer for Christ that God's Spirit of (eschatological) glory rests on them. For the present, until he returns, suffering with Christ remains a primary discriminant of the eschatological Spirit. The choice Paul places before the church for all time, until Jesus comes, is not for a theology of the Cross instead of a theology of resurrection-glory, but for his resurrection theology *as* theology of the Cross.

The question of Christian suffering needs careful and probing reflection, especially for the church in North America with its relative freedom and affluence, where suffering can seem remote and confined to the church elsewhere, but where we are surely naive not to be preparing for the day when that distance may disappear—perhaps much sooner than we may think.

Instructive is Romans 8:18ff., where Paul opens a much broader understanding of Christian suffering than we usually have. There, with an eye to the Genesis 3 narrative and the curse on human sin, he reflects on what he calls, categorically, the sufferings of the present time (v. 18), that is, the time, for now, until the bodily resurrection of the believer (v. 23). From that sweeping angle of vision, suffering is everything about our lives, as they remain subjected, fundamentally and unremittingly, to the enervating futility (v. 20) and bondage to decay (v. 21), which, until Jesus comes, permeate the entire creation.

Christian suffering, then, is a comprehensive reality that includes everything in our lives in this present order, borne for Christ and done in his service. Suffering with Christ includes not only monumental and traumatic crises, martyrdom and overt persecution, but it is to be a daily reality (cf. Luke 9:23: ". . . take up his cross *daily*" [NIV, emphasis added]); it involves the mundane frustrations and unspectacular difficulties of our everyday lives—when these are endured for the sake of Christ.

Philippians 1:29, I take it, is a perennial word to the church: "For it has been granted to you on behalf of Christ not only to believe on him, but also to suffer for him" (NIV). Here Paul speaks of the giveness of Christian suffering for the church as church. Probably we are not over-translating to speak of the gracious giveness of suffering; suffering is given to the church as a gift. At any rate, Paul is clear, the Christian life is a not only/but also proposition—not only a matter of believing but also a matter of suffering. Suffering is not simply for some believers but for all. We may be sure of this: Where the church embraces this inseparable bond between faith and suffering, there it will have come a long way toward not only comprehending theologically but also actually experiencing the eschatological quality of its resurrection-life in Christ, the life-giving Spirit.

Notes

1. In my judgment, the most instructive single summary treatment of issues related to biblical-theological method is still Geerhardus Vos, *Biblical Theology, Old and New Testaments* (Grand Rapids, Mich.: Eerdmans, 1948), 11-27.

2. See in greater detail my *The Centrality of the Resurrection* (Phillipsburg, N.J.: Presbyterian and Reformed, 1978; reprinted as *Resurrection and Redemption*, 1987), 33-74.

3. Geerhardus Vos, *The Pauline Eschatology* (Grand Rapids, Mich.: Baker, 1979), 45.

4. Grammatically, with the verb ἐγείρω used almost exclusively, Christ is either the direct object of (aorist) active forms (e.g., Rom. 4:24; 10:9), or the subject of (aorist and perfect) passive forms (e.g., 1 Cor. 15:20; 2 Cor. 5:15). In the case of the latter, an intransitive/active sense is excluded by the context.

5. Spiritual/physical is not an apt distinction, and is perhaps even misleading, at least if "spiritual" is used in its pervasive New Testament sense, referring to the activity of the Holy Spirit. The past resurrection of the believer is certainly spiritual in this sense, but so is the future, bodily resurrection—preeminently, climactically so (1 Cor. 15:44).

6. Missing, for instance, is a treatment of the forensic significance of the Resurrection, especially its relationship to justification. Briefly, Christ was raised for our justification (Rom. 4:25). The Resurrection vindicates Jesus in his obedience unto death (Phil. 2:8-9); it reveals that he embodies the perfect righteousness that avails before God. In that sense his resurrection is his justification and so, by imputation, through union with him by faith, our justification. Without the Resurrection, along with his death, there would be no justification of the ungodly (Rom. 4:5), our faith would be futile, and we would still be in our sins (1 Cor. 15:17); see further my *Resurrection and Redemption,* 114ff.

7. The absence of the article before πνεῦμα has little weight as a counterargument, if for no other reason, because of the tendency in koine Greek to omit the article before nouns designating persons when, as here, in construction with a preposition. See A. Blass, A. Debrunner, R. W. Funk, *A Grammar of the Greek New Testament* (Chicago: University of Chicago Press, 1961), 133f. (254, 255, 257).

8. This conclusion rests on a couple of interlocking, mutually reinforcing considerations that appear to me to be decisive.

a) πνεῦμα in verse 45 and πνευματικόν (spiritual, vv. 44a, b, 46) are cognate noun and adjective. The adjective, particularly as it is paired antithetically here with ψυχικόν, and in the light of the only other New Testament occurrence of this antithesis earlier (in 2:14-15), has in view the work of the Spirit and what is effected by him. This is further confirmed by Paul's consistent use of πνευματικός elsewhere; it never has an anthropological sense (e.g., Rom. 1:11; Eph. 1:3; Col. 1:9; the only exception appears to be Eph. 6:12).

In 2:6-16 the activity of the Spirit—his sovereign, exclusive work in giving and receiving God's revealed wisdom—is the primary focus of the immediate context. In contrast to the unbeliever (ψυχικὸς ἄνθρωπος, v.14), the spiritual man (ὁ πνευματικός, v. 15) is the believer (cf. vv. 4-5) as indwelt, enlightened, motivated, directed by the Spirit. The long-standing effort to enlist this passage in support of an anthropological trichotomy (with πνευματικός here referring to the human spirit come to its revived ascendancy), I take it, is not successful and ought to be abandoned; see, e.g., John Murray, *Collected Writings of John Murray,* vol. 2 (Edinburgh: Banner of Truth Trust, 1977), 23-33, esp. 23-29.

b) The participial modifier in 15:45b points to the same conclusion. The last Adam did not simply become πνεῦμα but "life-giving" πνεῦμα (πνεῦμα ζωοποιοῦν). Paul's use of this verb elsewhere with the Spirit as subject proves decisive, especially his sweeping assertion in 2 Corinthians 3:6: "the Spirit gives life." Few, if any, will dispute that here the Spirit (τὸ πνεῦμα) is "the Spirit of the living God" just mentioned in 3:3, in other words, the Holy

Spirit. And in Romans 8:11, a statement closely related to the 1 Corinthians 15 passage, the "life-giving" activity of raising believers bodily is attributed to the Spirit (cf. John 6:63).

9. See, e.g., various articles in the recent *Dictionary of Paul and His Letters,* G. F. Hawthorne, R. P. Martin, eds. (Downers Grove, Ill.: InterVarsity, 1993), 12a and 263b (L. J. Kreitzer), 107b, 108a, 112a (B. Witherington), 349a (R. B. Gaffin), 407b (T. Paige), 435a (G. M. Burge), 554 (J. J. Scott). See further Vos, *Pauline Eschatology,* 10, 168-69, 184, 312; Herman N. Ridderbos, *Paul: An Outline of His Theology* (Grand Rapids, Mich.: Eerdmans, 1975), 88, 222-223, 225, 539; Gaffin, *Resurrection and Redemption,* 78-92.

10. Virtually all the standard English translations obscure the sense of verse 45 by rendering spirit in the lower case. Notable exceptions are The Living Bible (and now The New Living Translation) and Today's English Version; they, correctly I believe, capitalize Spirit.

11. To deny that πνεῦμα in verse 45 is the Holy Spirit at the very least undercuts a reference to his activity in the cognate adjective *spiritual* in verse 44 and ends up giving it a more indefinite sense of something like *supernatural.* That easily tends toward the widespread misunderstanding that it describes the (immaterial) composition of the Resurrection body. Also, it has to be asked: Within the first-century Mediterranean thought-world of Paul and his readers, what is a life-giving spirit with a lower-case s? What would that likely communicate, at least without further qualification, such as is lacking here, other than the notion of an angel or some other essentially immaterial being or apparition? But πνεῦμα in that sense is exactly what Jesus, as resurrected, denies himself to be in Luke 24:37-39.

12. The flow of the reasoning in chapter 15 makes that virtually certain. It would make no sense for Paul to argue for the Resurrection of believers as he does if Christ were "life-giving" by virtue of, say, his preexistence or incarnation— or any consideration other than his resurrection. This is in no way to suggest that his preexistence and incarnation are unimportant or nonessential for Paul; they simply lie outside his purview here.

13. With the immediate context in view, this prepositional phrase is almost certainly an exaltation predicate, not a description of origin, say, out of preexistence at the Incarnation. As such ("from heaven," "the man from heaven," v. 48, NIV), he is the one whose image believers ("those who are of heaven," v. 48, NIV) will bear (fully, at the time of their bodily resurrection, v. 49; cf. Phil. 3:20-21).

14. The resurrection body is "spiritual" (v. 44), it bears emphasizing, not in the sense of being adapted to the human πνεῦμα or because of its (immaterial) composition or substance (to mention persisting misconceptions) but because it embodies (!) the fullest outworking, the ultimate outcome, of the work of the Holy Spirit in the believer (along with the renewal to be experienced by the entire creation, e.g., Rom. 8:19-22). That eschatological body is the believer's hope of total, (psycho-)physical transformation, and in that sense, our bodies, too, enlivened and renovated by the Spirit.

15. Herman Bavinck's way of stating this truth is striking: "But the Holy Spirit has become entirely the property of Christ, and was, so to speak, absorbed into Christ or assimilated by Him. By His resurrection and ascension Christ has become the quickening Spirit." *Our Reasonable Faith* (Grand Rapids, Mich.: Eerdmans, 1956), 387.

16. Prior to this time, already even under the old covenant, Christ preincarnate and the Spirit were conjointly present and at work; 1 Corinthians 10:3-4, whatever its further exegesis, points to that. Cf. 1 Peter 1:10-11: The Spirit comprehensively at work in the Old Testament prophets is specifically "the Spirit of Christ."

17. On the once-for-all significance of Pentecost—along with the death, resurrection, and ascension of Christ—see Richard B. Gaffin, Jr., *Perspectives on Pentecost* (Phillipsburg, N.J.: Presbyterian and Reformed, 1979), 13-41.

18. Although, as noted earlier, there is involved a real change/transformation experienced by Christ in terms of his true humanity. By virtue of the Resurrection, he now possesses what he did not previously possess, a *glorified* human nature (cf. 2 Cor. 13:4).

19. In more recent literature, Paul's clearly trinitarian understanding of God is admirably demonstrated by Gordon D. Fee, *God's Empowering Presence: The Holy Spirit in the Letters of Paul* (Peabody, Mass.: Hendrickson, 1994), 825-845, esp. 839-842.

20. A growing number of exegetes currently argue that the "Lord" in verse 17a applies Exodus 34:34, just cited in verse 16, to the Spirit, and they minimize or even eliminate any christological reference from verses 17b-18; e.g., Linda L. Belleville, *Reflections of Glory* (Sheffield, England: Sheffield Academic Press, 1991), 256ff.; J. Dunn, "2 Corinthians III.17—'The Lord Is the Spirit,'" *Journal of Theological Studies* n.s. 31, no. 2 (Oct. 1970): 309-320; Fee, *God's Empowering Presence*, 311-314; Scott J. Hafemann, *Paul, Moses, and the History of Israel* (Tübingen: J. C. B. Mohr, 1995), 396-400; Richard B. Hays, *Echoes of Scripture in the Letters of Paul* (New Haven, Conn.: Yale University Press, 1989), 143-144; N. T. Wright, *The Climax of the Covenant* (Edinburgh: T. and T. Clark, 1991), 183-184. But verse 17b ("the Spirit of the Lord") already distinguishes between the Spirit and the Lord, so that the latter likely refers to Christ, in light of what immediately follows in verse 18. There, "the Lord's glory" (NIV) is surely not the glory of the Spirit in distinction from Christ, but the glory of Christ; in beholding/reflecting that glory, Paul continues, believers are being transformed into "the same image," and that image can only be the glory-image of the exalted Christ. In the verses that follow, 4:4 ("the light of the gospel of the glory of Christ, who is the image of God," NIV), especially, points to that conclusion (note as well Rom. 8:29 and 1 Cor. 15:49). The only transforming glory believers behold with unveiled faces, which Paul knows of, is the glory of God in the [gospel-] face of Christ (4:6), mediated, to be sure, to and within them by the Spirit.

21. That here, too, Paul does not intend an absolute identity, denying the personal distinction between Christ and the Spirit, is clear later on in the passage: the Spirit's interceding *here*, within believers (vv. 26-27), is distinguished from

the complementary intercession of the ascended Christ *there,* at God's right hand (v. 34).

22. I leave to the side here the treatment of sanctification in the Lutheran and Reformed confessions of the sixteenth and seventeenth centuries, and the extent to which they counteract and serve to correct this practical tendency.

23. See further especially the penetrating discussion of John Murray, *Collected Writings,* vol. 2, 277-284 ("Definitive Sanctification"); 285-93 ("The Agency in Definitive Sanctification").

24. See, in greater detail, my comments in Wayne A. Grudem, ed., *Are Miraculous Gifts for Today?* (Grand Rapids, Mich.: Zondervan, 1996), 56-59.

25. To highlight this point by way of contrast, in terms of metaphors Paul uses for the Spirit: The arrival of the rest of the harvest does not involve the removal of the firstfruits (Rom. 8:23); the payment of the balance hardly results in subtracting the down payment or deposit (2 Cor. 1:22; 5:5; Eph. 1:14). Or, going to what is surely the heart of the Spirit's activity, the resurrection of the body at Christ's return will certainly not mean the undoing of the resurrection, already experienced, of the inner man.

26. Contemporary discussion of this passage (on all sides, I would observe) too frequently obscures or even misses Paul's primary concern: For the present, until Jesus returns, it is not our knowledge (along with the prophetic gifts that may contribute to that knowledge), but our faith, hope, and love that have abiding, that is, eschatological, significance. In contrast to the partial, obscured, dimly mirrored quality of the believer's present knowledge brought by such gifts, faith in its modes of hope and especially love has what we might call an eschatological "reach" or "grasp" (vv. 12-13).

Index